Spiritual Science as a Foundation
for Social Forms

Spiritual Science as a Foundation for Social Forms

Rudolf Steiner

The address and seventeen lectures presented here were given between August 6 and September 16, 1920 in Dornach, Switzerland, and on September 17 and 18, 1920 in Berlin. In the Collected edition of Rudolf Steiner's works, the volume containing the German texts is entitled, *Geisteswissenschaft als Erkenntnis der Grundimpulse Sozialer Gestaltung* (Vol. 199 in the Bibliographic Survey). They were translated from the German by Maria St. Goar and edited by Alan Howard.

Published in the United States by the Anthroposophic Press.

Copyright © 1986 by Anthroposophic Press, Inc.

Library of Congress Cataloging-in-Publication Data

Steiner, Rudolf, 1861–1925.
   Spiritual science as a foundation for social forms.

Lectures and addresses given in 1920 in Dornach, Switzerland and Berlin, Germany.
   Translation of: Geisteswissenschaft als Erkenntnis der Grundimpulse sozialer Gestaltung.
   1. Anthroposophy—Addresses, essays, lectures.
I. Title.
BP595.S894G4513   1986   299'935   85-28703
ISBN 0-88010-153-9
ISBN 0-88010-152-0 (pbk.) } Anthroposophic Press

Cover: Graphic form by Rudolf Steiner
Title lettering by Peter Stebbing

All rights reserved. No part of this book may be reproduced in any form without the written permission of the publishers, except for brief quotations embodied in critical articles and reviews.

Printed in the United States of America

Contents

Foreword by Carlo Pietzner vii
Lecture 1—August 6, 1920, Dornach 1
Lecture 2—August 7, 1920, Dornach 21
Lecture 3—August 8, 1920, Dornach 37
Lecture 4—August 14, 1920, Dornach 56
Lecture 5—August 15, 1920, Dornach 75
Lecture 6—August 20, 1920, Dornach 92
Lecture 7—August 21, 1920, Dornach 106
Lecture 8—August 22, 1920, Dornach 126
Lecture 9—August 27, 1920, Dornach 143
Lecture 10—August 28, 1920, Dornach 163
Lecture 11—August 29, 1920, Dornach 178
Lecture 12—September 3, 1920, Dornach 192
Lecture 13—September 4, 1920, Dornach 208
Lecture 14—September 5, 1920, Dornach 226
Lecture 15—September 10, 1920, Dornach 241
Lecture 16—September 11, 1920, Dornach 257
Address *On the Occasion of the General Meeting of the Berlin Branch*—September 17, 1920, Berlin 276
Lecture 17—September 18, 1920, Berlin 285
Notes 303

FOREWORD

This volume contains seventeen of the more than 6000 lectures given by Rudolf Steiner (1861-1925) during the early part of this century. As with many of his lectures Steiner assumes a certain familiarity with his basic writings on the part of his listeners, a familiarity which can be gained by reading one or more of his introductory works. Chief among these are four books: *The Philosophy of Spiritual Activity*, *An Outline of Occult Science*, *Theosophy*, and *Knowledge of the Higher Worlds and Its Attainment*. The readers unfamiliar with the above works might be well advised to consider first reading one or more of them before attempting this volume both as a way of increasing their appreciation and comprehension of this work and in fairness to Steiner who explains in detail how he came to his knowledge in these four volumes.

Some of the volumes of Steiner's lectures are known as cycles because they addressed a single theme and were delivered over a short period of time to the same audience. The seventeen lectures collected in this sequence do not, strictly speaking, constitute a cycle. They are strung together along a definite path stretching between the dates of August 6 to September 18, 1920; but two were delivered before a very different audience, in Berlin. Added to these lectures is an address to the General Assembly of the Berlin branch of the Anthroposophical Society.

To the careful student of Rudolf Steiner's work it may seem, however, as if these lectures indeed form a definite cycle. They transmit a powerful appeal to all those who are deeply concerned with the condition of the social fabric, irrespective of political partisanship; but who look to its cultural and philosophical basis as a means for social action and renewal.

The range of these lectures is enormous, and thereby symptomatic of Rudolf Steiner's contribution to the civilization of our time. We only need look at some of the themes of the lectures:

Spiritual science must be a knowledge of action.

The twelve senses of the human being in their relation to Imagination, Inspiration, Intuition.

The science of initiation and the impulse for freedom.

Viewpoints for the forming of a healthy social judgment.

The lectures turn to profound and deeply stirring observations concerning the inherent tasks and intentions of the peoples in the West and East, and describe the diverse influences upon them through various spiritual powers. To this stream a talk is added in honor of Hegel's 150th birthday, making us aware of the pervasive, albeit mostly unconscious, influence of this thinker upon the West, and by no means only in the form in which Communism claimed him.

The lectures which follow belong perhaps to the most exciting ones we can find in Rudolf Steiner's lectures on the fundamentals for a social renewal. Like a slow-growing plant they begin to open only gradually into full significance.

The initiative to make this volume available in English arose out of a circle of people, including this writer, who have long concerned themselves with social renewal. We are a group who have chosen to live and work with handicapped people all over the world in special communities, the Camphill communities.

The social forms developed by these Camphill communities are new types of villages or related forms of communal life. In these villages we have enabled exciting relationships, new ways and new values of labor to emerge and for these strivings this volume might become a constant source of strength and encouragement. Just as there exists a curative course* by Rudolf Steiner which provides insight and inspiration for educators of handicapped children, so these lectures can be regarded as a source of inspiration for the whole range of activities which unfold as social therapy. The practical labor arising therefrom thus could give the right background for applying the indications given in these lectures. The lectures would then provide truly new ways of understanding the impulses and efforts of community life. They would demonstrate what it means to become free from those often highly developed thoughts which have, nevertheless, led the actions of individuals, groups and nations into catastrophic situations for several hundred years. And they still continue to do so despite increasingly desperate calls for change! But do we truly want to change? Without insights of a spiritual nature we cannot and will not attempt to change. Neither can it be expected to be an easy task or to be done by the mere acceptance of some creed.

Rudolf Steiner says in the 10th lecture:

> We come closer and closer to total decline precisely because our intellectuals will not venture to construe the tasks in this world by utilizing ideas other than those gained from waking life, from what lies between birth and death.

At the same time we must be aware of the slow, though fundamental process to which we can aspire when we take seriously what Rudolf Steiner has to say at the very beginning of the 12th lecture:

Curative Education, Rudolf Steiner Press, London, 1984.

One becomes acquainted with the same things from ever-changing viewpoints; thus, conviction increasingly gains in strength.

This growing conviction becomes firmer, the more flexible the standpoint, the deeper and the more truthful the shift from one to another perspective is, and it brings that certainty we can see in the planetary companions of the sun as they move in their regular orbits, in that galaxy to which they belong, to which we ourselves belong. Ultimately, this is the cosmos of love and truth.

The practical-minded expert will either smile or get angry at this. What role shall such lofty sentiments play in a world of brutality, deceit and despair? In the midst of such conditions (where the practitioners of old vices and their political and power-seeking responses continue to be at work, Rudolf Steiner spoke the following, describing neither a wish nor an ethical utopia, but describing rather his sober insight into a law, that is akin to a law of nature.

> This will be the healthy social relationship in the future. You can see it already today. Labor will be a free activity out of the insight into the necessity that labor has to take place. Men labor because they look at the human being and recognize that he needs labor. What was labor in the ancient world? It was a tribute; it was done because it had to be done. And what is labor today? It rests upon self-satisfaction, and that kind of enforcement which is exerted upon us by egoism. Because we are where we are, we want to be paid for our labor. We work for our own sakes, for our own wages. In the future we will labor for the sake of our fellow human beings, because they need what we can work for. This will be the reason for our work. We will clothe our fellow human beings, we will make our work available to them for what they are in need of—as a completely free activity. Wages have to be completely separated from this. A tribute was labor in the past—an offering it will be in the future. Labor has nothing to do with self-satisfaction, nothing to do with payment. If I allow my work to be dictated

by the needs of my brothers with a view to what mankind really needs, then I will find myself in a free relationship to it, and my work becomes an offering for mankind. Then I shall work with all my strength, for I love mankind and put my strength at its disposal.*

Who cannot imagine the unbelieving, if not contemptuous, faces raised upon hearing this—the cynicism and impatience? For all those who at times play at intellectual games with Rudolf Steiner's indications, another paragraph of the same lecture shall be quoted. Rudolf Steiner continues:

> This must become possible and will only be possible when life's requirements are separated from work. And this will indeed happen in the future—no one will be the owner of the products of his own labor. Mankind must be educated for free labor, one for all and all for one. Each one will have to act accordingly. Today, if you would found a small community in which each one throws into a communal account what he earns and each one works as best he can, then his very life's existence—his needs—will be brought about out of the communal consumption. This will cause a greater freedom than the ordering of wages according to production. When that happens we shall turn in the right direction. Today, this could flow into law, into each regulation; of course, not in absolute terms, but approximately. One could today build up factories in this way. But it will require healthy, clear and sober thinking in the sense of anthroposophy.*

A deeper understanding of all this can be obtained from the present volume of lectures.

If Rudolf Steiner's printed work needs a preface or an introduction at all, it is to emphasize that it cannot be read like other books. It belongs to the type and quality of his

---

*These two quotations come from a public lecture given by Rudolf Steiner in Berlin on October 26, 1905. This lecture was published only recently for the first time in Beitrage zur Rudolf Steiner Gesamtausgabe, St. John's Time 1985, #88.

thoughts that they have the characteristics of living things: the inherent power of growth and potential for change which lies in the unfolding of all living things. We are not accustomed to such activity with thoughts, with thinking as a force akin to doing. Yet such is the nature of Rudolf Steiner's thoughts. They appeal to an otherwise dormant participation in us and offer an invitation to social activity. No doubt, this is an unusual demand. Conceivably it can cause offense. But the request is emphasized here and with good cause.

In our time, no one can be free from grave concerns for the future, which is reaching with its tentacles right into the present. Much good will and increasing desperation is spent on finding "solutions," on seeking, on organizing, on imploring to try different ways; ways of amelioration, of appeasement, of change with a truly human face—with few results. It would not be, then, a wasted effort to enter into the reading of these lectures with more than that intellectual scanning to which we have become accustomed, but instead to hear, almost from the first words, the intonation of a selfless voice, selfless even in search for knowledge. This voice speaks with the tone of hope and of insight and with the aspirations of all of us. Its familiarity should, in the encounter with its message, lead us securely—and far more deeply than we usually listen—to those places of the will in us which alone can bring about change and evolutionary responsibility.

Carlo Pietzner
Michaelmas 1985

Lecture I
Dornach, August 6, 1920

I must begin with the gratifying observation that upon my return[1] I encountered a great many friends who are here in Dornach for the first time. They have come to inform themselves about what goes on in Dornach and what is meant to proceed from here into our anthroposophical movement. I cordially welcome all the newly arrived friends and hope that because of their stay with us they can carry back with them many new inspirations. Among the friends we can greet once again are many we have not seen for years. This fact along with much else undoubtedly indicates the difficulties of the age in which we live. I have just returned from a visit in Stuttgart, which was filled with the manifold tasks generated within our anthroposophical sphere of work. Among other matters, it included the ending of the first academic year of the Waldorf School[2] founded in Stuttgart. This Waldorf School belongs to those establishments which manifest most prominently the ideas of our anthroposophical spiritual movement. Even though one sets high standards for it, the completion of the first school year has demonstrated that there is cause for satisfaction. I can say this because it is possible to remain objective even if one is wholeheartedly involved in the project and even if, in a certain sense, one has been its instigator.

Above all it is gratifying to see how the Waldorf School teaching staff definitely understood how to proceed from a completely anthroposophical basis, as had always been the intention. Present-day conditions necessitated that this basis in anthroposophy should not produce a school that teaches a certain world view, a school in which anthroposophy would be taught. That was never the intention. With this in mind, therefore, we arranged the religious instruction so that children of Protestant parents, who wished them to have Protestant religious instruction, could be taught by a Protestant minister; Catholic children, by a priest. Only those who did not care to be numbered among the existing denominations were separately taught a form of anthroposophical religious instruction. Except for this, we certainly never considered the founding of an institution that teaches a specific world outlook. All efforts were directed toward the creation of a school in which the practical teaching impulses arising from the viewpoint and will of our spiritual science could for once be directly applied in the education and instruction of youth. It was our aim that the anthroposophic impetus should be expressed not in the content of the classes but in the way classes were taught, in the manner in which the whole school system was handled; that this impetus be manifested in the specific kind, and the different methods, of instruction. Once an anthroposophist has stimulated his classes through his anthroposophic will, the fertilization of the teaching process shows precisely what a vitalizing effect anthroposophy has when it is implemented in this way.

Throughout its first year, I always had the opportunity to observe the progress at the Waldorf School. Again and again, I was there for one or two weeks. I could supervise instruction and was able to watch the development of the different classes. I could see, for instance, how our friend, Dr. Stein,[3] succeeded in enlivening his history class for older students by bringing anthroposophic impulses into history. Anthropology, as taught by Fraeulein Dr. von Heydebrand[3] in the fifth grade, was lifted from the tedium prevailing ordinarily in our schools by imbuing it truly with anthroposophic will. I could cite many other instances from which you could clearly see that without in any way teaching abstract anthroposophy the subject matter comes alive by the method and the way it is treated and fertilized by anthroposophy. This practical application of anthroposophic strength of purpose shows that anthroposophy need not remain an abstract, remote philosophy, but can definitely influence human activity, even though we unfortunately have little opportunity to penetrate human affairs, except in limited areas like the Waldorf School. Now, when we ended the first year something happened that seemed to be only an exterior matter, but, as I am about to explain, it was an event that had great inner significance. A complete innovation took place. It concerned the report cards.

The report card system is truly one of the most miserable aspects of our schools. In a superficial, groping manner, teachers must grade their students from 1, 2, 3, 4 to 5 and so on,* a procedure that stifles the very nature of schools in a most appalling way. *Our* report cards are based on actual educational psychology, on an absolutely practical application of human psychology. At the end of the first school year, the teachers were at the point where they were able to write a report card for every child corresponding to its own character and capabilities, individually indicating the possibility for continued growth and progress. No report card was like any other. There were no numbers indicating grades. Instead, through the teacher's individual insight into his pupil, the student received a characterization of his personality. Already in the course of the first school year, the teachers had so intimately sought to deepen their understanding of every child's soul that they were able to write

---

*Note by translator: In the German educational system, the grade of 1 is equivalent to an A; 4 is a D and 5 would indicate a failing grade.

into the report card an accompanying verse suited to each recipient's individual character.

These report cards are an innovation. Do not conclude, however, that it can be imitated or readily introduced somewhere else, because this change has been brought about by the whole spirit of the Waldorf School and is based on the fact that the most intensive educational psychology was practiced during the first school year. We carefully studied what was causing certain intimate manifestations in the faster or slower progress of a class, and already in the course of the first school year, we made a few discoveries that were in some ways surprising. We learned, for example, that the whole configuration of a class takes on a specific form if the number of boys and girls in that class is equal. The configuration is a quite different one if boys are in the majority and girls in the minority, and it changes again when there are more girls than boys in a class. We have had all these examples in our classes. These imponderables, which elsewhere are not taken into consideration at all, are in many ways the essential element in a class.

When one attempts to express certain aspects of psychology, trying to define them in so many words, he is then already past the point that really matters. It is just the predominant and nonsensical custom of our time that one attempts to express things too rigidly in words. One cannot study matters thoroughly if one wants to express them in this constrictive word structure. One must be aware that by expressing things in this manner they can only be indicated approximately.

Of course, we always find ourselves in an odd position when we talk about the results of our anthroposophically oriented movement of spiritual science. The Waldorf School, whose teachers have proven themselves eminently suited to their tasks, could only justify itself because a group of human beings was gathered together who were most competent and pedagogically most qualified. It is unfortunate that in any effort to carry something out in a practical sense today, one encounters, much more than is generally realized, the one great obstacle, namely, a lack of qualified people. Today, the world has a paucity of people who are qualified for any real tasks in life. In our case the difficulty would be compounded should a second school be established. To find suitable, really proficient individuals capable of working in the spirit of anthroposophically oriented spiritual science would be much more difficult because the one existing school has, of course, already attracted all those who could seriously be considered. Yet there can be no doubt that, for once, something has been accomplished in a certain area. I must say, however, that this is like an island. There, in the course of the first school year, a spiritual system of education has become manifest which truly evolved from the fundamentals of anthroposophy. It is an island, however, enclosed within its shores. Beyond these shores, the financial and economic connections of the school are affected by the great decline in the economic and political life of the present. This is where the problems lie. We can see that our prospects are not what they should be; they are not as good as they should be considering the nature of our achievement. Yet does anyone have even a slight understanding of what the Waldorf School has created based on the spirit?

The Waldorf School was founded by our friend Molt[2] so that the children of the Waldorf Astoria Works could receive an education. Already in the first year, many children from the outside, who were unconnected to the factory, became students at the school; there must have been around 280 of them. Now, many new students have been registered, but from the Waldorf Astoria Works we have no more than were previously here, as well as the few who have meanwhile reached school age. If everything goes really well, and if economic and other problems can be solved, we shall, judging from the present applications, have more than four hundred students in our school. This means we shall have to build, hire more teachers, establish parallel classes. All this must happen! In a certain sense it will be a crucial test as to whether the financial understanding of our needs by those involved can keep pace with what induces so many people from the outside to bring us their children. It was somewhat ironical to me when the mother of one of our students was introduced to me in the school corridor as Frau Minister So and So. Even those connected with the present government are bringing their children to the Waldorf School now!

Some of these matters actually should be studied more closely in their social context as well. Then, perhaps, it would be possible to perceive the real needs of our society and how they are met by institutions such as the Waldorf School.

Now and then the Waldorf School was beset by a certain superficiality that is a characteristic of our times, as I have often pointed out. The leadership of the school was naturally confronted with people here and there who wanted to visit for a while, that is to snoop around a bit. Yet there is really not all that much to see. What does matter is the whole spirit at work in the school, and that is simply the anthroposophical spirit. People who can't make the effort to read anthroposophic books and who hope to get something from scouting round in the Waldorf School would be better served by deepening their knowledge of anthroposophy. For what bestows spirit on the Waldorf School and lies at its very foundation can only be seen in the spiritual impulses that are the basis of anthroposophical spiritual life. I have often pointed out to those who have been attending my lectures for some time that today the anthroposophic spiritual life is not directed only toward the individual who seeks the way out of his soul's distress and life's afflictions in the spiritual forces of the world. Today, spiritual science must address itself to the need and decline of our time. Then, however, the comprehension of what spiritual science has to offer will be met by that special kind of understanding that a person today can generally bring to anything of a spiritual nature. When talking about spiritual science, it is often necessary to speak in an entirely different language than is customary. One could say that in a certain sense words acquire a new meaning through spiritual science. It is absolutely necessary to feel and to sense this.

Today I would like to acquaint you with some things that can illustrate how essential it is not only to be willing to hear a somewhat different world view expressed in customary terminology, but to learn to receive the words differently with one's feelings.

Let us begin with a specific case. When speaking about any ideology today, it is designated by an abstract name: materialism, idealism, spiritualism, and so forth, and people are quite sure that they can say which is correct, and which is incorrect. A materialist comes to a spiritualist, for example, and explains to him his way of thinking, how he sees man's thoughts and feelings as products of the brain. The spiritualist answers, "You think incorrectly. I can refute that logically!" Or, perhaps, "That is contradicted by the facts!" In short, the crux of the matter is that today, when people talk about issues concerning world views, one ideology is said to be right and the other one wrong. The spiritualist presumes that only he has the correct philosophy, and wishes to prove the materialist wrong and convince him that he would be better off if he became a spiritualist.

Spiritual science has nothing to do with such a way of proceeding. It does not wish to lead to a different logical insight from that of other world views. Spiritual science, if it really fulfills its task, must become action based on insight. In spiritual science, knowledge must turn into action, action in the whole cosmic world context. I will explain this by using a few definite examples. Today, when people look at the world naively but with a slight materialist tendency, when they direct their eyes and ears outward, hear sounds, notice colors, experience warmth and similar sensations, they perceive the external material world. Should they become scientists, or merely absorb through popular means what science wishes to represent, they will then form or simply accept certain concepts that have originated through the combination of all the color, sound and warmth elements and others that are to be observed in the external world. Now, there are people who maintain that everything one sees is, in the first place, only an external phenomenon. Yet this idea is generally not gone into thoroughly enough. People see a rainbow, for example. As a result of their education, when they look at the rainbow, they are already convinced that the rainbow is only an apparition, that they cannot go to the place where the rainbow is, neatly put a foot on it and march along the rainbow bridge as if it were a solid object. People are sure that it cannot be done, that the rainbow is merely an apparition, a phenomenon that arises and then disappears again. They are convinced that they deal only with apparitions because they cannot come into contact with this aspect of the external world through their sense of touch and feeling. According to their view, as soon as something can be grasped or touched, it is no longer a phenomenon to the same degree, even though recent philosophy may in some instances claim that it is. In any case, the impressions of the sense of touch, for instance, are intuitively taken as something that guarantees a different external reality than the phenomenal realities of the rainbow.

This notwithstanding, all that our external senses perceive comprises merely a world of phenomena, modified perhaps in respect to the apparition of the rainbow, but a world of phenomena nevertheless. Regardless of how far we direct our gaze, how far we can hear, in whatever is seen, heard or otherwise perceived, we deal only with phenomena. I have attempted to explain this in the introduction to the third volume of Goethe's scientific writings.[4] We deal with a tapestry of phenomena. Whoever makes an effort through experimentation or any combination of pure reasoning to find matter in the realm of appearances is pursuing a dead end.* There is no matter out there. One deals only with a world of phenomena.

This is precisely what the whole spirit of spiritual science reveals: In the external world, one deals only with a world of appearances. An exponent of a current world outlook will therefore conclude that it is wrong to look for matter at all in the realm of phenomena. Anthroposophy cannot agree with this attitude; it must put it differently by saying: Because of the whole configuration of man's mind, he comes to the point where he wants to seek for matter in the moving tapestry of phenomena, to seek out there for atoms, molecules and so on, which are resting points in the phenomenon. Some picture these as tiny, miniature pellets, others imagine them to be points of energy and are proud of the fact; others, prouder still, think of them as mathematical fiction.

What is important, however, is not whether one thinks of them as small pellets, sources of energy, or mathematical fiction, but whether one thinks of the external world in atomistic terms. This is what is important. For a spiritual scientist, however, it is not merely wrong to think atomistically. The kind of concept determining rightness or wrongness may be sound logic, but it is abstract, and spiritual

---

*Note by Translator: The "dead end" alluded to here is the translation of the German expression "Holzweg," literally, "wooden path." Like all such expressions in a language, it springs from real experience. The "Holzweg" is a rough timber road, or a system of such roads, proceeding into the forest and used by woodcutters. It leads nowhere and may dead-end suddenly. Hence, it would be easy to get lost on it.

science has to do with realities. I urge you to take it very seriously when I say that spiritual science has to do with realities!

This is why certain concepts that have become merely logical categories for today's abstract world-view must be replaced by something real. This is why, in spiritual science, we not only say that one who seeks atoms or molecules in the external world thinks in the wrong way; we must consider this manner of thinking an unhealthy, sick thinking. We must replace the merely logical concept of wrongness with the realistic concept of sickness, of unhealthiness. We must point to a definite sickness of soul—regardless of how many people it has seized—which expresses itself in atomistic thinking. This condition is one of feeblemindedness. It is not merely logically wrong for us, it is an expression of feeblemindedness to think atomistically; in other words, it is feebleminded to seek in the external world something other than phenomena which, when it comes right down to it, are on a par with the phenomenon of the rainbow. It is relatively easy for people with other world outlooks to set things straight: they do it by refutation. To have been able to refute something is considered an accomplishment. Yet, in a spiritual-scientific sense, no final conclusion has been reached by refutation; it is important to refer to the healthy or unhealthy soul life, to actual processes expressed in man's whole physical, soul and spiritual being. To think atomistically is to think unhealthily, not merely erroneously. An actual unhealthy process takes place in the human organism when we think atomistically. This is one thing we must become clear about regarding the phenomena of the external world and its character of appearance.

We must also become clear about our inner life. Many people seek the spirit inwardly. To begin with, the spiritual cannot be found in the inner realm of man. Truly objective evaluation of every abstract form of mysticism bears this out. What today is sometimes—nay, often—called mysticism consists of brooding over one's inner self, attempting to seek self-knowledge by introverted brooding. What is discovered by practicing such one-sided mysticism? One certainly finds interesting things. When we look into the human being and find all those inwardly pleasant experiences arising which we call mystical—what are they really? They are just the very things that point us toward material existence. We do not discover matter in the external world where the sense phenomena are found; we come upon matter in our inner being. This brings us to the point where we can characterize these things correctly. Regarded from the most comprehensive point of view, it is the body's metabolism that seethes and boils there within the human interior and which flames up into consciousness as one-sided mysticism, mistaken by many to be the spirit that can be found in the inner self. It is not the spirit, it is the flame of metabolism within man. We find matter not in the external world, we find it in ourselves. We find it precisely through one-sided mysticism. That is why a great many people who do not want to be materialists deceive themselves. They excuse their not wanting to be materialists by saying, "Out there is base matter; I shall rise above it and turn to my inner being, for there I will find the spirit."

Actually, spirit is neither without nor within. Outside are the interweaving phenomena; within ourselves is matter, constantly seething and boiling substance. This metabolic processing of matter kindles the flames that leap into consciousness and form the mystic impressions. Mysticism is the inwardly perceived corporeal matter of the metabolism. It is something that cannot be logically refuted, but must be traced back to actual processes when man yields in a one-sided way to the metabolism.

Just as the belief that it is possible to find traces of matter in the external world indicates feeblemindedness—that is, a real illness of the spirit, soul and bodily being of man—so does one-sided preoccupation with mysticism indicate a corporeal indisposition. It points toward something that sounds somewhat insulting if put bluntly. Yet we must use an expression that is, as it were, spoken from yonder side of the Guardian of the Threshold and means, "Childishness." In the same way that one incurs feeblemindedness through atomistic thinking concerning the outer world, one becomes childish when yielding to a mysticism that wants to feel the spirit in the seething of the inner metabolism.

Childishness, of course, has a good side, too. When we observe the child we see a lot of spirit in it, and geniality in many instances consists in man's preserving the childlike spirit all the way into advanced age. When we look at the world from the other side of the threshold we can see that it is the spirit which, for instance, forms the child's brain, that spirit which accompanies us from the spiritual world when we enter the physical world through conception or birth. This spirit is most active in the child. Later, it is lost. Therefore, the word childishness is not meant as an insult in this instance, it merely denotes that spirit which forms the brain out of a more or less chaotic mass. Later on, however, if this spirit, which actually shapes the child's brain, does not pour itself sufficiently into logicality, into experience, into what life presents; if, instead, it acts in a one-sided manner and excludes the individual physical experiences; if it goes on working in the way it did during the first seven years, then instead of becoming intellectually mature one becomes childish. Childishness is frequently found to be a characteristic of a great many mystics, particularly arrogant ones. They wish to weave and live in that spirit which is really what should be active in the child's organism. They have retained this spirit, however, and, greatly impressed by their own accomplishment, they gaze at it in wonder in their consciousness, believing, in their one-sided, abstract mysticism, that they are perceiving a higher spirituality, when it is only the matter of their own metabolism.

Again, we do not need merely to refute the one-sided mystic if we are really well grounded in an anthroposophically oriented spiritual science. We must show that it is the sign of an ailing constitution of the spirit, soul and body when man broods one-sidedly within his inner being, thereby attempting to find the spirit.

I have drawn these two examples, familiar to you from anthroposophical literature, in order to point out to you how serious from a certain viewpoint matters can become when, leaving the ordinary spiritual life of today, one immerses oneself in anthroposphical spiritual life. There, one no longer deals with something as insignificant as "right" or "wrong." It now becomes a question of "healthy" or "sick" conditions in the organic functions. Thus, on a higher level, something that goes in one direction must be considered healthy, while something going in another direction must be considered sick. I would like you to understand from these implications how spiritual science is an active knowledge; how it cannot stand still on the level of the nature of ordinary knowledge but becomes something real. The process of knowledge, insofar as it expresses itself in spiritual science, is something that actually takes place in the human organism.

In a similar manner we must define the element that lives in the realm of will. When we talk of the realm of will in our age—an age permeated by that grandiose decline we have often discussed—when we speak of what develops into human will impulses and try to define their character, then we say: Man is good or evil. Again, we are dealing with ethical categories—good and evil—which are just as necessary, of course, as logical categories. Yet, from what arises out of the impulses of spiritual science, it is not merely a question of what is meant when one action of man is designated as good and another as evil. When one calls a human action good, even in a karmic connection, it is a question of balancing in some way or other the good with the evil. We refer to something that pertains to an ethical judgment of man.

Whenever we rise into the realm of the spiritual scientific, it is much more a question of recognizing that what is at work there is a certain manner of thinking, feeling and willing for human beings which leads upward to a fruitful development, to progress in evolution. On the one hand, we have abstract goodness. It is of outstanding moral value, but even that is ethically abstract. When it is a matter of spiritual-scientific impulses, however, man must not only do good, or only do the good which lets him appear as an ethically good person. He can do, think or feel only that which advances the world in its development in the external sense world; or he can do something that is not merely evil, leading to an ethical condemnation, but has a destructive effect on the world forces. This was already meant to be indicated in the *Portal of Initiation*,[5] where Strader and Capesius are speaking and the following is pointed out: Everything that is done here in the sense world and is subject to ethical judgments of good and evil turns into phenomena behind the curtains of existence, having either a progressive, constructive effect or a destructive one, leading to decline. Just try to experience this entire scene that is permeated with thunder and lightning, where things are happening in a most realistic manner in the soul world while Capesius and Strader are discussing one or the other matter. Try to re-experience this scene and you will see how what we experience as the ethical sphere here on the physical plane is in reality very different there.

All this is to show you how serious world aspects become in that instance when, upon leaving today's customary way of judging by logical or outward human categories only, one ascends to the realities that confront us when we view the world from the spiritual scientific standpoint. Things become serious, yet they must be mentioned today because the world now demands a new kind of spiritual life. Things are happening in the world today that everyone sees but that nobody wishes to comprehend in their actual significance because one cannot take the step from external abstraction to reality. I want to give you a few other examples.

You find today that you live in a world where, among much else, there exist, for example in the social field, a great many party organizations—liberal, conservative and many other parties. Human beings are unaware of the actual nature of these parties. When they have to vote, they decide on one or the other party. They do not give much thought to what it really is that exists as party policy, pulsating through all of public life. They are incapable of taking these things seriously. There are quite a number of people who, in the nicest superficial manner, repeat all sorts of Orientalisms about the external world as Maya, but when it really comes to doing something in this external world they do not stick to what they repeat so abstractly. Otherwise, they would ask, "Maya? Then these parties must be Maya too. Then what is the reality to which this Maya points?"

If this matter is pursued in a spiritual-scientific way in more detail—and tomorrow we shall go deeper into this topic—one finds that these parties exist in the external world by having programs and principles, that is, they pursue abstract ideas. Everything that lives in the external physical world, however, is always the replica, the reflection of what is present as a reality in a much more intense form in the spiritual world. Here is the physical world (see drawing, red), but everything in it points toward the spiritual, and only above, in the spiritual world, can the actual reality of these physical things be found (red). Down here, for instance, you find the parties (orange). On the earth, they oppose each other, seeking to gather a great number of people under the umbrella of an abstract program. Then what are these parties a

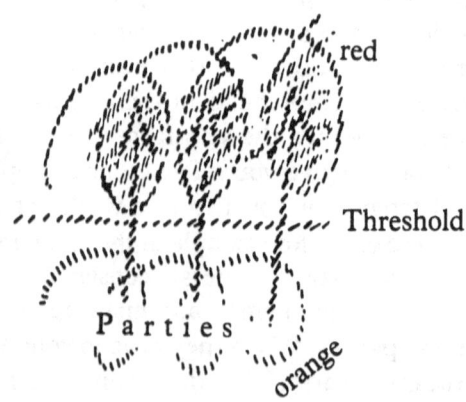

reflection of? What is up there in the spiritual world if these parties down here are Maya? No abstractions exist in the spiritual world above, only beings. Yet, political parties are rooted in abstraction. Above, one cannot profess adherence to a party program; there one can only be a follower of this or that being or hierarchy. There one cannot just subscribe to a program on the basis of the intellect; that cannot happen there. One must belong with one's whole being to another entity. What is abstract down here is being above— that is, the abstract below is only the shadow of beingness above. If you consider the two main categories of parties, the liberal and conservative, you know that each has its own program. When you look above to see what each is a reflection of, then you discover that ahrimanic being is projected here (see drawing, lower part) into the conservative views, luciferic being in the liberal thoughts. Down here, one follows a liberal or conservative program; up there, one is a follower of an ahrimanic or a luciferic being of some hierarchy.

It can happen, however, that the moment you pass across the threshold it becomes necessary really to understand all this clearly, and neither be fooled by words nor succumb to illusions. It is quite easy to assume that one belongs to a certain good being. Just because you call a being good, however, does not make it so. Anyone can say, for instance, "I acknowledge Jesus, the Christ," but in the spiritual world, one cannot follow a program. The whole manner in which the concepts and images of this Jesus, of Christ, fill such a person's soul indicates that it is merely the name of Jesus, the Christ, that he has in mind. Actually he is a follower of either Lucifer or Ahriman, but calls whichever it is by the name of Jesus or Christ.

I ask you: How many people today know that party opinions are shadows of realities in the spiritual world? Some do know and act according to their knowledge. I can point to some who know. The Jesuits, for instance, they know. Do not think that the Jesuits believe that when they write something[6] against anthroposophy in their journals, for instance, they have hit upon something special and logically irrefutable. Refutations are not what counts there. The Jesuits know very well how their refutations could be countered. They are not concerned with a rational fighting for or against something, but with being followers of a certain spiritual being which I do not wish to name today, but which they call Jesus, their leader, to whom they belong. Whoever this being may be, they call it Jesus. I do not wish to go into the facts more closely, but they call themselves soldiers and him their leader. They do not fight to refute, they fight to recruit adherents for the companies, the army of Jesus—that is, the being they call Jesus. And they know very well that as soon as one looks across the threshold, abstract categories, logical approval or disapproval no longer matter, only the hosts following one or the other being. Down on earth it is a matter of mere figures of speech. This is what mankind today is hardly willing to understand, namely, that if we wish to escape from the decline of our age it can no longer be a question of abstractions or merely of what one may think, but that we must deal with realities. We shall begin to ascend to realities when we stop talking about right or wrong and begin speaking about healthy or sick. We begin to rise to realities when we cease talking about programs of parties or world views, and instead speak about following real beings whom we encounter as soon as we become aware of what exists on yonder side of the threshold. It must be our concern today actually to take that serious step that leads from abstraction to reality, from merely logical knowledge to knowledge as deed. This alone can lead us out of the chaos now gripping the world.

The world situation, about which we shall speak tomorrow and the day after, can be judged in a sound way only by someone who examines it with the means that spiritual science is prepared to give him. Otherwise one will be unable to see in the right light the significant, existing contrasts between East and West. All that outwardly manifests itself in visible realities—what else is it but the inherently absurd expression of what lives as thoughts in people's heads? How, then, do these thoughts manifest themselves to us?

To answer this question and to conclude today's presentation, I would like again to call our attention to an obvious example. More than once, I have pointed out how Catholic clerical factions, especially here in Switzerland, are now resorting to a web of lies in order to destroy spiritual science. Those of you who have been here have witnessed a number of examples of what the Catholic Jesuits come up with in the attempt to destroy anthroposophy. Consider the attacks made by Jesuit seminarists with weapons that are certainly not nice. I need not characterize this; those who have not informed themselves can easily do so.

For Switzerland and Central Europe, where these things happen, are all part of the world. So, too, is America. I recently received a magazine published in America in which anthroposophically oriented spiritual science is characterized, while, at the same time, the Jesuits in Europe denounced spiritual science as a threat to the Catholic Church and to Christianity. You know by now that Reverend Kully[7] stated that there are three evils in the world. One is Judaism, the other Freemasonry, but the third—worse than all of them, even worse than Bolshevism—is what is taught here in Dornach. This originates from the Catholic side, and is how anthroposophy is characterized.

What about America? I want to read you a small paragraph from an American publication written at the same time Catholic journals over here printed their view of anthroposophy:

> Just as the Catholic hierarchy has always insisted that the Roman church is the only one with any authority,

—Protestant sects do not come into consideration; according to the Roman church, these sects stand outside the gates; they are viewed merely as a great number of heretics—

> so it is self-evident that the church which Steiner's glib tongue alludes to can be none other than the Roman Catholic church. This assumption is reinforced and indeed any doubt about the matter ceases, when one reads Steiner's other occult books. They all point to the same thing, namely, his writings are purely misleading; the sheepskin of a superficial occultism covering the wolf of Jesuitism.

So you see that in America anthroposophy is taken for Jesuitism, while in Europe the Jesuits strongly oppose anthroposophy as the biggest enemy of the Catholic church. That is how the world thinks today! That, however, is also how people think in Europe where they are living side by side; they are just not aware of it.

The American article concludes with several more nice sentences:

> Steiner claims to be an initiate. That may be; but whether he is of the White Lodge or belongs to the Brothers of Shadow is

something one can only decide when it is realized that he stood on the side of men of "blood and iron" . . . and that a number of his students here (in America) were interned as German spies.

So you see, sometimes the wind blows from the Roman Catholic corner, sometimes from the American side! It just shows you how things are inside the heads of our contemporaries. Yet, from the thoughts hatched inside human heads, there developed what has led into the decline of the present, and the ascent must truly be sought in a different direction from the one where many seek it today.

Tomorrow, we shall continue with the subject.

Lecture II
Dornach, August 7, 1920

Yesterday, I indicated in a certain context what it is that party opinions here on the physical plane actually represent. Since life today is actually ruled by party programs of all different shadings, it is essential to become more aware of their nature. I also mentioned that in this abstract age certain people are inclined at least to profess the maxim: All the phenomena that can be perceived with the senses or comprehended with ordinary reasoning are Maya. Yet, when it becomes a matter of comprehensively applying to life such a general, abstract truth, which people claim to embrace, the vital link connecting most persons' souls to life's realities today tears apart, as it were. Party opinion, too, must be regarded as a reflection of something that is of supersensory nature, having its reality in the spiritual world. It only has its image here in the physical world, just as natural phenomena, for example, even the most complex ones, must be acknowledged as such in regard to physical man. I already explained yesterday that party opinions are formed because a group of people flock to a more or less clearly defined abstract party program. A number of demands are raised; they are supposed to be fulfilled by one or another means; people do one thing or another—mostly, they talk about this or that—to help such programs, such party views, to become reality. Groups of people gathering under the flag of an abstract idea which they hope can be realized, that is what constitutes a party.

One who examines all this more closely, particularly

from the spiritual-scientific standpoint, is not so much concerned with the nature of the programs, because he first has to examine this aspect in its context with the world. His primary concern is with the external phenomenon of people forming into groups.

I said yesterday that when ascending from the physical plane into the higher worlds beyond the threshold, no abstractions exist, no abstract demands exist as posed in party programs. Instead, as soon as one has crossed the threshold, having passed the Guardian of the Threshold without lingering there as so many are inclined to do, one finds that only beings exist beyond the threshold. It is not possible to follow a program; one can only follow one or another being. One cannot group around an abstract idea, only around this or that being. While mankind is in great need of such knowledge, it is precisely this insight that men are vehemently rebelling against. At present, to gather under the umbrella of an abstract idea and to yearn for the realization of abstract programs is dear to people's hearts. To understand that abstract programs can only exist in the physical world and that something that can be grasped in abstract ideas can only be subject to the physical realm is something that people do not wish to comprehend, for it would be troublesome. I draw a line here, denoting the threshold (see drawing). Here are the party groups (*blue circles*) and here, their programs (X). This illustrates how people gather under party programs. Yet, since these programs correspond to certain beings in the supersensory world (orange), all those adhering to a party view link themselves with certain beings of the higher world. What is merely an image in the physical world corresponds to groupings around a being in the supersensible world (*red circles*).

It must be emphasized that this knowledge is an absolute necessity for a prosperous development in the future, because instinct must be replaced increasingly by awareness, if

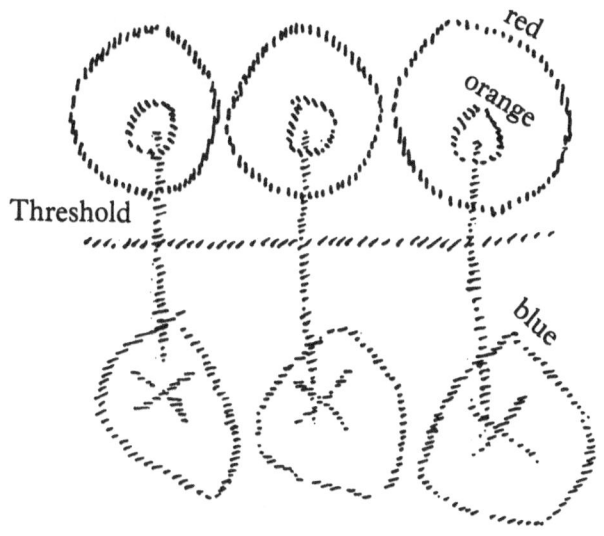

humanity is to progress in its evolution. A remnant of an old instinctive group mentality causes men today to congregate under the umbrella of party programs. They believe that by what they do in such groupings, by massing together and professing to the corresponding program, by actions or mostly words done or spoken for the sake of realizing this program, all possible avenues have been explored. People claim to belong to a certain party, a socialist, a liberal party, a women's movement, or a party of a spiritualistic nature, and so on. If I were to enumerate just a small segment of all the parties existing today, my lecture this evening would become much too drawn out. Because people nurture the belief that the nature of their activities here on the physical plane is fulfilled by what they do and say within a party, they unconsciously follow a being in the supersensory world whom they do not wish to know. Just because men do not know something does not make it any less real. Even if neither the liberal professing to liberal party views nor the one belonging to a women's rights group knows that he follows certain supersensory beings, this does not mean that he is not actually doing so. In reality, he is part of their entourage. Thereby, he counteracts the whole spirit of progressive evolution in our age, for that spirit demands the transformation of all instinctive, unconscious and subconscious elements into fully conscious intentions, into conscious action, word and thought.

Of course, we are also familiar with older groupings of people, groups with racial connections; and we know, too, of other groups, leading even today an ephemeral, shadowy, but nevertheless noisy and deluded existence—the groupings into nations. We know them well! If you recall the lecture cycle on the nature of folk souls which I gave in Kristiania in 1910,[8] you will find that one cannot remain on the physical plane if one wishes to examine carefully these relationships of races and nations. It becomes necessary to ascend into the higher worlds. We outlined in those lectures how such groups of people are held together and guided by beings from the hierarchy of archangels. We saw also that in such groupings into nations, supersensible entities are present among human beings.

If we now picture in our minds the difference between the relationship of racial and national groups of people to their supersensible beings, and the relationship of parties to their supersensible beings, we find that the former are able instinctively to manifest and transform into reality the impulses given them by the beings belonging to them in the higher world. In this case, it is fully justified that instinctive observance of the impulses of these supersensible beings holds sway. Mankind had to struggle to rise above this instinctive obedience to supersensible beings. It goes without saying that humanity could not consciously follow the folk spirits, the archangels, from the beginning, but instinctive forces instead had to permeate this allegiance. In a sense, human beings could only be educated gradually to a conscious state.

The farther back one traces mankind's evolutionary history, the more one discovers that ancient people had a clearly defined, albeit instinctive, awareness in following such supersensible beings as a group, a nation or a race. Certainly, during the middle epoch preceding our present age, such awareness was partially lost. More and more, men had to forgo their knowledge of the supersensible worlds, but the farther we go into ancient history, the more we find that men instinctively interpreted their sense of belonging together as a race by the fact that they recognized a spiritual, supersensible entity as their leader. In former times, even if a human leader was recognized by groups of men, the greatest part of his followers clearly sensed that the folk spirit was embodied in him. They felt that what they beheld as the external human form was in a sense possessed by their supersensible leader. One may view this any way one likes, one may even consider it an old superstition. Those, however, who think differently about so-called superstitions need only wait and see whether, by the year 3000, our zoology, chemistry and botany may not also be viewed as a nineteenth- and twentieth-century superstition by those whose mentality is on par with those who speak of these other matters today as old superstitions.

Now, what is the difference between the way these groups stand in regard to their spiritual guidance, and the position party opinions find themselves in with respect to their spiritual counterpart? The ancients did not have party programs that were derived by outlining abstract ideas. It would have ill behooved a Ghengis Khan or a Timur Khan, and others like them, to present their people with something like an abstract party program such as the present Ghengis Khan, who is called Lenin today, interposes between himself and his cohorts. There is a significant contrast. The great khans of the former Mongols were without programs, but those possessing insight perceived in them the living incarnations of supersensible beings. The great khans of the present, Lenin[9] and Trotsky,[9] carry within their souls an abstract party program, not an awareness of being heralds of a higher being. This makes a considerable difference because it indicates that the yes-men below the leaders in the party affairs have only abstract ideas in their minds and consciously deny to themselves that they are part of the fellowship of a higher spiritual being.

Only a few groups of men do not function on that level. I introduced one of them, the Jesuits, to you yesterday. The Jesuits do not get involved in childish nonsense such as party programs. Read the series of lectures I delivered in Karlsruhe, *From Jesus to Christ*,[10] a series that has somehow come into the hands of the local clergy. There, you can read about the exercises a Jesuit must subject himself to before he can properly assume his post. The Jesuit is not charged with any party program, no demands are dressed up for him in abstract formulations. He is shown through exercises how to follow his spiritual leader; he is trained to know himself to be in the entourage of a supersensible being. This is also the case in a few other more or less secret modern groups. It also holds true for those involved in the major political activities of the West, political activities which are literally, step by step, turning out just as these exponents of certain Western occult politics have envisioned them for a long time. What really matters, however, is that we pay heed to the spirit of progress in our age, that an awareness is regained of the link between man and the spiritual world and of the relationship between all that man does here on earth and events and living beings of that realm. We should seek out those beings in the spiritual world who participate in the constitution and guidance of our world so that we can know into whose following we enter through our various actions. Today one cannot do anything that benefits the actual progress of mankind if, apart from becoming aware of the connection to the spiritual world regarding egotistic inner soul needs, one does not become fully aware that through one's outward actions, expressed for example in party opinions and the like, a connection with the higher worlds is created as well. Spiritual science should not merely reassure our souls, so to speak, concerning the narrowly confined affairs of our individual personality; it is supposed to produce impulses for shaping all of life. This was the recurrent theme of my recent lectures. Humanity has arrived at abstraction and must find its way out of it. We are deeply enmeshed in abstraction, particularly in regard to the so-called practical sides of life, especially in party functions. We must shed this abstract nature if the recent European debacle is not to become a total catastrophe. In all areas, it is a matter of looking in the right direction.

We must above all consider something I mentioned before my trip to Stuttgart to a number of you sitting here. It is something that I would like to repeat today for the sake of the numerous foreign guests who are present, and also because every opportunity must be seized to lend a voice to those ideas that have to pervade human souls in our age. Yesterday I said that what is practiced as spiritual science must be a completely different form of knowledge from the one customarily called knowledge. It must be knowledge that is action. One must be conscious of the fact that in that one strives after spiritual knowledge, one has to do with realities, not mere logical schemes. I also said that people today are used to saying: This person is an advocate of materialism; materialism is wrong; hence, he must be refuted. One believes that something has been proven by refutation. I cited examples of how such concepts of right and wrong must yield to the much more real concepts of healthy and sick in the realm of anthroposophically oriented spiritual science. "Healthy" and "sick" indicate actual conditions in human life. We do not merely recognize right or wrong knowledge, we recognize healthy and sick knowledge. By shedding the proclivity for abstraction we enter deeply into the sphere of concrete reality.

We must consider all this from a still higher perspective. We know from the many books on anthroposophy that man is composed of a soul-spiritual part (blue) and a physical part (red), as illustrated in my sketch. We know that certain

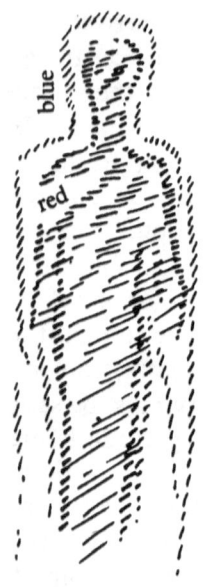

theoretical materialists of the nineteenth century felt that it was entirely unnecessary to speak of soul and spirit elements because they had nothing to do with human knowledge. They held that what dwells as thinking, feeling, and willing in the so-called human soul is merely the result of the physical nervous system and the brain. You know that we must differentiate between this theoretical materialism and the practical materialism which, to this day, still holds sway in a particularly crass form. It differs entirely from theoretical materialism which reached its peak in the nineteenth century. A person who is only used to the ideas prevalent today will disagree with the sort of materialism which maintains that human thoughts, feelings and impulses of will are merely the product of the nervous system and the brain. He feels that this opinion must be refuted. Once he has done so he believes that he has proven that man does not merely consist of a physical body with a nervous system and brain, but that he also has a soul and spirit. Spiritual science, however, cannot be content merely with this refutation, for it is not only a science bent on a logical course, but one dealing with realities. All that lives in the physical world is a replica of the world of soul and spirit, but not only in the sense of a picture one paints upon a wall. The physical world in all its activities and expressions of life is also a reflection of the higher world.

In the case of the human being, we observe that man descends from the soul-spiritual world through conception and birth into the physical realm. The configuration of forces that he brings along from the world of soul and spirit goes to work on the physical body which is taken over from the hereditary stream. This body with its entire configuration is developed by the descending soul and spirit forces. Not only is it developed in regard to its outer form but also in that of its inner functions. Consequently, everything surrounding you in the external sense world can be thought about very well simply with the brain. For, in regard to its faculties, this brain is also an image of soul and spirit. One who only confines himself to the absorption of what the outer sense world or modern science offers thinks only with the brain; he is merely matter that thinks. No objection can be made about this; he is just thinking-matter. Today, the time has come to transcend the state of being merely thinking-matter. One can accomplish this by thinking thoughts that have not been acquired from the sense world, such as anthroposophically oriented thoughts. Those who wish to adhere exclusively to the sense world consider these anthroposophical thoughts to be crazy, unreal and fantastic. This is because the moment they are called upon to think these thoughts they have to make a strenuous effort. They have to break free in their thinking, but they wish to think these thoughts with their brain. Yet, with the brain, one can only think the external physical thoughts, thoughts about the physical realm. One can think about atoms and molecules quite well with this brain in the feebleminded manner I outlined yesterday. By means of this brain, however, it is not possible to think the thoughts presented in such a book as *Occult Science, an Outline*.[11] Thus, anthroposophy is regarded as sheer fantasy. A considerable effort of will must be made to free the soul-spiritual. Then, one can think those thoughts and no longer finds them absurd or fantastic, but in full harmony with life.

In the course of the last centuries, however, since the middle of the fifteenth century, mankind reached a point where, in a sense, it increasingly sank down into itself. It permitted the soul-spiritual aspects to fall asleep and allowed itself to become immersed in the substantiality of the corporeal element. People were content to think merely with the physical brain, to set the brain on an automatic course, just as the brain of the professor, sitting at his lectern, functions automatically. The brain automaton above is followed below by the brain automata of the students. Whole groupings of human beings switched over to this merely automatic materialistic functioning of the brain, namely, physical thinking. They sank deeper and deeper into the corporeality, and did not activate themselves from within to quicken the comprehension for what is derived from the supersensible world. This has been the growing trend among the people of the so-called civilized world since the middle of the fifteenth century. And by the middle of the nineteenth century, just that particular segment of humanity which is called intellectual in the civilized parts of Europe and America had turned into physical thinkers.

Now, when Buechner, Moleschott or the weighty Vogt[12] appeared on the scene and began to think a little, unaware of the fact that behind their own thinking was something that should have given them a jolt, they observed their contemporaries and, interpreting them quite correctly, concluded: Individualism, spiritualism—wrong; it is the brain that thinks! Indeed, it was only brains that were thinking; materialism was quite correct. This is just the secret; the theoretical materialists of the nineteenth century stated nothing wrong; on the contrary, they were right. It would even have been an insult for colleague X to have claimed that colleague Y was endowed with soul and spirit, because in all truth X could only say concerning Y that a brain was thinking automatically. Nineteenth century materialism was therefore basically correct, for it referred to a certain stage of human evolution characterized by the fact that human beings have become body-bound and that their thinking, along with feeling and willing, arises out of materiality. Then even mystics came along who had steeped themselves in their inner being, but these mystics actually only observed the inner seething of substance within the skin until it became flames and flared up into consciousness.

Spiritual science would be in the wrong if it were now to take a merely logical standpoint. It may not say that materialism is incorrect and needs to be refuted. Such refutation is the favorite pastime of our age of abstraction. Spiritual science must do things by its knowledge. Hence, first of all, the mere refutation of materialism does not hold true for people who have become body-bound. Secondly, nothing is accomplished by merely disproving materialism. Instead, it is a matter of motivating people to shake themselves free of the bonds of materiality and to nurture and cultivate thoughts that follow the course of supersensible results of research. Materialism is not to be disproved, it is to be overcome! Human beings must once again become soul-spiritual by awakening their own soul-spiritual being. It must be through action that real materialism is overcome; not through some sort of erroneous refutation. The sad fact is not that materialism is a mistaken world-view, but that it has become right for the recent cultural development. It therefore cannot be a matter of contradicting a false world-view. Rather, it is a matter of giving human beings the means whereby they may perform soul deeds that overcome the body-bound condition of humanity so that they break free of materiality. The knowledge referred to here must be action, not mere logic. This is the issue.

However, people have a hard time comprehending the difference between mere bantering in negations or affirmations while remaining in the sphere of abstract concepts, and the element of action that flows directly from the wellspring of the spirit. Just try to clarify to yourselves that it is one thing merely to refute materialism logically because you are of the opinion that it is wrong, and quite another to facilitate the healing process through spirituality by overcoming the quite real materialism which has gripped mankind as a disease. This difference must be recognized, for what matters today is that spiritual deeds are accomplished and carried into social life as well. There is a fundamental difference between self-satisfaction in a theoretical world-view and the active involvement in knowledge that turns into action.

Attention must be focused on this matter so that we become aware of the difference between anthroposophically oriented spiritual science and other similar endeavors; for this spiritual science must be comprehended as something that actually relates to the tangible forces of ascent and decline in social life.

If we turn our attention to Eastern Europe we can see how the Russian character, concerning which Western and Central Europeans hardly form any proper concepts, is being infiltrated by something that Europeans can very well understand even though they abhor the Leninism and Trotskyism that are spreading out over Russia. There are many people who believe that this Leninism and Trotskyism have something in common with what is to arise eventually in the East. Far from it! These movements only have something in common with the decline of the East and its further ruin. They are purely destructive forces and what is to arise in the East must develop in opposition to these forces of annihilation. Let me illustrate this. Here, in the East, we have something fundamental (see sketch, green) which is given little attention today. During the past few years, Bolshevism, Leninism and Trotskyism have spread over the East as destructive forces (white). What I have indicated here in

green is trying to surface. Leninism and Trotskyism are merely the continuation of the old czarism and, as I have mentioned before, Lenin is the new czar, only in different attire, but basically the same thing. Czarism becomes Leninism, although as czarism it dies in Leninism. In the East, elements opposing czarism have for centuries tried to work their way to the surface. These elements only misunderstand their own existence if they make concessions, in any form, to Leninism and Trotskyism. This is happening all the way into Asia. People have yet to realize the magnitude of the coming upheavals; this is only a lull between the last catastrophe and the next one. The souls sleeping during this respite will have a rude awakening one day; they will rub their eyes and pull off their sleeping caps when the catastrophe continues on its course. Yet, what will work its way to the surface despite all this is the village community. Only a person who understands the nature of the individual village communities comprehends what is trying to emerge in the East as a social constitution. The village community is the only reality in the East. All the rest is but an institution that is perishing.

It will be the task of people in the West to understand the means by which this aggregate of the village community can be organized. Indeed, it is only by the threefold social organism that the crumbling web of Western opinions in single human individualities can also be organized.[13] On the one hand, the threefold social organism must incorporate the individual members of the Eastern village communities. On the other hand, it must save from ruin the crumbling Western organisms that are becoming individualized and which, as aggregates, are splitting up into their separate components.

In regard to the immediate future, the so-called civilized world faces only two options: Bolshevism on one side, and the threefold social order on the other. He who does not recognize that only these two alternatives exist in the near future understands nothing of the course of events on a grand scale. Yet a real comprehension of these matters can only be attained by trying to apply the inner training, acquired by man through spiritual science, to the observation and the management of public social conditions.

Nowadays, one is always truly sorry when one sees people squander their spiritual potential in antiquated party programs. It is sad to see that people are so unwilling to understand that something truly new is needed in order to overcome the last remnant of the old, the ultrareactionism and conservatism, namely, Bolshevism. It will certainly not be overcome through the programs devised by today's statesmen from Middle and Western Europe. For these programs contain nothing of the element that must indwell any impulse of the future; nothing of the new spirit lives in them. Yet, this new spirit is needed. And if this new spirit is not present in the great political and cultural endeavors, then these efforts only serve to let mankind slide into further catastrophes. Likewise, if this new spirit is not contained in the party views, humanity will slip down into more calamities.

It is this that must now be considered and thought over in all sorts of forms. One is asked the following question again and again, "Well, the threefold social order is fine, but how will this or that turn out when this order has actually been introduced into the social organism?" The grocer, for instance, wonders how he will sell his wares when the threefold order comes into being, and so on. Only a while back, here in this auditorium, the question was raised how ownership of a·sewing machine would be affected by the threefold social organism. If one is incapable of tackling the questions on the grand scale and is unable to realize that if they enter generally into the social life, the details will arrange themselves accordingly and assume their proper shape; if one is not in a position to handle the major questions on a grand scale, one will never reach the summit of this age, which is a time of hard trials for mankind. For this reason, it is necessary today to be able to envisage a spiritual metamorphosis of the old cherished notions. In this connection, it is probably still so that if one were to examine the essay books of Middle European students at the end of a school term to see what sort of essays they had written, one would find among a large number of them the following essay title: "Each one must choose his hero in whose footsteps he works his way up to Olympus."[14] Young ladies of private schools, middle and high school students write beautiful essays on this theme. In real life, however, people run after abstract party programs. But even something poetic like the above, which certainly has its justification in the context of the poetic work from which it was taken, must also be read here in a spiritual metamorphosis. We must discover the way of looking into the spiritual world that leads to the spiritual beings under whom we gather together.

What was introduced as a conservative or a liberal program in earlier years and is seen today as a social-democratic or an agrarian program is all so much chitchat. It is all abstract formulation, as are the programs of all women's clubs and vegetarian organizations, etc. The really important thing is that one knows how the world process pulsates through the world's course and that one has an answer for what holds sway in the supersensible sphere above when, for example, a certain group of people gathers together under some program for women's rights and so forth. Today, everything must be raised with the necessary earnestness to the vantage point of the spiritual, supersensible world, for only by viewing the higher world together with the sense world is it possible to find what it is that can truly bring about progress for us in our age of great affliction and bitter trials.

Lecture III
Dornach, August 8, 1920

Today, I should like to add depth to what has recently been discussed by linking it to an old theme already familiar to many of you. Years ago, I once characterized the totality of the human senses.[15] You know that in speaking of the senses one usually lists sight, hearing, smell, taste and touch. In more recent times, even some scientists have been driven to refer to other senses that are located, as it were, further within man, a sense of balance, and so on. This whole concept of the human senses lacks coherence, however, and, above all, inner integration. When we focus on the conventionally enumerated senses, we actually are always dealing only with one part of the human sense organization. It is not until twelve senses are taken into consideration that we have completely explored the sensory organization of man. First of all, we wish today to enumerate and to describe briefly these twelve senses.

Since one can begin anywhere with the enumeration and characterization of the senses, let us start, for instance, by considering the sense of sight. First, we will consider its nature in an external way that everyone can substantiate for himself. The sense of sight transmits to us the surface of external corporeality which confronts us in color, brightness or darkness. We might describe these surfaces in a great variety of ways to arrive at what the sense of sight mediates. If we now penetrate through sense perception into the inner being of external corporeality, if, through our sense organization, we convey to ourselves what does not lie on the surface but continues more into the interior of the body, then this must take place through the sense of warmth. Again, drawn more closely to us, linked to us, inclined towards us from the surface of the corporeality, we perceive certain qualities through the sense of taste. It is located, as it were, on the other side of the sense of sight. When you consider colors, brightness and darkness, and when you consider taste, you will realize that what confronts you on the surface of corporeality is something mediated by the sense of sight. What meets you in the interplay with your own organism, what frees itself in a way through sensation from the surface and moves towards you, is mediated by the sense of taste.

Now let us imagine that you go still further into the inner corporeality than is possible through the sense of warmth and that you focus not only on what permeates a body from outside, but on what inwardly pervades it like warmth, that by its very nature is an inner quality of bodies. You strike a metal plate, for example, and hear its sound. You then perceive something of the substantiality of this metal plate, that is, of the inner metallic essence. When you perceive warmth the sense of warmth conveys to you what permeates the bodies as general warmth but certainly is within them; you perceive through the sense of hearing what is already bound up with the inner nature of things. If you go to the other side, you arrive at something that the body in question exercises upon you as an effect, but which is a much more inward quality than what is perceived through the sense of taste. Smelling is, materially speaking, much more inward than tasting. Tasting comes about by bodies just stimulating, as it were, our secretions which then unite themselves superficially with our inner being. Smelling signifies quite an important change in our inner being, and the mucous membrane of the nose is organized in a much more inward way, materially speaking of course, than the organs of taste.

If you penetrate still further into the interior of the outer bodily nature to where the external corporeality becomes more soul-like, you enter then through the sense of hearing into the nature of the metallic element; you arrive at what is, in a way, the soul of the latter, but you penetrate still further, particularly into the external, when you perceive not only with the sense of hearing but with the word sense, the speech sense. It is a total misconception to believe that with the sense of hearing we exhaust the contents of the word sense. One may well hear something but need not grasp the content of the words to the point where they are understood. Even in regard to the organic organization, a difference exists between the mere hearing of sounds and the perception of a word. The hearing of sound is transmitted through the ear; the perception of a word is mediated through other organs that are as much of a physical nature as are those transmitting the sense of hearing. We also penetrate deeper into the essence of something external when we understand it through the word sense than when we merely hear its inner nature through sound.

Mediation through the sense of touch is still more inward, already quite separate from the objects, much more so than is the case with the sense of smell. When you touch objects, you actually perceive only yourself. You touch an object and if it is hard it presses forcibly on you; if it is soft its pressure is only slight. You perceive nothing of the object, however; you sense only the effect upon yourself, the change in yourself. A hard object pushes your organs far back into you. You perceive this resistance as a change in your own organism when you perceive by means of the sense of touch. You see, do you not, that as we move in there with our inner sensing, we are going out of ourselves. With the sense of taste, we are only outside ourselves to a slight degree; with the sense of sight, we are further outside and on the surface of objects. Through the sense of warmth, we already penetrate into the body. We enter into its being even more so with the sense of hearing, and we are poured into its essence through the word sense. By contrast, we penetrate our own interior already somewhat with the sense of taste; this is more the case with the sense of smell and still more with that of touch. Then, if we press still further into our interior, we come upon a sense which is usually no longer mentioned, at least not often. It is a sense by which we differentiate between our standing up or lying down, and through which we perceive when we are standing on our two feet, that we are in a state of balance. This experience of equilibrium is transmitted by the sense of balance. There, we penetrate completely into our interior; we perceive the relationship of our own inner being to the world outside, within which we experience ourselves in a state of equilibrium. We perceive this, however, entirely within our inner being.

When we penetrate further into the external world than we can by means of the word sense, this occurs through the sense of thought. To perceive the thoughts of another being actually requires another sense organ differing from the mere word sense. On the other hand, if we penetrate still further into ourselves we find a sense that inwardly reveals to us whether we are at rest or in movement. We don't only observe whether we are remaining still or moving simply by virtue of the external objects moving past us; through the extension or retraction of our muscles and through the configuration of our body insofar as the latter changes when we move about, we can inwardly perceive to what extent we are in motion, and so forth. This happens through the sense of movement.

When we confront human beings, we not only perceive their thoughts but the ego itself. The ego, too, is not yet perceived when one merely perceives the thoughts. For the same reason that we separate the sense of hearing from that of sight, we must recognize a special ego sense upon entering into the more subtle configuration of the human organi-

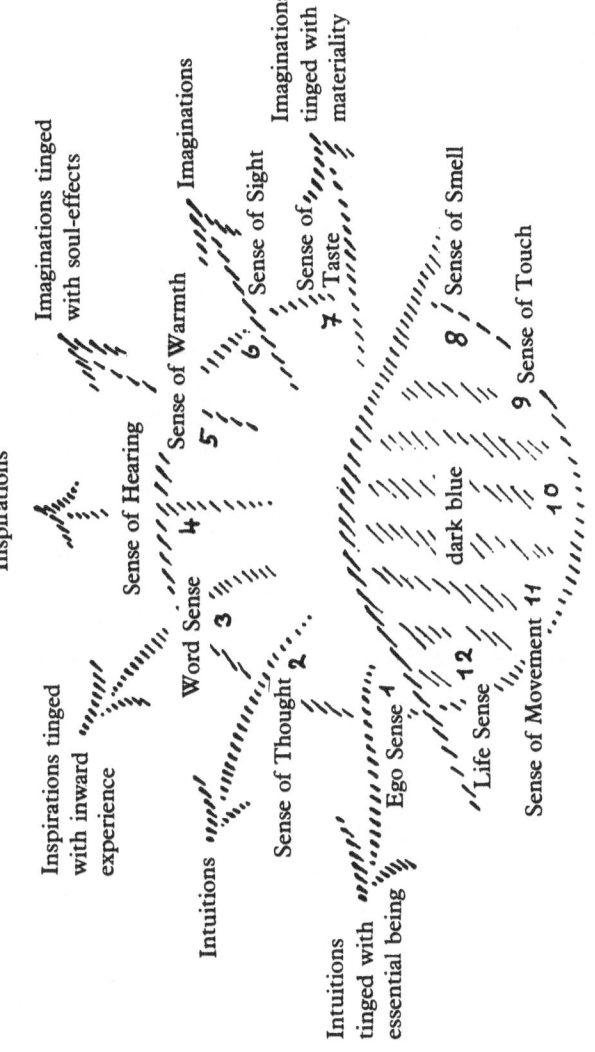

zation—a sense with which to perceive an "I" or ego. When we penetrate the ego of another person with our perception, we go out of ourselves the most.

When do we enter the most into ourselves? When, within the general feeling of life, we perceive what we always have as our consciousness in the waking condition; when we perceive that we *are*; when we experience ourselves inwardly; when we sense that we are we. All this is mediated by the life sense.

Here I have written down for you the twelve senses that constitute the complete sensory system. You can readily see from this that a certain number of our senses are directed more toward the outside, adapted more for penetrating the outer world. When we consider this circle (see drawing) the extent of our sense world, we can say: Ego sense, sense of thinking, word sense, sense of hearing, sense of warmth, sense of sight and sense of taste are the outwardly directed senses. On the other hand, where we predominantly perceive ourselves through the things and where we perceive more the effects of things in us, we have the remaining senses: Life sense, sense of movement, sense of balance, and the senses of touch and smell. They form more the sphere of man's inner being. They are senses that open themselves in an inward direction and, through perception of what is within, transmit to us our relationship to the cosmos (see dark blue area in drawing). Thus, when we have the complete system of the senses we can say: We have seven senses that are directed more toward the outside. The seventh sense is already doubtful—the sense of taste that stands right on the boundary between what refers to the external bodies and what they exercise upon us as an effect. The other five senses are senses that show us completely inward processes taking place within us, which are, however, effects of the external world upon us. Today, I should like to add the following to this systematic arrangement of the senses which is familiar to most of you.

You know that when man rises from the ordinary knowledge of the senses to higher knowledge he is able to do that by emerging out of his physical body with his soul-spiritual part. Then the higher forms of cognition appear, namely, Imagination, Inspiration and Intuition. They have already been described in my *Occult Science, An Outline* and in my book *Knowledge of the Higher Worlds and Its Attainment*.[16] You will easily be able to represent to yourselves, however, that since we have this membering of the senses before us, we are able to arrive at a special characterization of what perception of the higher worlds is. We emerge out of ourselves. But what boundary do we cross over then? If we remain within ourselves, our senses form our boundary. When we emerge out of ourselves, we penetrate outward through the senses. It is, of course, a matter of fact that when our soul-spiritual part leaves the corporeal sheath, it penetrates outward through the senses. We therefore pass through the external senses in an outward direction, through the senses of taste, sight, warmth, hearing, the word sense, the thought and ego senses. We shall see later what we reach when we pentrate inward through the other boundary where the senses open in the inward direction. So we penetrate through the senses to the outside when we leave our bodily boundary, as it were, with our soul-spiritual entity. Here, for example (indicating the drawing), we pass outward by the sense of sight. It signifies that we penetrate outward with our soul-spiritual being by leaving behind our organs of sight. Particularly, when we leave our corporeality through the eyes and move about the world, seeing with our soul eyes, yet leaving the physical eyes behind, we arrive in that region where Imagination holds sway (see drawing).

And when, through initiation, we are actually capable of

penetrating through the eye in particular out into the spiritual world, then we attain to pure Imaginations, imaginations that are pictures, so to speak, just as the rainbow is a picture—pure pictorial imaginations weaving and living in the soul-spiritual realm.

When we pass out through the organ of taste, the pictures appear tinged with the last remnants of material existence. We can say that the imaginations are then colored, literally touched here and there with materiality. We do not have pure images as in the rainbow; we get something that is tinged, containing in a kind of image something like a last residue of material substance. We come to ghosts, real specters, when we depart the physical body through the organ of taste.

When one leaves the physical body through the sense of warmth, one also receives pictures that are tinged. The images that are otherwise as pure as the rainbow, for instance, appear so that they affect our soul in a certain way. This is what their tinge now consists of. In case of the organ of taste, the image becomes condensed, so to speak, into something spectral. On the other hand, when we emerge through the sense of warmth, we also attain to imaginations but to a kind that have sympathetic and antipathetic soul effects, affecting us with warmth or coldness of soul. These images, therefore, do not appear passively, as did the others; they appear warm or cold in terms of the soul.

Now when we leave our body through the ear, through the sense of hearing, we come out into the soul-spiritual world and experience Inspiration. Previously, here (indicating the drawing) we experienced imaginations tinged by what affects our soul. When we leave our body through the sense of hearing, we penetrate into the sphere of Inspiration. Although these senses are directed more to the outside, now, when we leave the body, what passes over from the sense of warmth to the sense of hearing penetrates more into our soul-spiritual inner being, for inspirations belong more to the inner nature of soul and spirit than do imaginations. We are closely touched, not only emotionally, but we feel ourselves permeated by inspirations. Just as we feel ourselves permeated corporeally by the air we inhale, so we feel our soul permeated by inspirations when we enter those regions where they are to be found upon leaving the body through the sense of hearing.

The inspirations are once again tinged when we leave the body through the word sense, the sense of speech. It is of particular importance for anyone who acquires a feeling for the sense of speech to become familiar with this organ, which is just as real in the physical organization as is the sense of hearing. When the soul and spirit leave the physical body through this organ, Inspiration is tinged with inner experience, with a feeling of oneness with the foreign being.

When we leave the body through the sense of thinking, we penetrate into the sphere of Intuition. And when we leave the body through the ego sense, the intuitions are tinged by the beingness of the spiritual outer world.

Thus, we penetrate more and more into the essence of the spiritual outer world as soon as we leave the body with our soul and spirit. More and more, we become aware that everything surrounding us is in fact the spiritual world. Man, however, is in a sense forced out of the spiritual world. What is behind the senses he only perceives when he leaves the body with his soul-spiritual being. What is perceived, however, is molded by the senses. Intuitions appear through the ego sense and the sense of thinking but only as impressions of intuitions; inspirations appear as impressions through the word sense and sense of hearing; imaginations appear through the sense of warmth and sight and, to a lesser degree, through the sense of taste, but toned down, taken and transformed into the sensory element. Schematically, one could sketch it like this. On the boundary is the perception of the sense world (red). If one emerges with one's soul and spirit, one penetrates into the spiritual world (yellow) through Imagination, Inspiration and Intuition. And what is to be perceived in imaginations, inspirations and intuitions is out there. Yet, as it penetrates us, it turns into our sense world.

You see, there are no atoms out there as materialists imagine. Out there is the world of imaginative, inspired and intuitive elements, and as this world affects us, the impressions of it arise in the outward sense perceptions. From this you realize that when we penetrate through our skin which encloses the sense organs to the outside, as it were, but in the various directions in which the senses are effective, we arrive in the objective soul-spiritual world. Through the senses, which we have recognized as the ones opening to the outside, we penetrate into the external world.

Thus you see that when the human being enters into the outer world through his senses, when he crosses over the threshold—which, as you can see from all this, is quite near —in the direction of the external world, he penetrates into the objective world of soul and spirit. This is what we try to attain through spiritual science, namely to enter into this objective soul-spiritual world. We come into a higher sphere by penetrating through our outer senses into that which is covered for us by a veil within the sense world.

Just as we penetrate outward through the outer senses, what happens when we now penetrate into our inner nature through the inner senses, the life sense, the sense of movement, of balance, of touch and smell? Here, the matter is very different. Let us write down these inner senses once again: Sense of smell, touch, balance, movement and life. In everyday life, we do not actually perceive what occurs in the realm of these senses; it remains subconscious. What we do perceive with these senses is already radiated upward into the soul.

If this is the external spiritual world of Imagination, Inspiration and Intuition (see drawing below, red), it shines its rays, in a manner of speaking, upon our senses. Through these senses, the sensory world is produced and placed before us. The external world of spirit is thus moved inward by one degree. What surrounds these senses, however, what stirs below in the corporeality (orange), is not directly perceived. Just as the objective outer world of spirit is not directly perceived but is perceived only in its condition of being pushed into our senses, so we do not directly perceive all that stirs in our body, but only what is pushed up into the

red

orange

soul region. One perceives the soul effects of these inner senses to a certain extent. You do not perceive the life processes themselves. What you do perceive of the life sense is what of it is expressed in a feeling of inner well-being pervading us in waking consciousness, which is something you are not aware of in sleep, and which is only disturbed when something within hurts us. It is the life sense normally radiating upward as a feeling of comfort that is disturbed through pain in the same way as an external sense is disturbed when a person has a hearing loss. Generally, however, the life sense is experienced in a healthy person as a feeling of being comfortable. This feeling of overall well-being, which is heightened after a good meal, and somewhat lowered by hunger, this undefined inner sense of self is the effect of the life sense that has rayed into the soul.

The sense of movement is expressed in what takes place in us when, through contraction and elongation of our muscles, we perceive whether we are walking or standing still, jumping or dancing. We perceive whether or how we are in motion through this sense of movement. When it is radiated into the soul, this sense results in that feeling of freedom which allows man to sense himself as soul, namely, the experience of one's own free soul element. The fact that you experience yourself as a free soul is due to the effects of the sense of movement. It is due to what streams into your soul from the muscular contractions and elongations, just as inner comfort or discomfort is brought about by the results, the experiences of the life sense flowing into your soul realm.

When the sense of balance streams into the soul, the soul element is already considerably detached. Unless we have just fainted and are completely unconscious, just think how little we actually become aware of how we are placed into the world in a condition of equilibrium. How then do we sense the experiences of the sense of balance which radiate into the soul? That is entirely a soul experience. We feel it as inner tranquility, that inner tranquility which brings it about that when I go from one place to another I do not leave behind the being contained within my body but take it along; it remains, quietly, the same. Thus, I could fly through the air and yet quietly remain the same person. This is what makes us appear to be independent of time. I do not leave myself behind today, I am the same tomorrow. This sense of being independent of the corporeality is the inpouring of the sense of balance into the soul. It is the sensation of experiencing oneself as spirit.

Still less do we perceive the inner processes of the sense of touch which, in fact, we project entirely to the outside. We can sense whether bodies are hard or soft, rough or smooth, made of silk or wool. We project the experiences of touch entirely into external space. What we have in the sense of touch is actually an inner experience, but what takes place within remains completely in the subconscious. Only a shadow of it is present in the properties of the sense of touch ascribed to the objects. The organ of the sense of touch, however, causes us to feel whether the things are silken or woolen, hard or soft, rough or smooth. This, too, sends it effects within. It radiates into the soul, but the human being is not aware of the connection of his soul experiences with what the sense of touch attains in touching, because the two aspects are greatly differentiated—namely, what streams to the soul within and what is experienced on the surface outside. What does, however, stream into the soul is nothing else but being permeated with the feeling of God. Without the sense of touch, man would have no feeling for God. What is felt by the sense of touch as roughness and smoothness, hardness and softness, is the element streaming outward. What is turned back as a soul phenomenon is the condition of permeation with universal cosmic substance, with being as such. It is precisely through the sense of touch that we ascertain the existence of the outer world. When we see something, we do not immediately believe that it is indeed present in space; we are convinced of its spatial existence when the sense of touch can grasp it. What permeates all things and penetrates into us also, what holds and bears all of you—this all-pervading substance of God—enters consciousness and is the inwardly reflected experience of the sense of touch.

You are familiar with the outward radiation of the sense of smell. When the sense of smell radiates its experiences towards man's inner being, however, he no longer takes note of how these inner experiences coincide with the external ones. When a person smells something, it is the extension of his sense of smell to the outside; he projects the images to the external realm. This effect is also projected within; man, however, is aware of it less frequently than of the outward effect. Many people like to smell fragrant things and experience the outward emanation of the sense of smell. There are also people who surrender themselves to what grips the inner being as the effect of the sense of smell so intensely that it not only pervades the human being like the feeling of God, but places itself in him in such a manner that he experiences it as the mystic oneness with God.

5. sense of smell   = mystical union with God
4. sense of touch   = permeation by the feeling of God
3. sense of balance   = inner rest, feeling oneself as spirit
2. sense of movement = experience of one's own free soul nature
1. sense of life   = feeling of well-being

Thus you see that if we penetrate to the heart of things as they really are in the world, we must free ourselves from a great deal of sentimental prejudice. Some aspiring mystics will certainly have a funny feeling when they hear what this mystical experience actually represents in relation to the sense world, for it is the experience of the sense of smell sending its effects into the soul's inner being.

There is no need to be alarmed by these things, for we shape all our sensations according to the external, conventional world of semblance, of Maya. And why should one cling to this Maya-conception of the sense of smell, even though the sense of smell is not, to begin with, considered to be a part of the most sublime aspects? Why shouldn't we be able to consider the loftiest aspect of this sense of smell where it becomes the creator of man's inner experiences? Mystics in fact are often inveterate materialists. They condemn matter and wish to ascend above it because it is so lowly. So they raise themselves above it by pleasurably surrendering to the effects of the sense of smell within.

When confirmed mystics of the sensitive kind, such as Mechthild von Magdeburg, Saint Theresa or Saint John of the Cross, describe their inner experiences—and such individuals give quite vivid descriptions—one who possesses a great sensitivity and susceptibility for such matters will "smell" or sense what is going on because of the particular nature of these experiences. The mysticism, even of Meister Eckhart or Johannes Tauler,[17] can be "smelled"—indeed, more adequately—as it can be absorbed sensually through the soul's experience. A person who perceives matters in an occult sense will sense a sweetish aroma within when he considers the descriptions of the mystic experiences, for instance, of Saint Theresa or Mechthild or Magdeburg. When he considers the mysticism of Tauler or Meister Eckhart, he experiences a scent reminiscent of rue, a herb with a tart, but not unpleasant, odor.

In short, the particular and striking thing we discover is that when we move outward through our senses we come into a higher world, an objective spiritual world. When we descend through mysticism, through permeation by the feeling of God, through the inner tranquility of experiencing oneself as spirit, through feeling oneself free in soul, and through inner comfort, then we come to corporeality, to material substance. I have already indicated this to you in these considerations. In terms of Maya, we attain to ever more lowly regions in our inner experience than those we already have in ordinary life. In lifting ourselves outward beyond the senses, we enter into higher regions. This can indeed show you how important it is not to harbor illusions concerning these matters. Above all, we should not delude ourselves into believing that we penetrate into a special kind of spirituality when we descend into our inner being through the mystical sense of union with the divine. No, there we merely descend into what our nose gives us within; and the most beloved mystics offer us something in their descriptions of what they felt within themselves through the sense of smell continuing its effects inwardly.

You can see that when one speaks from beyond the threshold, speaking out of the spiritual world about the affairs of this world, one must speak in words that differ completely from the conceptions about the physical world formed by people from this side. This really should not surprise you, for you ought not to expect the spiritual world beyond the threshold to be a mere duplication of the physical world. Such duplications are experienced in only one instance, namely, when you read the descriptions of the higher worlds given in Islamic esotericism, or those of the Devachan by Mr. Leadbeater.[18] There, with very few changes, you basically come across duplications of this world. People find this very comforting, especially among those who enjoy a certain elegant life style with fine clothes and sufficient satisfaction of their appetites here on the physical plane. One frequently notes that they expect to enter after death into a life style in Devachan that is not unlike the one here, as Mr. Leadbeater does indeed describe it to them. One who has to outline the truths concerning the spiritual worlds is not in this comfortable position. He has to tell you that permeation with the feeling of God leads to the inward projection of smell, and that the mystic actually reveals nothing more to the genuine occultist than the manner in which he smells within. There is no room for sentimentality in an actual observation of the world from the spiritual standpoint. I have mentioned it many times. If one really penetrates into the spiritual world, matters become serious to such a degree that even small things must be given different words from those applied to them here, and that words themselves acquire a completely opposite meaning. To penetrate into the spiritual world does not merely mean describing specters of this physical world. Instead, we have to brace ourselves, for much of what is experienced there is the opposite of the physical world here; above all, it is the reverse of what is pleasant.

I wished to place this viewpoint before you today in order to convey to you a more general feeling for what is really required for our age. When one listens to what is being said today in the West (it is somewhat different the farther east one goes), when a thought is interpreted in a Western manner, one frequently hears the following: One cannot express oneself this way in French; one cannot say that in English. The farther West one goes, the more prevalent is this opinion. But what does this opinion imply other than an attachment to the physical, the condition of having already become rigid in the physical as opposed to the real world? Of what consequence are words? What matters is that people go beyond words and arrive at a mutual understanding. Then, however, one must be capable of freeing the words from objects, but not only this, one must even be able to free the subjective feelings acquired in the sense world. If the sense of smell is looked upon as a lowly sense, this is a value judgment arrived at in the sensory world. Likewise, if the inner correlate of it, namely mysticism, is regarded as something nobler, this is also an opinion gained in the sense world. Considered from yonder side of the threshold, the organization of the sense of smell is of extraordinary significance, whereas mysticism, beheld from beyond the threshold, is nothing so sublime. This is because mysticism is in fact a product of the material, physical world, for it represents the manner in which human beings who actually remain materialistic try to penetrate into the spiritual world. They regard everything existing here on the physical plane as nothing but matter. It is all too lowly, too materialistic for them. If they were to penetrate into what does in fact exist outside, they would come directly into the spiritual world, into the realm of the hierarchies. Instead, they sink into their inner being, fumbling about in the pure matter within their own skin. It is true that this appears to them as the higher spirit. But it is not a question of our penetrating mystically into our body through our soul-spiritual phenomena; rather, it is a matter of penetrating through our material phenomena, the phenomena of the sense world, to the spiritual world, entering the world of the hierarchies, the world of spiritual entities. We shall never arrive at impulses that lead again to an ascent until humanity will accept opinions such as these and permit one to speak in different terms about the world than those of the last four hundred years. Nothing will be gained until our social views are also formulated out of such completely transformed concepts. If we wish to remain in what we have acquired so far, basing our social activity only on that, we shall slide deeper and deeper into decline, into the decline of the Western world.

On what is something like Oswald Spengler's[19] judgment based? It rests on the fact that although he has a brilliant mind, he can think only in terms of the ordinary concepts of the Western world prevalent today. These he analyses and thus figures out—and quite correctly in terms of these concepts—that by the beginning of the third millennium barbarism will have taken the place of our civilization. If one speaks to him of anthroposophy, he turns red in the face, for he cannot stand it. Were he to comprehend what can enter into men through anthroposophy and how it can invigorate them, then he would see that the decline can be prevented only through anthroposophy, that it is the one and only way to come to an ascent again.

Lecture IV
Dornach, August 14, 1920

By linking much of what has been said lately with various outside information, you will have gathered one thing, namely, that our anthroposophical movement has entered a state that expects of each individual seeking to participate in it that he associate this participation with a profound sense of responsibility. I have repeatedly alluded to this but it is not always envisaged thoroughly enough. Just because we are placed within our movement, we must not lose sight of the terribly grave time presently faced by European civilization and its American cousins. Even if we ourselves would say nothing about the connection between the impulses generated by anthroposophically oriented spiritual science and contemporary historical events—although it is certainly necessary to speak up—such events would make an impact on our activities and inevitably would play a part in them without our having a hand in the matter. Therefore, the point is not to shut our eyes to the importance of what is indicated by such words.

From the interpretations put forward by Dr. Boos[20] yesterday, a number of friends who had not realized it before may have understood the necessary and practical connection existing between the idea of the threefold social order and the aims of anthroposophy.

The course of world events presently resembles that of an unusually complicated organism, and from all the various phenomena that must be carefully observed, the direction being taken by this organism becomes obvious. Much is happening today that initially makes an insignificant appearance. These seemingly unimportant events, however, frequently point to something immensely incisive and drastic. Again, things go on that clearly show the extraordinary difficulty we have in freeing ourselves from old familiar ideas in order to rise to a perception of what is in keeping with the times.

You can see from a number of newspaper reports of the last few days[21] the effect made on the world by what issues forth from Dornach, how certain aspects of it are received by a number of persons. We should give these matters serious consideration, recognizing that every word we utter today must be well thought out. We should not say important things without assuming the obligation to inform ourselves about the course of world affairs in what is currently a most complicated organism. At the earliest opportunity I shall have to go into additional matters that have a bearing here; today I only wish to introduce the subject by saying that because of the connections of our movement with general world affairs it is above all else our duty to acquire a full understanding of the fact that we can no longer indulge in any sectarianism whatever in our movement. I have often mentioned this. The present time makes it necessary for us to rely on each individual co-worker, but each one bearing the full responsibility for what he represents in reference to our movement. This responsibility should take the form of an obligation never to say anything that does not appear through inner reasons to have the right relationship to the general course of contemporary world events. Sectarian activities are least of all in harmony with present-day world events. What is to be advocated today must be of a nature that can be represented before the whole world. It must be free in word and deed of any sectarian or dilettante character. We should never allow fear to deter us from sailing between Scylla and Charybdis.

Indicating a certain Scylla, many people may certainly say: How am I supposed to inform myself about what happens today when the course of events has become so complex, when it is so difficult to deduce the inner trends of facts from the symptoms? However, this should not lead to the Charybdis of doing nothing; it should induce us to steer the correct course, namely, to make us aware of our obligation to be in harmony with world events as far as possible, using all available means. It is certainly easier to say: This is anthroposophy and I am studying it; based on it, I engage in a little thinking, researching one or the other subject which I then represent before the world. If we wish to be active in the way indicated above without looking left or right, wearing blinkers in a sense in face of the great, important events of the present, we head straight for sectarianism. We are duty bound to study the contemporary course of events and, above all, to base our observations on the judgment we can acquire through the facts engendered by spiritual science itself.

Throughout the years, facts have been gathered together here for the purpose of enabling each individual person to form a judgment on the basis of these facts. They must not be left out of consideration when, based on our observations, a person wishes to give an opinion about something that is happening today. I mean to refer to this only in general terms, but plan to discuss it in greater detail at the first opportunity.

Today I should like to present something that will supplement what I said last Sunday about the nature of the human sense organism.[22] I shall begin by pointing out a certain contradiction that I have often dwelt on before. On the one hand, without the general public knowing much about it, but nevertheless thinking along these lines, there exists the condition today of being infected in a sense with the natural scientific mode of thinking. On the other hand, we have one type of person still holding to the old traditional belief regarding moral or religious ideals; another has only skepticism and doubt, while for a third it is a matter of indifference. This great contradiction basically stirs and vibrates through all humanity today: How is the inevitable course of natural events related to the validity of ethical, moral and religious ideals?

I now wish to repeat what many of you may have already heard me say.[23] On the one side, we have the natural scientific world concept. It supposes that by means of its facts it can determine something about the course of the universe, in particular, that of the earth. And although it may consider its assertions to be hypothetical, they are imprinted into humanity's whole thinking, attitude and feeling. Our earthly existence is traced back to a kind of nebular condition. It is thought that everything arising out of this nebula is brought about entirely through the compulsion of natural laws. Again, the final condition of our earth's existence is also viewed as being based upon inflexible imperative laws, and concepts are formed about how the earth will meet destruction. Scientists base this kind of view on a widely accepted fundamental concept—even taught to school children —that the substance of the entire universe is indestructible, regardless of whether it is pictured as consisting of atoms, ions or the like. It is thought that at the beginning of earth's formation this substance was in some way compressed, then changed and metamorphosed, but that fundamentally the same substance is present today that existed at the beginning of earth evolution and that it will be present at the end, although compressed in a different form. It is supposed that this substance is indestructible, that everything consists only of transformations of this substance. The concept of the so-called conservation of energy was added to this by assuming that in the beginning there were a number of forces which are then pictured as undergoing changes. Basically, the same sum of forces is again imagined to exist in the final condition of earth.

There have been only a few brave spirits who have rebelled against ideas of this kind. One of these I have often mentioned as a typical example, namely, Herman Grimm,[24] who has said: People talk of a nebulous state, of the nebulous essence of Kant-Laplace, at the beginning of the earth's or the world's existence. From it, it is supposed that everything on the earth, including the human being, has been compressed through purely natural processes. Furthermore, it is assumed that this undergoes changes until it finally falls back into the sun as a cinder. Now, Herman Grimm is of the opinion that a hungry dog nosing around the bone of a carcass presents a more attractive picture than this theory of Kant-Laplace concerning world existence, and that from a cultural and historical point of view people of the future will find it difficult to grasp how it had been possible for the nineteenth and twentieth century to have fallen victim to such pathological thinking. As I said, a few courageous individuals have opposed these ideas. The latter are so widespread today, however, that when somebody like Herman Grimm rejects them, it is said of him: Well, an art historian need not understand anything about natural science. When someone who claims that he is knowledgeable about natural science raises objections, he is regarded as a fool. These ideas are taken today as self-evident and the significance of this attitude is sensed by very few people. For, if this conception has even the slightest justification, all talk of moral and religious ideals is meaningless, for according to this conception these ideals are simply the product of human brains and rise up like bubbles. The social-democratic theorists label these ideals an ideology which has arisen through the transformations of substance, and which will vanish when our earth comes to an end. All our moral and religious concepts are then simply delusions. For the reality postulated by the natural scientific world-view is of a kind that leaves no room for a moral or religious outlook, if this scientific view of life is accepted in the way it is interpreted by the majority of people today. The point is, therefore, that, on the one hand, the time is ripe and, on the other, urgently requires that a world conception be drawn from quite different sources than those of today's education.

The only sources that make it possible for a moral and religious world concept to exist side by side with the natural scientific one are those of spiritual science. But they must be sought where they find expression in full earnestness. It is difficult for many people nowadays to seek out these sources. They prefer to ignore the glaring contradiction that I have once again brought to your notice, for they do not have the courage to assail the natural scientific world-view itself. They hear from those they look upon as authorities that the law of the conservation of matter and of energy[25] is irrefutable, and that anyone who questions it is a mere dilettante. Oppressed by the tremendous weight of this false authority, mankind lacks the courage to turn from it to the sources of spiritual science.

External facts also demonstrate that the well-being of Christianity, a true understanding of the Mystery of Golgotha, depends upon our turning to the sources of spiritual science. The external course of events does indeed show this. Look at the so-called progressive theologians and what is expounded by the more advanced representatives of Christianity. Materialism has, after all, fastened its hold even upon religion. One can no longer understand how the spiritual, divine principle that is indicated by the name, Christ, is united with the human personality of Jesus of Nazareth. For, today, it is only through the sources of spiritual science that insight concerning this union can be acquired.

Thus, matters have reached the point where even theology has grown materialistic and speaks only of "the humble man from Nazareth," of a man who is reputed to have taught something more sublime than others, but in the end is only to be considered as a great teacher. One of the most eminent among present-day theologians, Adolf Harnack,[26] actually coined the words: "It is the Father, not the Christ, Who belongs in the Gospel." In other words, the Gospel is not supposed to speak of Christ, because theologians such as Harnack are no longer familiar with the Christ; they know only the teacher from Nazareth. They are still willing to accept his teaching. The teachings concerning the Father, the Creator of the world, belong in the Gospel, but not a teaching about Christ Jesus himself!

Without doubt, Christianity would continue on this path of naturalization, of materialization, if a spiritual-scientific impulse were not forthcoming for it. In all honesty, no conception concerning the union of the divine and the human natures in Christ Jesus can be derived by humanity from what has been handed down to it by tradition. For that we require the uncovering of new sources of spiritual science. We need this for the religious life and also for giving the social conditions of our civilization the new structure demanded by current events. Above all, we need a complete reconstruction of science, a permeation of all scientific fields with what flows from the spiritual-scientific sources. Without this, we cannot progress. Those who think that it is unnecessary to be concerned with the course of the religious or the social life, the course of public events throughout the civilized world or the accomplishments of science; those who believe they can present anthroposophy in sectarian seclusion to a haphazardly thrown together group that is looked upon as a circle of strangers by the rest of the world, are definitely victims of a grievous delusion.

The sense of responsibility in face of the whole trend of present events underlies everything that I say here. It is the basis of every sentence, of every word. I have to mention this because it is not always understood with all seriousness. If people today continue referring to mysticism in the same manner as was done by many during the course of the nineteenth century, it is no longer in harmony with what the world currently demands. If the content of anthroposophical teaching is merely added to what otherwise takes place in the course of world events, this is also not in harmony with present-day requirements. Remember how the problem, the riddle of human freedom has been the central theme of the studies I have conducted for decades. This enigma of human freedom must be placed by us today in the center of each and every true spiritual-scientific consideration.

This must be done for two reasons. First, because all that has come down to us from the old Mysteries, all that has been presented to the world by the initiation knowledge of old is lacking in any real comprehension of the riddle of human freedom. Sublime and mighty were the traditions those mystery teachers could pass on to posterity. There is greatness and power in the mythological traditions of the various peoples that can indeed be interpreted esoterically, although not in the way it is usually done. Something grand is contained in the other traditions that have as their source the initiation science of ancient times, if only the latter is correctly understood. One aspect is lacking, however; there is no reference at all to the riddle of human freedom in the initiation science of the ancient Mysteries, in the myths of the various peoples—even when they are comprehended esoterically—or in the traditions deriving from this initiation science. For, whoever proceeds from a present-day initiation knowledge, from an initiation of today, knows how present initiation compares to that of the past. He knows that in the course of its worldwide evolution mankind is only now entering the stage of real freedom, and that formerly it was simply not necessary to give to human beings an initiation science impregnated completely with the riddle of freedom. Today, hardly anybody has an inkling of what this riddle of freedom includes, what condition the human soul finds itself in when it becomes clearly aware of the burden it shoulders due to this enigma. New light must be shed, after all, on all initiation knowledge due to this riddle of human freedom. We observe how certain secret societies carry on in direct continuation from former times, some of them being quite strongly involved in present-day life. They only preserve the traditions of the past, however, only imitating and continuing on in the sense of the old practices. These societies are nothing more than mere shadows of the past; indeed, they represent something that can only do harm to mankind if it is active nowadays.

We have to realize that if anyone today were to teach even the loftiest former mysteries, they would be detrimental to humanity. No one who understands the nature of present initiation can possibly teach in a timely sense applicable to our age what was once taught in the Egyptian, Chaldean, the Indian or even those still so near our time, the Greek mysteries. After all, what has been propagated up to now as doctrine concerning Christianity has all been produced by these traditional teachings. What is needed is that we comprehend the Mystery of Golgotha anew based on a new teaching. This is what must be considered on the one side.

On the other side, we see the course of world events. We see how the striving for the impulse of freedom rises up from subconscious depths of the human soul; how, at the present time, this call for freedom resounds through all human efforts. It does indeed pervade them, but there is so much that resounds in human striving that is not clearly understood, that only echoes up from subconscious levels yet to be permeated by clear comprehension. One might say that mankind thirsts for freedom! Initiation science realizes that it must produce an initiation knowledge that is illuminated by the light of freedom.

And these two, this striving of humanity and the creation of a new initiation wisdom, illuminated by the light of freedom, must come together. They must meet in all areas. Therefore, a discussion of the social question must not be based on all sorts of old premises. We can only speak of it when we view it in the light of spiritual science, and that is what people find so difficult. Why is that?

Mankind is indeed striving for freedom, freedom for the individual, and rightfully so. I emphasize: rightfully so. It is no longer possible for human beings to cooperate with group souls in the sense of the ancient group system. They have to develop into individualities. This striving, however, seems to be at variance with what is acquired by listening to initiation science, something that must obviously originate from individual persons in the first place. The ancient initiate had his own ways and means of seeking out his pupils and passing on to them the initiation wisdom, even of gaining recognition for them, himself and his Mystery center. The modern initiate cannot allow that, for it would necessitate working with certain forces and impulses of the group soul nature, something that is not permissible today. Thus, humanity's condition today is one where everyone, proceeding from whatever his standpoint happens to be, wishes to become an individuality. For that reason, he naturally does not care to listen to what comes from a human being as initiation science. Yet, no progress can be made until it is understood that men can become individualities only when, in turn, they accept the content of initiation science from other individualities. This is not only related to isolated ideological questions. It is connected with the basic nature of our whole age and its effects on the cultural, political and economic spheres. Humanity is yearning for freedom, and initiation science would like to speak of this freedom. We have, however, only just reached the point in the stage of mankind's evolution where sound human reasoning can grasp the idea of freedom. Today, we must gain insight into much that can be gathered from anthroposophical literature, and that I should like to summarize in turn from a number of viewpoints. It must be understood today what sort of being man is. All the abstract chatter concerning monism misses the point of true monism which can only be attained after one has gone through much else, but it cannot be proclaimed from the first as a world conception.

Man is a twofold being. On the one side, we have what may be called man's lower nature—the word leads to misunderstandings, but there are few words in our language that adequately express what one would like to convey from the spiritual-scientific standpoint—namely, the physical, corporeal organization of which he consists in the first place. I have described the latter to you in my last lecture in connection with the sense organization. Today, we shall not go into that but refer to it again tomorrow. Those of you, however, who have studied anthroposophical literature to any extent at all, have some idea of man's physical, bodily organization and know that it is connected to the surrounding environment. What constitutes the outside world and dwells out there in the mineral, plant and animal kingdoms, also constitutes us human beings in the physical, corporeal sense. In a way we are its concentration, elevated to a higher level, and figuratively one could say that we are the crown of creation. In the physical, bodily sense we are a confluence of the effects of forces and substances occurring outside and appearing before us through our sense perceptions.

On the other side, we have our inner life. We have our will, our feeling, our thinking and our conceptual capability. When we reflect upon ourselves, we can observe our own will, feeling and thinking, and permeate these with what we call our religious, moral and other ideals. Here, we arrive at what may be termed the man of soul and spirit. Again, this term may easily lead to misunderstandings, but it must be used. We cannot manage if we do not turn the gaze of our soul on one hand to this soul-spiritual human being, and on the other to the physical, corporeal man. But whether we study the facts of nature impartially or contemplate spiritual science, it is necessary to come to the realization: This physical, bodily organization is not really available to what human science, currently existing in the exoteric world, is able to grasp in any sense. If I am to clarify this schematically by means of a sketch, I should like to say: When I condense all that constitutes the human physical organization

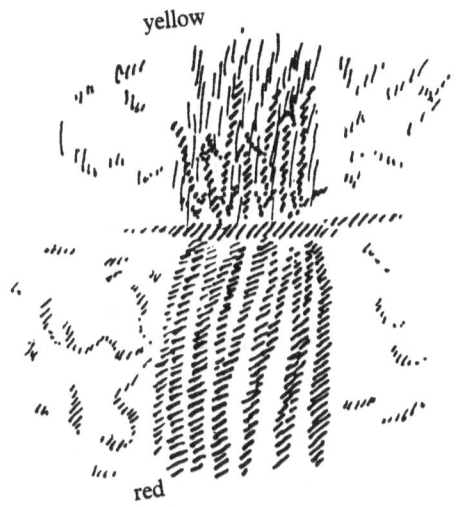

and its connection with the whole surrounding world (red in sketch), this continues to a certain point. I shall indicate that here by a line. Despite all modern amateurish objections of psychology, beyond this point and polarically differing from it, we have what may be called the soul-spiritual nature of man (yellow), that, in turn, is linked with a world of soul and spirit. That world appears most abstract to present-day human beings, because they grasp it only in the sense of abstract moral or religious ideals that have also become increasingly abstract conceptions. Yet, in regard to both sides of human nature, we are obliged to say: What is looked upon today as science encompasses neither man's physical body nor his soul-spiritual nature. We cannot recognize the physical corporeal nature of man. You can discover the reasons for this in my little book, *Philosophy and Anthroposophy*.[27] For, if man would penetrate into himself with inner vision, that is, if he were to look into the very depths of his being and perceive what is going on there, he would be able to do so exactly in the sense of what modern science deems "exact." Then, however, man could not be the being he is today, for he would have no memory, no facility of recollection. When we look at the world, we retain its pictures in our memory. This means that impressions of the world reach only as far as this barrier (see arrow in sketch). From there, they strike back into the soul and we remember them. What thus strikes back out of our own selves into memory conceals from us our physical bodily nature. We cannot look into it, for if we were able to do so all the impressions would merely be momentary, nothing would be thrown back to form recollections. It is only because this barrier acts as a reflector—after all, we cannot look behind a mirror either, its impressions are reflected back to us—that we cannot see inside ourselves. The impressions are reflected back to us unless we rise to spiritual science. If they were not thrown back, we would not have the reflected impressions of memory in ordinary life. We must be so organized as human beings in life that we have memories. Due to this, however, our physical bodily organization is concealed from us. Just as we cannot see through a mirror to what lies behind it, we cannot look behind or under the mirror of memory and behold the way the physical body of the human being is organized.

This is true psychology; this is the true nature of memory. Only when spiritual-scientific methods penetrate through this reflector in such a way that no use is made of the faculty of memory—as I have already mentioned in public lectures—and, instead, without recollection, one works each time with new impressions, only then are the true forms of body and soul discovered.

It is the same in the other direction. If, with our ordinary powers of cognition, we could penetrate the soul-spiritual—concerning which I told you last Sunday that this is what is in truth located behind the world of the senses rather than atoms and molecules—and if we were not prevented, so to speak, by the boundaries and barriers of natural science, there would not be present in us something that is, in turn, needed in human life and must be developed by us between birth and death, namely, the capacity for love. The human capacity for love is created in us by the fact that, in this life between birth and death, if we do not advance to spiritual science, we have to forego penetrating the veil of the senses and seeing into the spiritual world. We retain the capacity of memory only by renouncing all ability to see into our own physical body. Thereby, however, we are exposed to two great illusions. The dogmatic adherents of the natural scientific world conception are at the mercy of one of these illusions. They pay no attention to initiation knowledge and do not come to the realization—in the way I described it to you last Sunday[28]—that behind the veil of the senses there is no matter, no substance, no energy, of which natural science speaks, but soul-spiritual being through and through. Today, I must still reiterate with the same emphasis what I stressed in my commentary on the third volume of Goethe's scientific writings, namely, Goethe's *Theory of Color*.[29] Out there is the world's carpet of colors, the red, blue and green; out there are the other perceptions. No atoms and molecules are concealed behind it all, but spiritual beings. What is driven to the surface from these spiritual beings lives and expresses itself in the world's carpet of colors, in its relationships of sound and warmth and all the other sensations the world transmits to us.

Those, however, who are dogmatic followers of the natural scientific world view today do not realize this. They have no desire to listen to initiation science. In consequence, they begin to speculate about what is hidden behind color, warmth, and so forth, and arrive at a material construction of the world. However well founded this construction may seem—for example, the modern theory of ions—it is always the result of speculation. We must not speculate about what is behind the world of the senses; we may only gain experiences there by means of a higher spiritual world. Otherwise, we must content ourselves to remain within the phenomena. The sense world is a sum of phenomena and must be comprehended as such.

Thus, we are given a picture of nature today which is then extended to include the state of the earth at its beginning and at its end—a picture that excludes an ethical and religious world view for the honest thinker.

The victims of the second illusion are those who look within. For the most part, they do not go beyond what is reflected. Ordinary man in everyday life perceives the effects of memory—he recalls what he experienced yesterday and the day before, indeed, years ago. Someone who becomes a mystic today brings any number of things to the surface from within which he then clothes in beautiful mystical words and theories. But as I have recently pointed out,[30] these things are but the bubbling and seething of his inner organic life. For, if we penetrate this mirror, we do not come to what a Master Eckhart or Johannes Tauler have in their mysticism. We arrive at organic processes of which, it is true, the world today has scarcely any idea. What is clothed in such beautiful words is related to these organic processes as the flame of a candle is related to the flammable material —it is the product of these organic processes. The mysticism of a John of the Cross, of a Mechthild of Magdeburg, or of Johannes Tauler and Master Eckhart[31] is beautiful, but nevertheless, it is only what boils up out of the organic life and is described in abstract forms merely because one lacks the insight into how this organic life is active. He can be no true spiritual scientist who interprets as mysticism the inwardly surging organic life. Certainly, beautiful words are used to describe it, but we must be capable of taking a completely different viewpoint from that of the ordinary world when referring to these matters. We ought not to adopt the humanly arrogant standpoint and say: The inner organic life is the lower form of life. It is not elevated if its effects are designated as mysticism. On the contrary, we are impelled into the life of the spirit when we discern this organic life and its effects and realize that the more we descend into man's individual nature, the more we distance ourselves from the spiritual. We do not approach it more closely. We draw near the spirit only by way of spiritual science, not by descending into ourselves. When we do the latter, it is our task to discover how the collaboration of heart, liver and kidneys produces mysticism; for that is what it does.

I have often pointed out that the tragedy of modern materialism is that it actually cannot perceive the material effects, indeed, that it cannot even reach as far as the material effects. Today we have neither a true natural science nor a genuine psychology. True natural science leads to the spirit, and the kind of psychology progressing in the direction that we have in mind today leads to insight into heart, liver and kidneys, not the abstractions our modern, amateurish psychology speaks of. For what is frequently called thinking, feeling and willing today is an abstract set of words. People lack insight into the concrete aspects, and it is easy to accuse even sincere spiritual science of materialism just because it leads into the nature of material elements in order to guide us in this way to the spirit.

It will be the specific task of true spiritualism to unveil the nature of all matter. Then it will be able to show how spirit is effective in matter. It must be taken quite seriously that spiritual science ought not to be concerned with the mere logicality of knowledge, but has to aim for a knowledge that is action. Something must be done—with regard to knowing. What is taking place in the process of cognizing must become involved in the course of world events. It must be something factual. It was just this that I was trying to indicate last Sunday and the days before. It is a matter of arriving at the realization that spirit as such must be comprehended as a fact; no theory concerning the spirit may be developed. Theories should only serve to lead to living experience of the spirit. This is the reason why it is so often necessary for the true spiritual scientist to speak paradoxically. We cannot persist today in talking in the customary formulations when we speak about spiritual science; otherwise, we come to what an erroneous theosophy has led to. It mentions any number of the members of man's being—the physical man, the etheric and astral being—each one more tenuous than the last. Physical man is dense, the etheric is less so, the astral being is still more rarefied. There are utterly tenuous mental and other states that are increasingly delicate, a perceptible mist, but all remain a mist, they all remain matter! That, however, is not the point. What does matter is that one learns in substance itself to overcome material. This is why one must frequently employ words that have a different connotation from the one customary in everyday life.

Therefore, we must say—and that matter will become

clearer to us tomorrow: Take, on the one side, a person who is of a thoroughly materialistic mind and has been led astray, shall we say, by present-day materialism, one who cannot raise himself to a view of anything spiritual and, according to theory, is a complete materialist, considering any mention of the spirit pure nonsense. Suppose, however, that what he says concerning matter is intelligent and really to the point. This man, then, would have spirit. Although, by means of his spirit, he might uphold materialism, he would have spirit.

Then, let us look at another person who is a member of a theosophical society and adheres to the viewpoint: This is the physical body, then comes the more rarefied etheric body, followed by a more tenuous astral body, mental body, and so on. It does not take much spirit to make these assertions. Indeed, such a theory can be represented with very little spirit. The expounding of such a spiritual world is then, strictly speaking, a falsehood, because in reality one only pictures a material world phrased in spiritual terms.

Where would a person look who is genuinely seeking for the spirit? Will he seek it by turning to the materialistic theorist who has spirit, albeit in a logical manner, or will he turn to the one who makes plausible statements, so to say, but whose words refer only to matter? The true spiritualist will speak of the spirit in connection with the former, the one who represents a materialistic world conception, for there spirit can be present, whereas no spirit need be present in expounding a spiritual view. What is important is that spirit is at work, not that one speaks of spirit.

I wished to say this today merely to clear up certain matters that seem paradoxical. The spirited materialist may be more filled with spirit than the exponent of a spiritual theory who presents it spiritlessly. In the case of true spiritual science, the possibility no longer exists merely to dispute logically about ideological standpoints. It becomes imperative to grasp the spirit in its actuality. That is impossible unless one first comprehends some preliminary concepts such as those of which we have spoken today and shall be considering further tomorrow.

Lecture V
Dornach, August 15, 1920

Today, I would like to develop a number of themes, repeatedly presented as far as some of you are concerned. At the same time, this can serve as a preparation for what will have to be put forth tomorrow[32] concerning the formation of a social opinion. First of all, I would like to call your attention to the manner in which we proceed within the sphere of present-day academic habits when debating and forming opinions concerning ideological questions. Our main concern is to decide logically: What is true and what is false? This specific mode of inquiry is something that must change today. Johann Gottlieb Fichte[33] put it beautifully, "One's philosophy depends on what sort of person one is." Depending on a person's disposition, he forms a more materialistic or a more spiritualistic world conception, a realistic, idealistic, liberal or conservative, socialistic political world outlook; he develops a philistine or a progressive opinion concerning the emancipation of women. I could add indefinitely to the list. Opinions are formed and defended, because a person is convinced he possesses the only right view and that someone with an opposing idea is wrong. Right and wrong is something that is of special interest to us today in forming a judgment.

Already, it can be observed—as we shall make clear presently—that we have the beginning of a transition from these "true and false" judgments to something entirely different. First, however, we shall try to clarify that the concepts of "true" and "false" did not always mean what they do today. Even as late as in the early days of Christianity, but particularly in ancient Egyptian and Chaldean times, not to mention the periods that preceded these cultural epochs, something quite different was applicable when one wished to form a judgment. Logic was not the determining factor. Instead, one had the feeling that if a person judged something in a certain way, it was healthy, if he formed an opinion in another way it was unhealthy. Just as we judge a person to be healthy because he is chubby-faced, rosy and lively, and we judge someone to be sickly because he is emaciated, pale and has circles under the eyes, it was said that an individual was healthy or sick depending on the way he made judgments. In the manner in which he formed opinions one saw an expression of the whole human organization just as we do in the chubby-faced or drawn, pale appearance. A person was judged more on what he himself actually was, less in regard to what he represented concerning his surroundings about which he developed for himself conceptions of right or wrong.

I have already emphasized for a number of you who were present earlier that in a certain sense we must return again to this way of looking at things. The course of human evolution is such that certain instinctive atavistic truths, originating from the ancient Mysteries, gradually became intellectualized and abstract. To this day we live in this intellectualism and abstraction. The new initiation science, on the other hand, which must become established, has to revert in a certain sense to the former feelings in full consciousness. Hence, in the future—although in a more or less distant future in regard to general humanity—there will be no dispute concerning whether an opinion is right or wrong, if one is seriously endeavoring to work for the progress of human civilization. An individual who searches for atoms and molecules in the external world, for example, instead of envisioning spiritual beings behind the sensory veil, will be considered to have pathological opinions. People will think that he is suffering from a certain sickness of soul that can be designated as a mental deficiency. The view that the external world is not a "phenomenon" in Goethe's sense, but that behind it something like real atoms and molecules are concealed, will be considered feebleminded. Such a view will be called mentally defective, not wrong, because people will find that it proceeds from an inadequate organization of the whole human being. It would also not be called wrong but childish to describe what arises out of the body's organization as a result of the metabolic processes—the combustion processes arising from the liver, the stomach, the blood circulation, and so on as an exalted mystic does. It can be described accurately, but it is a matter of what standpoint one takes. However, if you consider it as something other than the flame that flares up out of the organization, it would be childish. I told you earlier that the word "childishness" has a different connotation on the other side of the threshold than on this side.* Seen from this side, you realize that the human being must mature in the course of his life between birth and death. He must become composed and sober and, unlike a child, cannot remain playful in his opinions. If, on the other hand, you look from yonder side of the threshold, from the supersensible world, into the sense world and observe the growing child, you see how the human being descended from the spiritual world and took hold of the physical body. You also see how the entity that descended works in a sculpturing manner on the corporeality in the physical world. In an entirely different way you then see that the soul-spiritual element is much more perfect than what we can develop in the life between birth and death as our reasoning power, our intellectuality.

---

*Note by translator: In German, the word for "childishness" is "Kindskoepfigkeit," literally meaning "child-headedness." Hence the references below to the head, etc.

I indicated earlier[34] that between birth and death the human being is capable of inwardly attaining to the wisdom which, out of the spiritual world, is actively involved in shaping the human brain and the remaining human organization. Philosophers such as Max Dessoir,[35] for example, took exception to these views, because when they mention the soul they have no idea what soul and spirit really are. Speaking from the other side of the threshold, "childishness" signifies that the soul-spiritual element of the child's head works on the physical head. What we designate as genius from this side of the threshold is nothing but the preservation of a portion of this "childishness," "child-headedness," throughout life. It is only when you retain too much of this childlike quality and you cannot realize how it surges forth out of the seething organism as the inner spark, the inner divine element, that genius turns into excessive "child-headedness," namely, "childishness." This is something that must be comprehended quite objectively. We must only be aware that on the other side these matters must be defined differently than on this side and that words receive another meaning. When we use the word "Kindskoepfigkeit" (childishness) on this side of the threshold, we really mean something negative. When we speak from the other side, we refer to the quality that remains in the human being in the right sense as genius and in the pathological sense as false mysticism.

Returning once again from the merely abstract and logical to reality, when we speak of right and wrong, we refer to something that exists in the human being only as thought, a mere discrepancy between the inner and the outer realm, but when we speak of an unhealthy opinion, we indicate that something is amiss in the human being. This is the case, for example, when a person takes the world of phenomena to be a real, material world, or mysticism to be a direct divine manifestation within, instead of the flickering of organic processes. Knowledge, then, must become real, factual. This is the essential point towards which we will have to aim through spiritual science, namely, to refer to the factual, the real, once more, not simply the logical, when we speak of what comes from the human being.

As I said, even in the early ages of ancient Greece such talk of right and wrong in the modern logical sense would not have been understood. The old Greeks still spoke of healthy and unhealthy opinions. The followers of Platonism then gradually worked to achieve logic, which reached its culmination during Roman civilization and continued on into later periods.

Under certain suppositions, the judgments of right and wrong received a special expression in Scholasticism, judgments that were like an echo of the Roman manner of judging, only in a different area. People are still far from regaining a spiritual comprehension of healthy and unhealthy opinions in our time; instead, they aim in a different direction. They have worked their way to something entirely apart from man insofar as making judgments is concerned. When I say that a person makes healthy or unhealthy judgments, I refer to his organization. When I say: This person makes right or wrong judgments, I only make a statement about his condition of soul and frame of mind. I mean thereby that he is either a simpleton or an intelligent person, referring to characteristics of his. Lately, however, people have departed from that. Already, a particular world conception has taken hold of a number of individuals. Among those who will not find their way to spiritual-scientific views, this world conception will become popular, will become ever more and more widespread. It is something that proceeds from America but already makes itself felt in Europe, although, to begin with, only among the philosophers who always seem to have the edge on such matters. I am referring to so-called pragmatism. It is no longer concerned with right and wrong in the sense of the logic of antiquity; it maintains that right is what enables a person to adjust well to life. A person who maintains something that is not advantageous to him in life says that it is damaging. On the other hand, if he holds a view whereby he cleverly masters life, then he calls it something useful. Among pragmatists the views of right and wrong are considered so much nonsense, an illusion that people succumb to. An entire school of philosophy has sprung up around pragmatism which, as I said, is more widely known in America than here, but is also beginning to show up in Europe in a variety of forms. This school of thought regards right and wrong as illusory, and believes that what is termed right or true is called that by man only because he finds it useful in life. Man judges something to be false or wrong because it is detrimental in life. In Germany where people are always the most thorough in such matters, this view has attained quite a special development in the so-called "philosophy of the as-if."[36] It originated from a man by the name of Vaihinger and has already found some popularity—I believe there is even an "as-if science," or something like that. The latter says that we cannot assert that atoms and molecules exist. We can, however, say that we view the world with an eye to what is useful. It serves our purpose to view the world "as if" there were molecules and atoms; it is useful to us to view the world's course "as if" ethical ideals were made manifest. We behold the world "as if" it were ruled by a God. This "as-if" philosophy is quite characteristic of our times. It is the German version of American pragmatism, which has found disciples here. One of them, for example, is Wilhelm Jerusalem,[37] who has gone so far as to say that the qualifications true and false originally signified nothing else but something useful or disadvantageous in a dialectical sense. When we have to conclude that a person has a wrong idea about something, but this simultaneously helps him to become rich and well adjusted to life, these logicians come and say, "His idea is true!" To us, this is an illusion. In reality, it is not true, but something that is beneficial to him, which is then reinterpreted and called "true," and whatever is disadvantageous is then considered incorrect, untrue.

In another passage by Jerusalem we find, "The evaluation, which is subject to an interpretation carried out on the basis of usefulness or disadvantage, and the measure taken on the same basis, is nothing else but the origin of the concepts true and false." Sorry, I cannot read it to you differently; this is philosophical style!

It really is almost legal jargon. You can see that here the concepts true and false are traced back to the concepts of usefulness and disadvantage. This is absolutely the lowest level. We proceed from the concepts of healthy and pathological and then find the concepts of right and wrong. These concepts still adhere to man. One who has a right opinion is called intelligent, one who judges wrongly is called stupid. But it is at least something that still points to human qualities. Now we go so far that we find truth only in what is useful, wrong only in what is detrimental. This is the truth of the present! Philosophers put it into words; others actually judge accordingly, but they are just not aware of it. Particularly social opinions, when voiced, are expressed from none other than this standpoint.

Evolution must again continue in an upward direction. In the presence of truth, we must be capable, first of all, of having a feeling, an inner experience that in itself gives us a feeling of salubriousness. We must feel happy, so to say, in the face of truth and unhappy in the presence of the false. Our age demands this; we must strive for this in a healthy manner. We have to return again to the concepts of true and false, but with feeling.

This is what must take hold of humanity as inner cultural education, namely, that the concepts of true and false are not treated in the complacent manner customary today, but that man can have an inward part in truth and error. When one has insight into the necessities of the present age, it is a very painful experience to see that people have gradually become so indifferent to one or the other assertion. Even just a century ago it was otherwise. You should have seen what would have happened if a gathering of people a hundred years ago had been told that, looked at from the other side, childishness signifies the same thing which, when seen from this side, is designated under certain circumstances as genius! A Wilhelm von Humboldt or a Fichte would have jumped up from their seats, if something like this had been stated in those days when man was still involved with all his being in such matters. Nowadays, people do not get stirred up when one or another contention is made. The souls are asleep today. To have to encounter these sleeping souls at every step is something that fills one who comprehends the demands of our age with pain. As the most extreme result of this drowsiness in our age, we now have the theosophical movement whose followers wish to feel an inner sensual pleasure. They like matters expressed in such a way that everybody is gently calmed down more and more. A harmonious mood is supposed to pour over the listeners, gradually lulling everybody to sleep. It is just then, when everything can slowly, gently drift into sleep, that the eternal mystical element is felt!

This is what must change again. What we require is that our hearts leap in one or the other direction depending on the kind of assertion that is made. Then, one will no longer analyze with mere logical neutrality whether something is right or wrong; one will feel well or sick depending on whether something is experienced as right or wrong. From that point, still further progress will be made. Spiritual science, however, has to cultivate this already now as an impulse that must penetrate us. We will have to return in full consciousness to where we judge something to be healthy or pathological. This, in turn, must affect the will. What we formerly experienced merely as true or false must now fill us inwardly with will, as it were. The will must be aroused. We must will the right; we must not will but rather destroy what is wrong, namely, what is sick. We must aspire to this change of attitude in man. It is not a matter merely of striving for another more or less correct view that can subsequently be discussed. Instead, we must aim for something that makes human beings sound inside. Our understanding must not merely aim for something concerning which we can then say that it is logically correct. It must lead to action, to reality, by means of which something happens.

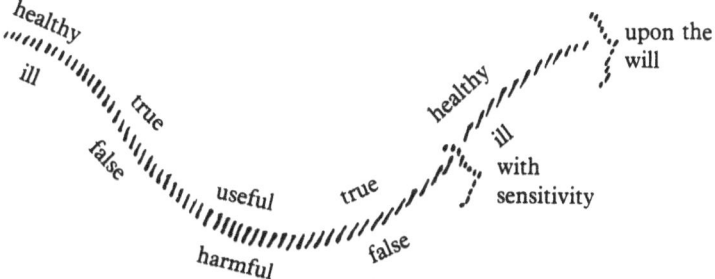

It is life that is of importance to true, genuine spiritual science, not something that inhabits the head of a professor who today sits in his chair and with complete indifference holds forth on truth and error, till his listeners, vexed by his neutrality, could climb the walls. Certainly, many people would now interject that it is precisely inner calmness and tranquility that should be developed. Such matters must not be misunderstood. Inner calm and equanimity signify balance. This implies that we are capable of taking the side of the sound opinion, but that we are also able to develop the counter-forces so as to remain in balance in spite of taking sides, meaning that we always have ourselves under control. Conscious balance differs from drowsy inner balance. Thus, you see that what we call an evolution in the spiritual-scientific sense must reach deeply into the innermost definitions of truth.

We cannot speak about man's faculties between death and a new birth if we do not become accustomed to using words in a way differing entirely from how it is done in today's spoken language. This is why people who wish to hear only what they already know will always find the language of spiritual science unintelligible. For not only would they have to accustom themselves to the fact that the words are connected in a different manner, but that a content other than the one heretofore understood is poured into the words. It is only when we thus look into human evolution that we acquire the ability to judge how different the human being was in prehistoric times; how he will change again in the far-off future, and how we must evaluate what presently confronts us in the intermediary stage of civilization. Our age is beset by such catastrophic dangers that it is imperative to come round to a real knowledge of man. At the moment, we in Europe find ourselves at a most important, decisive point. Most people have no inkling of what goes on in the complicated organism of public life. The present days are almost more significant for the continuing progress of European civilization than the days of the recent past. People will have to get used to the fact that the wish to cling to the old is destructive, and that only a firm reliance on the sources of spiritual science will lead us forward.

It is strange how a certain insight gained beyond the threshold in the spiritual worlds casts its shadows into this arch-materialistic age. Two or three years ago one became the subject of ridicule if one spoke about the impulses proceeding from certain secret Western societies that determine public affairs. I gave a whole series of lectures[38] here concerning these matters, and a number of you will have become familiar with their content in one way or another. One was laughed at, more or less, if one mentioned that public affairs are penetrated by forces whose origin is discovered when light is thrown upon certain secret societies that follow the traditions of ancient initiation wisdom but apply the latter in the wrong direction. Today, in a relatively short time, things have changed. For a week, the sober English press, which is indeed not inclined to lend itself to special capers, has brought out articles about the existence of secret societies. Even though these articles deal with starting points that are nothing but what is put out by the Jesuits, one nonetheless must admit that even though the wind blows from quite the wrong corner it still catches people's attention. What is discussed for as long as a week with, let me say, philosophical exactitude indicates how thoroughly the world has changed in this regard in the last few years. People easily overlook it, however, when the sober English newspapers[39] print compilations today such as the one showing that in 1897 the world was confronted with something like a description of future events. Something like this appears in the columns on the left-hand side while on the right side appear the programs of the Bolshevists and current events. What was known already in 1897 *is happening* today; one can prove philologically that today's events correspond to the earlier forecast. Naturally, people point to these matters journalistically without having any knowledge about the deeper relationships; hardly anybody today senses what he is dealing with. What this is all about is that there are individuals, standing far in the background of what happens on the surface, who with a firm hand manipulate the strings leading to current events. Yet they wish to remain unknown and therefore transfer to others what would otherwise be traced back to them. What is printed is a fabrication, but a carefully calculated one, especially when its origins are considered, because it is designed to lay the blame on others so that mankind will not suspect those who are actually pulling the strings. As I said, today one must feel the responsibility to face what is actually taking place.

I said to many a person in 1914: It is not permissible to write the history of that catastrophic war, which began in 1914, in the manner in which such events were reported in former days simply by drawing on the archives. If one really wishes to comprehend what had its start in 1914, one must resort to the occult means of thinking. One has to clearly understand that some of the most eminent individuals, who participated throughout the civilized world in bringing about the catastrophe, suffered from a benumbed, dimmed consciousness. Such moments, however, when people become benumbed in their consciousness, are the gateways through which the Ahrimanic powers enter the world, governing and taking charge. If a person occupies an important position but in a decisive moment suffers a dimming down of consciousness, he no longer rules; Ahriman rules through him. Spiritual forces extend their rule into this world, such as those I now refer to, in this case of Ahrimanic nature. The events of the last few years can only be understood if one is willing to trace these relationships in a spiritual-scientific manner. It will become increasingly impossible to comprehend what is happening throughout the civilized world unless one is ready to understand it on the basis of spiritual science. One can have endless discussions about what this or that person said three or four years ago or today. It is much more important to acquire a knowledge of man, so that it is possible to ascertain how sound or unsound a person was or is in a given position, for it depends on that whether benign or evil powers affect the course of events. It is true that the path to forming judgments in this manner is not strewn with roses. For when people are asked to form judgments in this manner concerning the interplay in the sense world of supersensory or subsensory powers, they are easily tempted to lose their heads in mystical arrogance.

He who would seriously nurture spiritual science requires not only the normal degree of sobriety but a higher form of it; no rapture, no losing of oneself, but a firm stand on a solid basis of reality. This is what is necessary. We must train ourselves toward reality if we wish to form judgments the way they really ought to be formed today.

It is a great danger when anyone says that his pronouncements are the result of higher powers, not of what he does or does not wish. Nothing but pure egotism is usually concealed behind that. Mystics who present themselves to the world as bearers of this or that spiritual entity are most frequently the biggest of egotists. This is why the first requirement on the path to a certain higher knowledge is the development of sobriety, the ability to disregard everything connected with egotism. As a rule, fanatical ecstasy is nothing but an alternate form of egotism. It is also particularly important that mankind cultivate a certain sense of humor on its path to spirituality. The world is far removed from such humor today. It is extraordinarily difficult to cope with the world's opinion in regard to these matters, because everything possible that organically exists and works in the depths of human nature adds its voice to it.

Perhaps a first indication has now been given of what has to be pointed out in order to stress the significance, on the one hand, of the path leading to the attainment of a spiritual opinion, on the other, the difficulty and danger of this path. We must be aware of these two aspects. We must not allow ourselves to be held back because of the dangers involved; we also may not become remiss in face of the efforts required truly to form an opinion in accordance with the spirit. These points must always be kept in mind when trying to understand the human being of the present time, and without understanding him in this way, we cannot arrive at a social opinion. Man must be comprehended in such a manner that he is fully appraised as a body, soul, and spirit; that not only his life between birth and death but also his life between death and a new birth is taken into consideration. Basically, judgments such as "useful" or "detrimental" have no validity for the life between death and a new birth; the opinions "healthy" or "unhealthy" make much sense for that period. There, human souls are either "healthy" or "unhealthy" due to the after-effects of earthly life. To consider the concepts "useful" or "damaging" as "right" or "wrong" in the sense that we explained it here implies limiting all world observation merely to a physical world. The existence in the present of pragmatism and a philosophy of the "as-if" is the surest sign that people have no feeling at all for what lies across the threshold from the physical world in the spiritual realm.

A sound social view, however, will only come about on the basis of this initiation science. Let us take one area of the threefold social organism, held by some to be the most material and prosaic, namely, the economic life. We know that the economy will only develop in a healthy direction when it evolves under the principle of associations. What does that imply? It means that in the future people will in no way acquire an economic opinion for themselves through the single individuality. Of course, epistemologically it will stem from the individuality, but it will not be developed by it. To a properly evolved mankind of the future, the forming of an economic opinion merely out of the individuality will seem like the famous sleeper, depicted by Jean Paul, who wakes up in the middle of the night in a dark room, sees nothing, hears nothing and ponders what time it is, trying to figure this out by thinking about it. One must be in harmony with one's surroundings if one wishes to form an idea of what time it is in the middle of the night. And in the future, if one is to arrive at an economic opinion—concerning, for example, prices or the number of workers that can be employed in a certain branch of the economy—one will have to be in close contact with associations, those active in production in this particular branch and those representing its consumers. As a result of such cooperation between associations it will be possible to form a valid judgment. The way one tries to do it today, proceeding from the individuality, is the same thing as what the above mentioned fellow does who has been asleep and attempts to calculate all by himself what time it is. Recent events have demonstrated how far one gets with an opinion that is not based on associative experience.

I have cited another example as well to a number of you already. In the nineteenth century learned discussions were held concerning the usefulness of the gold standard. From the middle well into the last third of the nineteenth century, representatives from all the parliaments of Europe, as well as from any number of practical spheres, always found the most beautiful and ingenious reasons why a gold standard should replace bimetalism.[40] What did they expect from it? They claimed that the gold standard would bring about free trade. What happened in reality? Protective tariffs everywhere—the opposite of what all those smart economists and parliamentarians had predicted! I am not trying to be funny when I say "those smart people." They were all in error, yet I am not calling them stupid or foolish; they really were smart. They did not have economic experience, however; for this sort of experience cannot be fabricated out of thin air or developed through pondering. It can only be attained when, in associative connections, one draws lines from one area to another. Just as we read time from the clocks, so, from the associations, we shall read the basics for an economic judgment that can lead to actions.

What does all this signify? You will recall my frequent references to the existence of a kind of group opinion, a group soul, at a certain starting point of our human evolution. Whole groups of people instinctively judged and felt alike. Indeed, languages would never have developed if people had not formed opinions as groups. There even existed a group memory, as I have outlined in some of my lecture cycles.[41] Thus, humanity's evolution proceeded from groups, from instinctive group opinions. It then descended to its lowest point, and will ascend again through associations, but consciously this time by uniting people once again in groups, in associations, that support and base themselves on their economic judgment. People once again ascend to an associative opinion. However, this will be accomplished by the conscious forming of such groups; what happened formerly out of atavistic instinct will now happen in full consciousness. Here, you again have one of the reasons that can be given on the basis of spiritual science for the necessity of a social development such as set forth in my book, *Towards Social Renewal*.[13] These matters are of such a nature that they can be established with absolute mathematical certainty if one turns to the sources of true perception. These matters are not made public recklessly and lightly; they are brought up from the very foundations of human life. What is necessary for our time is to build a world in a social manner that is based on insight into human nature. We cannot advance without that. All talk about leftist or rightist politics, all dogmatic dictates that men have for believing in a God, everything from a philistine to a liberal conception of women's rights, from the most reactionary to the Bolshevistic side, remains empty talk without such insight, talk not founded on reality, which will lead only into destruction. Reality will only be grasped by means of spiritual experience. Then, however, one must be capable of entering into a true knowledge of the human being. One must be able to see how this associative element, required in the economic life with full consciousness, will result in an ascending development in respect to what had been lost of the atavistic, instinctive judgment during the descent. We deal here with true, genuine, totally discernible science; a science that is as lucid as the Pythagorean theorem, even though today's scientists pay little heed to its lucidity. Yet we must have a sufficient number of human beings who can comprehend the crystal clarity of those judgments which alone are the only ones able to lead from our decline to an ascent by drawing on the sources of spiritual science.

instinctive group judgment — *judgment of associations*

I intended all this as a sort of introduction also for tomorrow, when we are going to speak in lectures and free discussions about the forming of social judgments and the necessities of doing that in the present-day social conditions.

Lecture VI
Dornach, August 20, 1920

Once again, I would like to sum up some of what has been presented here recently. We spoke about the external sense world in its relation to the inner world of the human being and I pointed out two things in particular. I stressed that the external sense world certainly must be understood as a world of phenomena and that it is a sign of the prejudices of our age not to interpret correctly this view of the world of phenomena. Certainly, here and there, a certain perception surfaces concerning the fact that the outer sense world is a world of phenomena, of appearances, not one even of merely material realities. Then, however, behind this world of external phenomena, one seeks for material realities, for example, for atoms and molecules, and the like. This search for atoms and molecules, in short, for any world of physical reality standing behind the world of phenomena, is just as if one were to seek for some kind of molecular materiality behind the rainbow that is obviously only an appearance, a phenomenon. This search for material reality in regard to the external world is something quite unfounded, as spiritual science points out from the most diverse directions. We have to understand clearly that surrounding us in what we perceive as the sense world is a world of phenomena, and we may not interpret the sense of touch differently from the other senses in regard to the sense world. Just as we see the rainbow with our eyes without searching for a material reality behind it, accepting it as appearance, so we must accept the entire external world as it is, namely, in the sense I depicted it decades ago in my introduction to the volume on color theory[42] in Goethe's natural scientific writings. The question then is posed to us: What is it that really stands behind this world of phenomena? The material atoms are not behind it; there are spiritual beings behind it—there is spirituality. This recognition signifies a lot, for it means that we admit that we do not live in a material world but in one of spiritual realities.

When we as human beings turn to the external world—this drawing representing, as it were, the boundary of our body—we have here the sense world and behind it the world of spiritual realities, spiritual beings (right side).

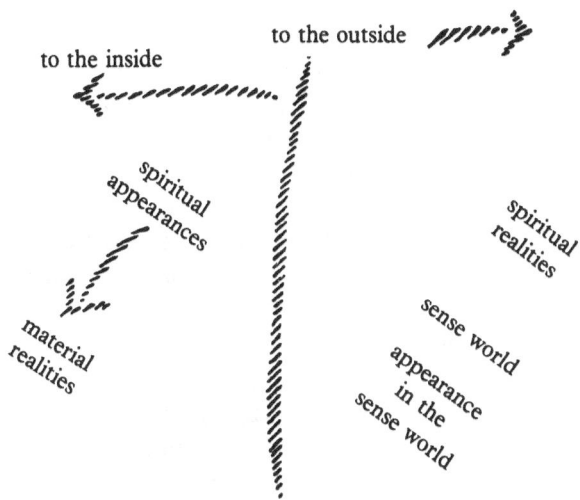

Now, when we turn to the human interior, when we move from our senses inward, we have first of all the content of our world of conceptions, our soul world. If we call the sense world the world of sense phenomena, of sensory appearances, we have the world of spiritual phenomena when we turn from our senses inward (left). Naturally, in the manner in which they are present within us, our thoughts, our conceptions, are not realities, they are spiritual phenomena. Now, if we descend from this soul world still deeper into our inner being, it is all-important for us not to believe that we thereby arrive at a special, higher world, something that mystic dreamers presuppose. There, we actually come into the world of our organism, the world of material realities.

This is why it is important not to assume that by inward brooding one could discover something spiritual; there, we should seek for the constitution of the material human organism. One should not seek for all manner of mystical realities within oneself, as I have pointed out from a number of viewpoints. Instead, behind what pushes up into the soul and thus turns into a spiritual phenomenon, especially when one penetrates more and more deeply into oneself, we should seek the interaction of liver, heart, lungs, and other organs that mystics in particular do not like to hear mentioned. There we become acquainted with the essentially material element of our earthly existence. As I have often emphasized, many a person who believes he has encountered mystical realities by descending deeply into his inner being only finds what is given off by his liver, gall bladder and other related organs. Just as tallow turns into flame, so everything that liver, lungs, heart and stomach give off turns into mystical phenomena when it lights up into consciousness.

The important point is that true spiritual science guides the human being beyond any sort of illusion. Materialists cling to the illusion that they can find physical, material realities, not spiritual realities, behind the sense world. It is the illusion of mystics that when they descend into their own being, they can find, not the world of the material organization, but different kinds of special divine sparks, and such like.

In genuine spiritual science, it is important that we do

not search for material substance in the outer world and do not seek the spirit in the inner world, which initially appears as such through inward brooding.

What I have now said is of significant consequence for our entire world view. Bear in mind that from the time man falls asleep until he wakes up he is outside his physical and etheric bodies with his astral body and I. Where is he then? This is the question we must ask ourselves. If we assume that out there is the world described by the physicists, it makes no sense whatever to speak about an existence of the astral body or the ego outside the physical body. If we know, however, that beyond the sense world lies the world of spiritual realities, out of which the sense world blossoms forth, then we are able to imagine that the astral body and ego move into the spiritual world which lies behind the sense world. Indeed, astral body and ego find themselves in that part of the spiritual world that underlies the sense world. Thus, we can say that in sleep man penetrates into the spiritual world which is the basis of the physical world. Of course, upon awakening, his ego and astral body first penetrate his etheric being and then what constitutes the realm of the material organization.

Clear concepts of an anthroposophical world-view can only be attained if one is able to form intelligible ideas concerning such matters. For, above all, one will not succumb to the illusion of seeking the divine, or the spiritual underlying our human condition, behind the sensory surroundings. There, only that spiritual element is found which, out of itself, brings forth the sense world. As human beings we have our roots in the spiritual world, but in which spiritual world? We have our roots in the very spiritual world that we leave when incarnating into our physical body. We come from the spiritual world that we live in between death and a new birth; through birth or conception we enter this physical existence. The world we inhabit between death and a new birth, which we then leave, is a different spiritual world than this one [behind the sense world], although, because it is a spiritual world, it is related to the latter from which springs forth our sense world. We will not grasp the spiritual world of which we are speaking—I have described it in the lecture cycle, *Inner Nature of Man and the Life Between Death and a New Birth*,[43] namely, the spiritual world we experience between death and rebirth which creates and brings us forth—if we seek it behind the sense world. We will not take hold of it if we seek it within ourselves. There, we only discover the material element of our own organization. We can only grasp it when we leave space altogether. This spiritual world is not within space. As I have often emphasized, we can only speak about it when we base it solely on time, thinking of it as a world of time. Consequently, it goes without saying that all the descriptions we have about this world between death and rebirth can only be images, merely pictures. We must not confuse these pictures, in which we must of necessity express ourselves, with the realities in which we dwell between death and a new birth. It is vital that on the basis of the anthroposophical world-view we do not merely talk about all manner of fantastic things, depicting them in the ancient terminology which actually does not designate anything new. What matters is that we enrich our world of concepts and ideas when we try to send our thoughts into the world in which we live between death and rebirth. Thus we can acquire a most important concept that can also give rise to profound, albeit uncomfortable, reflection. It is this: When we have absolved the life between death and birth, we incarnate here in space. We penetrate into space out of a condition that is not spatial. Space has significance only for our experiences between birth and death. Again, it is important to know that when we pass through the portal of death, not only do we leave the body with our soul, we also leave space behind.

This concept was quite familiar to people until the fourth, fifth, and sixth centuries A.D. Even a person like Scotus Erigena,[44] who lived in the ninth century, was fully conversant with it. Yet the modern age has completely lost the concept of the spirituality underlying human existence, within which the human being lives after death—as was thought then, only after death; today we must say: between death and rebirth we are outside space. The modern age is proud and arrogant regarding its thinking, yet it can actually think only of what is spatial, holding any and every thought in a spatial context. In order to conceive of spiritual matters, on the one hand, we must make the effort to overcome space within our thinking. Otherwise we will never reach the truly spiritual; above all, we will never attain to an even approximately correct natural science, much less a spiritual science. Particularly in our time it is infinitely important to become acquainted with these finer distinctions of spiritual-scientific knowledge. For, what we acquire through such concepts is not just any kind of world concept, any sort of thought concent. The acquisition of a thought content is, after all, the very least we can achieve through anthroposophically oriented spiritual science. For it is one and the same whether someone believes the world consists of molecules and atoms, or if he believes man consists of a physical body, a somewhat less dense etheric body, then something more nebulous and tenuous, the astral body, followed by whatever is next, say, a still finer mental body, or something even more and more rarefied; for one doesn't come anywhere near the etheric body by just thinking of something more rarefied. It is really the same thing whether one is a materialist picturing the world as atoms, or whether one harbors this coarsely materialistic conception that is the common factor of the so-called theosophical society teachings, or whatever they are called now. Something quite different is what really matters, namely, that we become capable of changing our entire soul constitution. We have to make every effort to think about the spiritual in a manner different from the one in which we are accustomed to think about the external sense world. We do not comprehend spiritual science if we conceive of something *other* than the sense world as being spiritual; we enter into spiritual science if we think about the spiritual in a different way than we think about the sense realm. We think of the latter in terms of space. We can think about the spiritual world in terms of time within certain limits, because we have to think of ourselves within this spiritual world. And we are in a certain sense spiritually conditioned by time, in that at a certain moment in time we are transposed from the life between death and rebirth into the life between birth and death.

As I have often indicated, it is this transformation of the state of mind that is so absolutely essential for mankind of today. For how did we become caught up in the calamities of the present? It is because, along with so-called modern progress, humanity has altogether forgotten to admit the spiritual into its conceptions. The theosophical teachings of the so-called Theosophical Society are actually the attempt to characterize spiritual facts in materialistic forms of thought, hence, to drive materialism all the way into the spirit. We do not attain to a spiritual concept merely by calling something spiritual, only by transforming our thinking to what is suited to the sensory realm.

Human beings do not live with each other only in purely spatial relationships that can be constructed by means of what has become the general thinking of natural science. We can no longer develop social concepts based on the present-day world view. The kind of thinking that humanity has become accustomed to owing to natural science cannot lead to a characterization of social life. In this way arise the aberrations we experience today as a variety of social ideologies that only come about because it is impossible to think realistically about the social problems based on the conceptions from which we proceed to regard something as right or wrong. Not until people are willing to penetrate spiritual science will it become possible again to think of the social life in the manner it has to be conceived if further decline is to be halted and, instead, progress is to ensue. The discipline brought about in us by spiritual science is more important than its content. Otherwise we shall finally reach the stage of demanding that spiritual matters be popularized, that is to say, that they be presented in coarsely sensory, realistic terms. Things that must be expressed in a certain manner if one doesn't want to fantasize but to speak of realities, as I have done in our anthroposophical presentations as well as in my book, *Towards Social Renewal*,[45] are found to be not graphic enough. Well, "graphic" is a word that has a peculiar connotation for people today. There are people today who have much to say about this longing of mankind to have everything presented in a *crudely sense-perceptible manner*. This is true all over the world, not just in certain countries.

I found an interesting passage, for example, in a recently published book, *Les forces morales aux Etats-Unis*,[46] written by a French lady. It has the following subdivisions: l'eglise, l'ecole, la femme. The book contains an interesting little episode which demonstrates how, in certain quarters, one tries "graphically" to describe matters pertaining to man's relationship with the spiritual world. The author relates:

> One evening a friend and I strolled down Broadway. I came to a church. A quick glance showed us the place was filled with men only. Offended by seeing this, we avoided moving further inside. A priest clad in a soutane saw us, approached and invited us to come in. Since we hesitated, he asked about our confession. "We are not Catholics," I said. He urged us to enter the church and, index finger pointing upward, he said with conviction "Come here and listen to me. If, for instance,

you wish to travel to Chicago, how would you go about it? You might go on foot, take a car, a boat, or travel by train. It stands to reason that you would choose the fastest and most comfortable means. In this case that's the train. Obviously, if you wish to get to the Garden of God you will choose the religion that will get you there in the fastest and safest way. That's the Catholic religion, which is the express train to Paradise."

The lady telling the story only concluded that she was so perplexed she did not think of telling him that he had forgotten the airplane in his graphic comparison, which he could have mentioned as a still quicker means of getting to Paradise.

You see, here was someone eager to counter people's prejudices, and he chose graphic conceptions. The description of the Catholic Church as the "express train to heaven" is a graphic image. It is indeed the tendency of our time to search for graphic images, meaning concepts that do not make any demands on people's thinking. It is precisely here that we must already discern the gravity of modern life which demands that we do away with such graphicness which turns into banality and triviality, thus pulling man down into materialism in regard to those matters that must be comprehended spiritually. Even in symptoms such as these we have to search for what is needed most in our age. It must be said again and again: Such symptoms cannot be ignored; we cannot afford to go blindfolded through the world, which is an organism asking to be understood by means of its symptoms. For these symptoms contain what we must comprehend if we wish to arrive at an ascent again from our general decline.

At this point, however, it is necessary to see a number of things in the right light. What has actually been produced from spiritual-scientific foundations in *Towards Social Renewal* truly has not been created out of some theory but out of the whole breadth of life, with the difference that this life is viewed spiritually. Mankind today cannot progress if people do not adjust to such a view of life.

I would like to put in here two points taken from life that once again showed me recently how necessary it is to lead humanity today to a life-filled comprehension of reality, but at the same time a spiritual comprehension of reality. Yesterday I read an article by a journalist whose name, so I am told, is Rene Marchand,[47] who, for a long time, was a correspondent for *Figaro, Petit Parisien*, and so on. He participated in the war on the Russian front, being a radical opponent of the Bolsheviks. He then had dealings with the general of the counter-revolution, becoming a follower of it. Overnight, he became converted to the idea of workers' councils, to Bolshevism. From an opponent of Bolshevism, so it says here, he turned into a protagonist, an unreserved supporter of the leadership and the ideology of workers' councils. Here is a man who belongs to the intellectual class, for he is a journalist, who, after all, lives with a deeper understanding of life, a deeper sensitivity for life, who dwells in the old traditions as do most of today's sleeping souls. It is interesting how such a person suddenly realizes: All this will assuredly lead to destruction!—and now the only goal worth aiming at for him appears to be Bolshevism! In other words, the man now perceives that everything that is not Bolshevism leads to ruin. I explained to you how Spengler described this.[48] Marchand sees only Bolshevism; initially, he believes that Bolshevism is merely a Russian affair. Then he discovers something quite different. He feels that Bolshevism is an international matter that must spread over the whole world. He says:

> It now became clear to me that peace can only be restored when the people in all the countries freely take their destiny into their own hands. The principles, hitherto proclaimed by the bourgeois governments merely to deceive the masses, can

only become reality when this new imperialism (that of the Entente powers) has in turn broken down.

He then relates how he has now arrived at the conviction that justice, unity, peace, and law will only rule when the world has become bolshevistic through and through; not till then will reconstruction be possible. This man now sees that all else leads to destruction. And basically he is quite correct in pointing out: If anything outside Bolshevism is to be cultivated further, it must turn into the dictatorship of the old capitalism, the bourgeoisie and its trappings. It must become the dictatorship of people like Lloyd George,[49] Clemenceau,[50] Scheidemann,[51] and so on. If one does not wish for this, if one does not want ruin, there is no other choice but the dictatorship of Bolshevism. He sees the only salvation in the latter.

In a certain sense this man is honest, more honest than all the others who see the approach of Bolshevism and believe they can oppose it with the old regime. At least Marchand sees that all the old ideas are ready to perish. A question arises, however, especially if one stands on spiritual scientific ground and experiences this; for a man like Rene Marchand is an exception. The question forces itself upon one's mind: Where has the man gained knowledge of all this? He has acquired such knowledge where most of our contemporaries have gathered it, namely, from newspapers and books. He does not know life. To a large extent, people living today know life only from newspapers and books. Particularly the people in leading circles know life just from newspapers. Think of all that we have experienced in this regard through newspapers, by means of books! We have witnessed that a few decades ago people still formed their world conceptions by reading French comedies, that they knew the events occurring in a comedy better than what takes place in life. They ignored the realities of life and informed themselves by what they had seen on the stage.

Later, we saw that people formed their view of life based on Ibsen, Dostoevsky, or Tolstoy. They did not know life; neither could they judge the books on the basis of life. Actually, people only assimilated the secondhand life printed on paper. From that they developed their slogans, founded societies for all manner of reforms without any real knowledge of life. It was a life which they knew only from Ibsen or Dostoevsky, or a life they knew in a manner that frequently could not help becoming quite obnoxious to a person when, in all the big cities of Europe, Hauptmann's "Weber" (weavers),[52] for example, was being performed. The lifestyle of weavers appeared on stage. People with no idea of what transpires in life, having seen only its caricature on the stage, observing the misery of weavers on stage, and because it was a time of social involvement—began talking about all sorts of social questions, having become acquainted with these matters only in this way. Basically, they are all people who do not know life except vicariously from newspapers or books such as exist today. I have nothing against the books; one must be familiar with them, but one must read them in such a manner that through them one is able to perceive life. The problem is that we live in an age of abstraction today, abstract demands by political parties, societies, and so on.

This is why it is interesting for me to encounter, on one side, such a realistic man like Rene Marchand who, being a journalist, is simultaneously an oracle for many people. It does not even occur to him to ask if this Bolshevism really leads to a viable life style. For he really does not know life; he only exchanges what he has become acquainted with and finds headed for destruction, with a new abstract formula, with new theories. On the other side, I must now compare a letter I received this morning with these utterances of an intellectual. Somebody who is fully grounded in life, who has experienced precisely what can be experienced today in order to form an opinion of the social condition, wrote to me. He wrote that my book, *Towards Social Renewal*,[13] had become a sort of salvation for him. This man, who has worked in a weaving mill, was thoroughly familiar with the practical aspects. One will only grasp what is meant with the book, *Towards Social Renewal*, when one judges it from the standpoint of practical life. It is a book depicting reality, but derived completely from the spiritual world, as must be the case with anything that is to serve life today. One will only know what is meant if one understands that every line, every word of this book is in no way theoretical, but taken straight from practical life; when one realizes that it is a book for those who wish to intervene actively in life, not for those who want to engage in socialistic chatter and babble about life.

It is this that causes one such pain, namely, that a book steeped in reality is called utopian by those who have no idea of reality. Those who have no inkling of the reality of life, being themselves addicted to literature, view even such a book that is truly taken from life as a piece of literature. Today, the "how" matters more than the "what." Everything depends on our acquiring thought forms that are suitable tools for the comprehension of the spiritual life, for in reality spiritual life is everywhere. We have spiritual realities here in our surroundings as well as from beyond the sense world. It is out of these spiritual realities that social reconstruction must come about, not out of the empty talk appearing in Leninism and Trotskyism, which is nothing but the squeezed-out lemon of old commonplace Western views that have no power to produce any viable kind of social idea. One may well ask: Where are the human beings today who are prepared to comprehend life with the necessary intensity? We will never penetrate life if we are unwilling to view it from the spiritual standpoint. The life between birth and death will not be understood as long as one is not willing to comprehend the life between death and rebirth. If people are unwilling to resort to the spiritual life, they will either become complete materialists or intellectuals living in theories that only enable them to comprehend life after having had it dramatically presented by an Ibsen, a Dostoevsky, or another writer. What matters is that we interpret library presentations as a kind of window through which we look out upon life. This will be possible for us only if we perceive the spiritual world, the world of spiritual entities, behind the sense world; if we finally dismiss all the fantasies concerning atoms and molecules from which present-day physics wishes to construct a world for us. It would follow from these fantasies that the whole present world in fact really consists basically only of atoms and molecules, effectively eliminating all spiritual, and with it, moral and religious ideas. I will say more about this tomorrow.

Lecture VII
Dornach, August 21, 1920

Genuine knowledge of the impulses holding sway in humanity, knowledge that must be acquired if we wish to take a position in life in any direction, is possible only if we attempt to go deeply into the differences of soul conditions existing between the members of the human race. In respect to the right progress for all mankind, it is certainly necessary that human beings understand one another, that an element common to all men is present. This common element, however, can only develop when we focus on the varieties of soul dispositions and developments that exist among the different members of humanity. In an age of abstract thinking and mere intellectualism such as the one in which we find ourselves, people are only too prone to look only for the abstract common denominators. Because of this they fail to arrive at the actual concrete unity, for it is precisely by grasping the differences that one comprehends the former. From any number of viewpoints, I have referred in particular to the mutual relationships resulting out of these differences between the world's population of the West and East. Today, I should like to point to such differentiations from yet another standpoint.

When we look at the obvious features of present general culture, what do we actually find? The form taken by the thoughts of most people in the civilized world really shows an essentially Western coloring, something originating in the characteristic tendencies of the West. Look at newspapers today that are published in America or England, in France,

Germany, Austria or Russia. Although you will definitely sense certain differences in the mode of thinking, and so on, you will also notice one thing they have in common. If this is the Western region here (see sketch), this the middle one and that the Eastern, this common element, which comes to

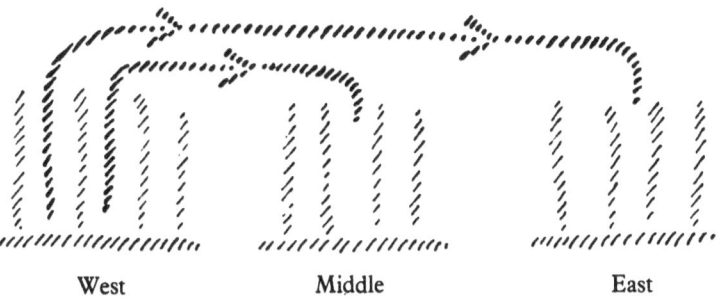

West　　　　　Middle　　　　　East

light everywhere, say, in newspapers as well as in ordinary popular literary and scientific publications, does not derive its impulse from the depths of the national characteristics. In a St. Petersburg paper, for instance, you do not find what arises from the heritage of the Russian people. You do not discover the heritage of Central European peoples by reading a Viennese paper or one from Berlin. The element determining the basic configuration and character (of all publications) has basically arisen in the West, and then poured itself into the individual regions. The fundamental coloring of what has come to the fore from among the peoples of the West has, therefore, essentially spread out over the civilized world.

When things are viewed superficially, one might doubt this; but if you go more deeply into the matters under discussion here, you can no longer doubt them. Consider the attitude, the basic sentiment, the conceptual form, expressed in a newspaper from Vienna or Berlin, or a literary or scientific work from either city. Compare this with a publication from London—quite aside from the language—and you will discover that there is a greater similarity between the publication from London and the book from Vienna, Paris, or even New York or Chicago than there is between the present thoughts and ideas in literary and scientific works from Vienna and Berlin, and the special nuance which Fichte,[53] for example, poured into his thoughts as an enlivening element. I shall demonstrate this to you by citing just one example.

There is a saying by Johann Gottlieb Fichte, the great philosopher who was born at the turn of the nineteenth century, that is so characteristic of him that no one today understands it. It goes, "The external world is the substance of duty become visible." The sentence means nothing less than this. When we look out into the world of mountains, clouds, woods and rivers, of animals, plants and minerals, all this is in itself something devoid of meaning, without reality, it is merely a phenomenon. It is only there to enable the human being in his evolution to fulfill his duty. For I could not carry out my obligations in a world in which I would not be surrounded by things that I could touch. There must be wood, there must be a hammer. In itself, it has no significance and no materiality. It is only the substance of my duty which has become sense-perceptible. Everything outside exists primarily for the purpose of bringing duty to light.

This saying was coined by a man a century ago out of the innermost sentiments of his soul and character as well as his folk spirit. It did not become generally known. When people talk about Johann Gottlieb Fichte today, when they write books about him and mention him in newspaper articles, they only perceive the external form of his words. No one really understands anything about Fichte. You may take everything you find on him today, either literary or scientific, but it has nothing whatever to do with Johann Gottlieb Fichte. It does, however, have a great deal to do with what arose out of the Western folk spirit, and has spread over the rest of the civilized world.

These more delicate relationships are not discerned. That is the reason why nobody even thinks of characterizing in a deep and exhaustive manner the essential feature of what arises from the spirit of the various nationalities. For it is all inundated today by what arises from the West. In Central Europe, in the East, people imagine that they are thinking along their own ethnic lines. This is not the case, they think in accordance with what they have adopted from the West.

In what I am now saying lies the key to much of what is really the riddle of the present age. This riddle can be solved only when we become aware of the specific qualities arising from the various regions of the world. There is, first of all, the East that today certainly offers us no true picture of itself. If untruthfulness were not the underlying characteristic of all public life in our time, the world would not be so ignorant of the fact that what we call Bolshevism is spreading rapidly throughout the East and into Asia; that it has gone far already. People have a great desire to sleep through the actual events, and are glad to be kept in ignorance. It is therefore easy to withhold from them what is really taking place. Thus, people will live to see the East and the whole of Asia inundated by the most extreme, radical product of Western thought, namely Bolshevism, an element utterly foreign to these people.

If we wish to look into what it is that the world of the East brings forth out of the depths of its folk character, it becomes obvious that it is possible to discover the fundamental nuance of feeling in the East only by going back into earlier times and learning through them. For, in regard to its original character, the East has become completely decadent. Forgetting its very nature, the East has allowed itself to be inundated by what I have described as the most extreme, radical offshoots of Western thought. Certainly, it is true that what was once there is still living within Eastern humanity, but today it is all covered up. What once lived in the East, what once vibrated through Eastern souls, survives in its final results where it is no longer understood, where it has turned into a superstitious ritual, where it has become the hypocritical murmurings of the popes of the Orthodox Russian ritual, incomprehensible even to those who believe they understand it. A direct line runs from ancient India to these formulas of the Russian church ritual, which are now only rattled off to the multitudes in the form of lip service. For this whole inclination which thus expressed itself, which bestowed on the Eastern soul its imprint and also does so today in a suppressed form, is the potential for developing a spiritual state of mind that guides the human being towards the prenatal, to what exists in our life before birth, before conception. In the very beginning, the nature of what permeated the East as a world conception and religious attitude was connected with the fact that this East possessed a concept which has been completely lost to the West. As I have said here before, the West has the concept of immortality, not that of "not having been born," of "unbornness." We have the word immortality, we do not have the term "unbornness." This implies that in our thinking we continue life after death, but not into the time before birth. On the other hand, the East possessed that special soul inclination it had that still included Imagination and Inspiration in its thoughts and concepts. By means of this particular manner of expressing the conceptual content of its soul world, the East was far less predisposed to pay heed to the life after death than to that before birth. In regard to the human being it viewed life here in the sense world as something that comes to man after he has received his tasks prior to birth, as something that he has to absolve here in the sense of the task given him. He was disposed to regard this life as a duty set human beings by the gods before they descended into this earthly body of flesh. It goes without saying that such a world conception encompasses both repeated earth lives and the lives between death and birth; for one can quite well speak of a single life after death, but not of only one before birth. That would be an impossible teaching. After all, one who refers at all to pre-existence would then not speak of *one* earth life only, which is something that should be obvious to you upon reflection. It was the way they had of looking up into the supersensory world, which was brought about by the whole predisposition of these Eastern souls, but it was one that focused their attention on the life we lead between death and a new birth prior to being drawn down to earthly life. Everything else, everything in the way of political, social, historical and economical ideas was only the consequence of what dwelt in the soul due to the orientation towards the life between birth and conception.

This life, this mood of soul, is particularly fitted to turn the human soul's gaze to the spiritual, to fill man with the supersensible world. For even here on earth, man considers himself entirely a creation of the spiritual world, indeed, as a being who, in the world of the senses, is merely pursuing his supersensible life. Everything that became decadent in later ages, the establishment of kingdoms, the social structure of the ancient Orient and its very constitution, developed from this special underlying mood of soul. This soul condition might be said today to be overpowered, because it became weak and crippled, because it was only promulgated as if out of what I would like to call "rachitic" soul members, as for example, in the works of Rabindranath Tagore,[54] which are like something that is poured into vague, nebulous formulas. In actual practice, we are today inundated by what expresses itself in Bolshevism as the most extreme, radical wing of Western thinking. The West will have to experience that something it did not wish to have for itself is moving over into the East, that in a not very distant future, what the West pushed off on the East will surge back upon it from there. This will result in a strange kind of self-knowledge.

What has this remarkable development in the East led to? It has led the people of the East to employ the holy inner zeal they once utilized to foster the impulse for the supersensory world and to apprehend the spiritual in all its purity, to accept the most materialistic view of outer life with religious fervor. Even though Bolshevism is the most extreme consequence of the most materialistic view of the world and social life, it will, as it moves further into Asia, increasingly transform itself into something that is received there with the same religious zeal as was the spiritual world in former times. In the East, people will speak of the economic life in the same terminology once used to speak of the sacred Brahma. The fundamental disposition of the soul does not change; it endures, for it is not the content (of the soul) that matters here. The most materialistic views can be approached with the same fervor formerly used to grasp the most spiritual.

Let us now turn and look at the West. The West has given rise to the human soul's most recent development. It must be of special interest to us because it has brought forth the view which, rising like a mist, has since spread over the whole civilized world. It is the manner of conception that already found its most significant expression in Francis Bacon and Hobbes; in minds of more recent times, in the economist Adam Smith, for example; among philosophers, in John Stuart Mill, and among historians, in Buckle, and so on.[55] It is a form of thinking that no longer contains any Imagination and Inspiration in its conceptions and ideas, where the human being is dependent on directing his conceptual life entirely outwards to the sense world, absorbing the impressions of the latter according to the associations of thoughts resulting from that same world. This came to its most brilliant philosophical expression in David Hume, also in other such as Locke.[56]

There is something very strange here that must, however, be mentioned. When we focus on the West, we must pay heed to how minds like John Stuart Mill, for example, speak of human thought associations. The term "association of ideas" is in fact a completely Western thought form, but in Central Europe, for instance, it has been in such comon use for more than half a century that people speak of it as if it had originated there. When psychology is taught in John Stuart Mill's sense, one says, for instance, that in the human soul, thoughts first connect themselves by means of one thought embracing another, or by one thought attaching itself to another, or by one permeating another. This implies that people look upon the thought world and view the individual thoughts as they would little spheres that relate themselves to each other (see drawing). To be consistent

one would have to eliminate everything to do with the ego and astral body, inwardly referring only to a mere thought mechanism, something that a great number of people do, in fact, speak of. The soul of man is disemboweled, as it were. When you read a book by John Stuart Mill with its deductive and inductive logic, you feel as if you were mentally placed in a dissecting room where a number of animals hang that are having their innards taken out. Likewise, in the way Mill proceeds, one feels as if man's soul-spiritual being were disemboweled. He first empties the human being of everything within, leaving only the outer sheath. Then, thoughts do, indeed, appear only like so many associated atomistic formations that coalesce when we form an opinion. The tree is green. Here "green" is the one thought, "tree" is the other, and the two flow together. The inner being is no longer alive; it has been disemboweled and only the thought mechanism remains.

This manner of conceiving of things is not derived from the sense world; it is imposed upon it. In my book, *The Riddles of Philosophy*,[57] I have drawn attention to how a mind such as John Stuart Mill's is in no way related to the inner world; it is simply given to behaving like a mere onlooker in whom the external world is reflected. Our concern here is that this method of thinking brings about what I have often described as the tragedy of materialism, which is that it no longer comprehends matter. For how can materialism fathom the nature of matter—and we have seen that, by going deeply into the human being, one penetrates into the true material element of the earth—if it first eliminates in thought what actually represents matter? In this regard, an extreme consequence already has been reached.

This extreme consequence could easily be traced today if it were not for the fact that people never look at the whole context of things, only at the details. Imagine where it must lead if all the actual inner flexible aspects of the ego are eliminated, if the human being is emptied of the very element that can enlighten him in the sense world concerning the spirit. Just think, where must this finally lead? It must result in the human being feeling that he no longer has anything of the actual content of the world. He looks outside at the sense world without realizing the truth of what we said yesterday, namely, that behind the external world of the senses there are spiritual beings. When he gives himself up to illusions, he assumes that atoms and molecules exist outside. He dreams of atoms and molecules. If man has no illusion concerning the external world, he can say nothing but that the whole outer world contains no truth, that it really is nothing. Inwardly, on the other hand, he has found nothing; he is empty. He must talk himself into believing that there is something inside him. He has no grasp of the spirit; therefore, he suggests spirit to himself, developing the suggestion of spirit. He is not capable of maintaining this suggestion without rigorously denying the reality of matter. This implies that he accommodates himself to a world view which does not perceive the spirit but only suggests it, merely persuading itself into the belief of spirit, while denying matter. You find the most extreme Western exponent of this in Mrs. Eddy's Christian Science[58] as the counterpart of what I described just now for the East. This was bound to arise as the final outcome of such conceptions as those of Locke, David Hume or John Stuart Mill. Christian Science as a concept is, however, also the final consequence of what has been brought about in recent times by the unfortunate division of man's soul life into knowledge and faith.

Once people start restricting themselves to knowledge on one side and faith on the other, a faith that no longer even tries to be knowledge, this leads in the end to their not having the spirit at all. Faith finally ceases to have a content. Then, people must suggest a content to themselves. They make no attempt to reach the genuine spirit through a spiritual science. In their search for the spirit, they arrive at Mrs. Eddy's Christian Science, this spirit which has come to expression there as the final consequence. The politics of the West have for some time been breathing *this* spirit. It does not sustain itself on realities; it lives on self-made suggestions. Naturally, when it is not a matter of an in-depth cure, one can even effect cures with Christian Science, as has been reported, and accounts are given of its marvelous cures. Likewise, all kinds of edifying results can be achieved with the West's politics of suggestion.

Yet, this Western concept possesses certain qualities, qualities of significance. We can best understand them when we contrast them with those of the East. On looking back to the ages when the Eastern qualities came especially to the fore, we find that they were those which, first of all, were capable of focusing the soul's eye on the prenatal life. They were therefore preeminently fitted to constitute what can represent the spiritual part, the spiritual world, in a social organism. Fundamentally speaking, all that we have created in Central Europe and the West is in a certain sense the legacy of the East. I have already mentioned this on another occasion. The East was particularly predisposed to cultivate the spiritual life. The West, on the other hand, is especially talented at developing thought forms. I have just described them in a somewhat unfavorable light. They can, however, be depicted in a favorable light as well, namely, if we consider all that has originated with Bacon of Verulam, Buckle, Mill, Thomas Reid, Locke, Hume, Adam Smith, Spencer, and others of like mind, for example, Bentham.[59] On the one hand, we admit that these thought forms are certainly not suited to penetrate into a spiritual world by means of Imagination and Inspiration, to comprehend the life before birth. Yet, on the other hand, we are obliged to say, particularly when one studies how this manner of thinking has pervaded and lives in our Western science, that all this is especially appropriate for economic thinking; and one day, when the economic life of the social organism will have to be developed, we shall have to become students of Western thought, of Thomas Reid, John Stuart Mill, Buckle, Adam Smith, and the rest. They have only made the mistake of applying their form of thinking to science, to epistemology, and the spiritual life. This thinking is in order when we train ourselves by means of it and reflect on how to form associations, how best to manage the economy. Mill should not have written a book on logic; the spiritual capacity he applied to doing this should have been used for describing in detail the configuration of a given industrial association. We must realize that when anyone today wishes to produce a book such as my *Towards Social Renewal*, it is necessary for him to have learned to understand in what manner one attains to the spiritual sphere in the Oriental sense, and in what manner—although following a much more erratic path—one arrives at economic thinking in the West. For both directions belong together and are necessary to one another.

As far as a view of life is concerned, this Western thinking then does lead to pseudo-sciences like the one by Mrs. Eddy, her Christian Science. We must not, however, look at matters according to what they *cannot* be, but consider what they can be. For unity must come about through the cooperation of all human beings on earth, not by some abstract, theoretical structure of ideas that is simply laid down, and then viewed as a unity.

At this point, one may ask from where in the human organization this particular thinking of Mill, Buckle, and Adam Smith originates. We find that Oriental thinking has basically arisen from a contact with the world, especially when looking back to the more ancient forms of Oriental philosophy. It is a thinking, a feeling, which gives the impression that, out of the earth itself, the roots of a tree grow and produce leaves. In just this way, the ancient Indian, for example, seems to us to be united with the whole earth; his thoughts appear to us to have grown out of earthly existence in a spiritual manner, just as a tree's leaves and blossoms appear to have grown out of it by means of all the forces of the earth.

It is precisely this attachment to the external world in the Oriental person, the absorption of the spirituality, that I have referred to as lying beyond the sense world. In the West, everything is brought out of the instincts, the depth of the personality—I might say, from man's metabolic system, not the external world. For the Oriental, the world works upon both his senses and spirit, kindling within him what he calls his holy Brahma. In the West, we have what arises from the body's metabolism and leads to associations of ideas; it is something that is particularly suited to characterize the economic life, something that does not apply until the next earth incarnation. For, with the exception of the head, what we bear as our physical organism is something that does not find its true expression, as we have outlined, until the following life on earth. We have been given our head from our previous earth life; our limbs and our metabolic system are borne by us into the next earthly incarnation. This is a metamorphosis from one life on earth to the next. Hence, in the West, people think with something that only becomes mature in the following earth life. For this reason, Western thinking is particularly predisposed to focus on the life after death, to speak of immortality, not of eternity, not to know the term, "unbornness," but only the word, "immortality." It is the West which represents life after death as something that the human being should above all else be concerned about. Yet, even now, something I might call radical, but in a radical sense something noble, is preparing itself in the West out of the totally materialistic culture. One with the faculty to look a little more deeply into what is thus trying to evolve makes a strange discovery. Although people strive in the most intimate way for life after death, for some kind of immortality, hence, for an egotistic life after death, they strive in such a manner that, out of this effort, something special will develop. While a large part of humanity still harbors an illusion in this regard, something quite remarkable is, oddly enough, developing in the West. Since individual elements of the ideas concerning life after death being developed by the West are reflected to a certain extent in a great majority of Europeans, they, too, have especially perfected this preoccupation with the postmortem life. The European, however, would prefer to say, "Well, my religion promises me a life after death, but in this transitory, unsatisfactory, merely material earth life I need make no effort to secure the immortality of my soul. Christ died to make me immortal; I need not strive for immortality. It is mine once and for all; Christ makes me immortal."—or something to that effect.

In the West, particularly in America, something different is preparing itself. Out of the most diverse, occasionally the most bizarre and trivial religious world conceptions, we see something trying to arise which, although it has quite materialistic forms, is nevertheless connected with something that will be a part of life in the future, particularly in regard to this world-view of immortality. Among certain sects in America, the belief is prevalent that one cannot survive at all after death if one has made no effort in this earthly life, if one has not accomplished something whereby one acquires this life after death. A judgment concerning good and evil is envisioned after death that does not merely follow the pattern of earthly truth. He who makes no effort here on earth to bear through the portals of death what he has developed in his soul will be diffused and scattered in the cosmic all. What a person wishes to carry with him through death must be developed here. A man dies the second death of the soul—to use the saying of Paul—who does not provide here for his soul to become immortal. This is something that is definitely developing in the West as a world concept in place of the leisurely, passive, awaiting what will happen after death. It is something that is emerging in certain American sects. Perhaps today it is still little noticed, but there is a great deal of feeling in favor of viewing life here in a moral sense, and to arrange the conduct of life in such a manner that by means of what one does here, something is carried through the gate of death.

As I said, in the East, the particular attention to the life before birth developed long ago. This made it possible for life on earth to be viewed as a continuation of this prenatal, supersensory life in the spirit. Earthly life thus received its content, not out of itself, but out of the spiritual life. In the West, an attitude is developing today for the future that will have nothing to do with a passive, indifferent life of waiting here for death because the life beyond is guaranteed; instead, the knowledge is growing that man carries nothing through the portal of death unless care is taken on earth to make something out of what one already has here.

Thus, Western thinking is adapted, on the one hand, to organizing economic matters within the social organism; on the other hand, it is suited to develop further the one-sided doctrine of life after death. This is why spiritualism has had a special opportunity for developing in the West, and from there, could invade the rest of the world. After all, spiritualism was only devised to give a sort of guarantee of immortality to those who could no longer attain to any conviction concerning immortality by means of any kind of inner development. For, in most instances, a person actually becomes a spiritualist in order to receive by some means or the other the certain guarantee that he is immortal after death.

Between these two worlds lies something that is implied in Fichte's words, "The external world is the substance of my duty become visible." As I said before, people really have no understanding for this mode of thinking, and what is written today about Fichte could well be compared to what a blind man might say about color. Particularly in the last few years, a tremendous amount of talking and lecturing has been done about this saying by Fichte, but it was all accomplished in such a way that one is disposed to say that Fichte, that out-and-out Central European mind, has really been americanized by the German newspapers and writers of literature. One is confronted with americanized versions of Fichte. There, we find the nuance of human soul life which, in a special way, is supposed to develop the middle member of the social organism, the one that arises from the relationship of man to man. It would be of benefit if some of you would for once make an in-depth study—it isn't easy—of one of Fichte's writings where he speaks as though nature did not exist at all. Duty, for example, and everything else is deduced by first proving that external human beings actually exist in whom the materialized substance of duty can become reality. Here, all the raw material is contained, so to speak, from which the rights and state organism of the threefold social order have to be put together.

What, then, is the actual cause of the catastrophic events in the past few years? The basic reason is that there was no living perception, no feeling, for such matters. Berlin's policies are American. This is fine for America, but it is not suitable for Berlin. This is why Berlin's politics amount to nothing. For, just imagine, since American policies were constantly carried out in Berlin or Vienna, we could just as well have called Berlin, New York, apart from the difference in language, and Vienna, Chicago for all the difference there would have been otherwise. When, in Central Europe, something is done that is completely foreign to it, something originating in the West where it has its rightful place, then the primal essence of the folk spirit is aroused and gives it the lie without the people being aware of it. This was basically the case in recent decades. This was the underlying phenomenon of what happened, the phenomenon that consists, for instance, in the fact that people have trampled Goethe's thinking underfoot, and as another example, have read Ralph Waldo Trine[60] out of a sort of instinct. Actually, all our aristocratic dandies in politics have shown an interest in Trine, and received their special inner stimulus or whatever from that direction. When affairs came to the boiling point, they even turned to Woodrow Wilson;[61] and he[62] who would now again like to be President of the German Republic still has that frame of mind that allows his brain automatically to roll out Woodrow Wilson's Fourteen Points. Thus, in recent times, in the Grand Duchy of Baden, we experienced how a formerly truly representative German personality spouted forth americanisms. This is the best and most immediate example of how matters really stand at present. Indeed, we must be able to see through these archetypal phenomena if we wish to understand what is actually happening today. If we merely pick up a newspaper and read Prince Max von Baden's speeches, simply studying them out of context, then this is something absolutely worthless today. It is a mere kaleidoscope of words. Only when we are able to place such things into the whole context of the world can we hope to understand anything about the world. No progress can be made until people realize how necessary it is today that world understanding be acquired if one wishes to have a say. The most characteristic sign of the time is the belief that when a group of individuals have set up some trashy proposition as a general program—such as the unity of all men regardless of race, nation or color, and so forth—something has been accomplished. Nothing has been accomplished except to throw sand into people's eyes. Something real is attained only when we note the differences and realize what world conditions are. Formerly, human beings could live in accordance with their instincts. This is no longer possible; they must learn to live consciously. This can be done only by looking deeply into what is actually happening.

The East was supreme in regard to life before birth and repeated earthly lives that are connected with it. The greatness of the West consisted in its disposition in regard to life after death. Here, in the middle (see drawing on next page), the actual science of history has originated, although today it is as yet misunderstood. Take Hegel[63] as an example. In Hegel's works, we have neither preexistence nor postexistence; there is neither life before birth nor after death, but there is a spirited grasp of history. Hegel begins with logic, goes from there to a philosophy of nature, develops his doctrine of the soul, then that of the state, and ends with the triad of art, religion and science. They are his world content. There is no mention of preexistence or an immortal soul, only of the spirit that lives here in this world.

Preexistence, postexistence—this is really life in the present state of mankind, the permeation of history. Read what has been drawn up particularly by Hegel as a philosophy of history. In libraries, one generally finds the pages of his books still uncut! Not many editions have appeared of Hegel's works. In the eighties of the last century, Eduard von Hartmann[64] wrote that in all of Germany, where twenty universities exist that have faculties of philosophy, no more than two of the instructors had read Hegel! What he said could not be refuted; it was true. Nonetheless, it hardly needs to be said that all the students were ready to swear to what they had been told about Hegel by professors who had

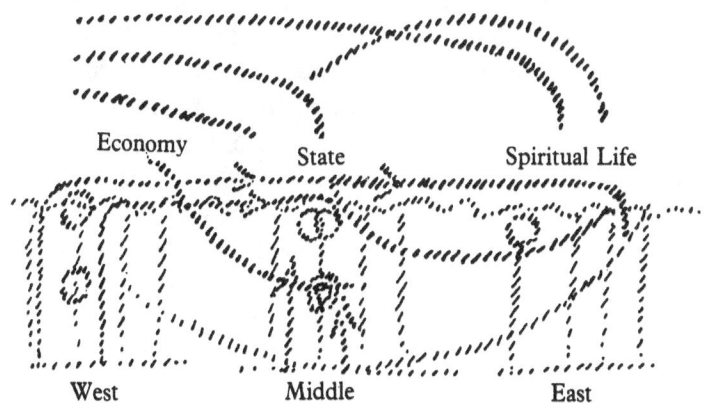

never read him. Do familiarize yourselves with his work and you will find that here, in fact, historical conception has come about, the experience of what goes on between human beings. There you also find the material from which the state, the rights sphere of the threefold social organism, has to be created. We can learn about the constitution of the spiritual organism from the Orient; the constitution of the economic sphere is to be learned from the West.

In this way, we have to look into the differentiations of humanity all over the whole earth, and can gain an understanding of the matter from one side or the other. If the goal is approached directly, namely, if the social life is studied, one arrives at the threefold order as developed in my book, *Towards Social Renewal*. By thus studying the life of mankind throughout the earth, we come to the realization that there is one part with a special disposition for the economy; there is another with a special aptitude for organizing the state; and yet another with a specific inclination towards the spiritual life. A threefold structure can then be created by taking the actual economy from the West, the state from the Middle, and from the East—naturally in a renewed form, as I have often said—the spiritual life. Here you have the state, here the economic life and here the spiritual life (see above sketch); the two others have to be taken across from here. In this way, all humanity has to work together, for the origins of these three members of the social organism are found in different regions of the earth, and therefore must be kept properly apart everywhere. If, in the old manner, human beings wish to mix up in a unified state what is striving to be threefold, nothing will result from it except that in the West the state will be a unity where the economic life overwhelms the whole, and everything else is only submerged into it. If the theorists then take hold of and study the matter, meaning, if Karl Marx moves from Germany to London, he then concludes that everything depends on the economic life. If

Marx's insanity triumphs, the three spheres are reduced to one, the one being of a purely economic character. If one limits oneself to what wishes to be merely the state or rights configuration, one apes the economic life of the West, which for decades has been fashioning an illusory structure, which then naturally collapses when a catastrophe occurs—something that has indeed happened!

The Orient, which possesses the spiritual life in a weakened state in the first place, simply has adopted the economic life from the West and has inoculated itself with something that is completely alien to it. When these matters are studied, we shall see particularly that blessings can only fall upon the earth when, everywhere, one gathers together into the threefold social organism through human activity what by its very nature develops in the various regions.

Lecture VIII
Dornach, August 22, 1920

I would like to sum up once more what I said yesterday concerning the differences of the soul constitutions among the various nations and of human beings generally all over the world. I have indicated that various predispositions and soul qualities exist among people in different parts of the earth. Thus, the population of each region on earth can contribute to what all humanity accomplishes in regard to the whole of civilization. Yesterday we had to point out that the Oriental nations and all the people of Asia are especially predisposed by their nature to develop that element which makes its contribution to the spiritual life of the social organism. Oriental people are especially gifted for everything pertaining primarily to the spiritual development in mankind, hence to knowledge and formulation of the supersensible realm. This is connected with the fact that Oriental people are particularly inclined to develop concepts and ideas on how the human being has descended into this earthly existence from spiritual worlds, in which he has lived since his last death until this birth. The realization or the doctrine of preexistence, which is based on the fact that the human being has undergone a spirit existence before entering into a physical body here, is a principal aspect of these Oriental predispositions. There is therefore also the capability of comprehending repeated earth lives. It is possible for a person to adhere to the view that life goes on after death, continuing on forever without his returning to the earth. It is not logically possible, however, to hold the view that life on earth is a continuation of a spiritual existence without also being obliged to take for granted the thought that this life must repeat itself. Thus, the Oriental was particularly predisposed to understand that he dwelt in spiritual worlds prior to this earth life, that in a sense he received the impulses for this life on earth from the divine spiritual world.

This is connected with the whole way in which the Oriental arrived at his knowledge, his whole soul constitution. I have already indicated this to some of you. Now there are a number of other friends present here, and I would like to characterize something once more that I have already outlined for some of you.

We know that man is a threefold being, that he is divided into the nerves-and-senses man, the rhythmic man—who includes the activities expressed in breathing, blood circulation, and so on—and the third, the metabolic man, everything that has to do with man's metabolism. Now these three members of the human organization do not come to expression in the same manner everywhere on earth; they are expressed in different ways in different parts of the world.

Speaking of the East, all this is in decadence in a sense; it is suppressed and slumbers today in the Oriental human being. We are not concerned now with his present soul condition. Instead, we must become principally acquainted with a soul state that he possessed in a distant past. For the very reason that this soul condition has diminished, Asia humanity is about to adopt Bolshevism with the same religious fervor and devotion with which it formerly received the teaching of the holy Brahman—something that Europeans and Americans will become aware of before very long to their horror. Which of the three members of human nature came to special expression in the Oriental? It was the metabolic man. It was particularly the ancient Oriental who dwelt completely in the metabolism. This will not appear a repulsive view to anyone who does not conceive of substance in terms of lumps of matter, but who knows that spirit lives in all matter. The lofty, admirable spirituality of Orientals was brought about by what rose out of their metabolic process, and radiated into consciousness. What occurs in the human metabolism is, of course, intimately related with what the external sense world is. From the latter, we receive what then turns into matter within us. We know that behind this outer sense world there is spirit. In reality, we consume spirit and the consumed spirit *becomes* matter first within us. Yet, what we consume in this manner produced spirit in the Oriental even after it had been consumed. Thus, a person who understands these things views the remarkable poetic achievements of the Vedas, the greatness of the Bhagavad Gita, the profound philosophy of the Vedas and Vedanta and the Indian philosophy of Yoga without admiring them any less—because he knows that they have emerged from the inner process as a product of metabolism, just like the blossoms of a tree are the result of its metabolism. Just as we look at the tree and see in its blossoms what the earth pushes toward air and light, so we view what human beings in ancient India produced in the Vedas, in the Vedanta and Yoga philosophies, as a blossom of earthly existence itself. What we see as a product of the earth in tree blossoms is, in a way, offered up to air and light. Nevertheless, it is a product of the earth in the same sense as are wheat and grain growing in the fields, and fruits on trees, which are then cooked, enjoyed and digested by the human being. Within the special nature of the ancient Indian, this —instead of turning into plant blossoms and fruits—became the marvelous formulations of the Vedas, the Vedanta and Yoga philosophies. One who must view the ancient Indian as one would a tree. Both are examples of what the earth is capable of producing in its metabolism—in a tree, through its roots and sap, in man through his nourishment. Thus, one learns to recognize the divine in something that the spiritualist scorns, because he finds matter to be of such a low order.

Moreover, the ancient Indian had an ideal. It was his

ideal to go beyond this metabolic experience to the higher member of human nature, namely, the rhythmic system. This is why he did his Yoga exercises, his special breathing exercises, practicing them consciously. What the metabolism brought forth from him as a spiritual blossom of earth evolution came about unconsciously. What he did consciously was to bring his rhythmic system, the system of breathing and blood, into a regulated, systematic movement. What did he do by thus advancing himself, for this was his specific form of advancement. What did he accomplish? What happened in this rhythmic system? We inhale the air from outside; we give to this air something that comes from the human metabolism, namely, carbon. Within us, a metabolic process takes place between something that is a result of our metabolism and something contained in the air that we breathe in. Today's materialistic, physical world-view finds nitrogen and oxygen—ignorant of the true nature of both—mixed together in the air and considers it something purely material. The ancient Indian perceived the air as the process which occurs when the element derived from the metabolism unites in the human being with what is inhaled and is then absorbed. When he fulfilled his ideal inherent in Yoga philosophy, the ancient Indian perceived in the blood circulation the mysteries of the air, that is, what exists spiritually in the air. Through Yoga philosophy he became acquainted with what is spiritual in the air. What does one learn to know there? One comes to recognize what has come into us, insofar as we have become beings that breathe. We learn to perceive what entered into us when we descended from spiritual worlds into this physical body. Knowledge of preexistence, of life before birth, is then cultivated. Therefore, it was in a sense the secret of those who practiced Yoga to penetrate the mystery of life before birth.

We see that the ancient Indian dwelt within his metabolism, notwithstanding the fact that he produced much that was beautiful, grandiose, and powerful, and he artificially raised himself to the rhythmic system. All this has, however, fallen into decadence. Today, all this sleeps in Asia. It only makes itself felt nebulously in abstract forms in asiatic souls when enlightened spirits, such as Rabindranath Tagore,[54] speak of and revel in the ideal of the Asians.

Going from Asia to Central Europe, we find that the European, provided that he really is one, can be characterized as in Fichte's statement which I pointed out to you yesterday: "The external material world is the substance of my duty become visible; on its own, it has no existence. It is there only so that I might have something with which to fulfill my duty." The human being who lived and lives in the central regions of the earth on this basis, dwells in the rhythmic system, just as the ancient Indian lived in the metabolic system. One remains unconscious of the element in which one lives. The Indian still strove upward to the rhythmic system as to an ideal, and he became aware of it. The Central European lives in the rhythmic system and is not conscious of it. Dwelling in this way in the rhythmic system, he brings about all that belongs to the legal, democratic governmental element in the social organization. He forms it in a one-sided way, but he forms it in the sense I indicated yesterday, because he is especially talented in shaping matters dealing with relationships between people, and between a person and his environment. Yet he, in turn, also has an ideal. He has the ideal to rise to the next level, to the man of nerves and senses. Just as the Indian considered Yoga philosophy to be his ideal, the artistic breathing that leads to insight in a special manner, so the Central European considers it his ideal to lift himself up to conceptions that come from the being of nerves and senses, to conceptions that are pure ideas, attained through an inner elevation, just as the Indian by advancing himself attained to the Yoga philosophy.

Therefore, it is necessary to realize that if one really wishes to understand individuals who have worked from such a basis as did Fichte, Hegel, Schelling and Goethe, one must understand them in the same way an Indian understood his Yoga initiates. This special soul disposition, however, tones down the real spirituality. One still gets a clear awareness of it, for instance, in the way Hegel takes ideas as realities. Hegel, Fichte and Goethe possessed this clear awareness that ideas are truths, realities. One even comes to something like Fichte says: "The external sense world has no existence of its own; it is only the visible substance of my duty." But one does not reach the fulfillment of ideas which the Oriental had. One can reach the point of saying, as did Hegel: "History begins, history lives. That is the living movement of ideas." Yet one limits oneself only to this external reality. One views this external reality as spirit, as idea. Yet, particularly if one is in Hegel's place, one can speak neither of immortality nor of unbornness. Hegelean philosophy begins with logic; this means that it starts with what the human being thinks of as *finite*; then it extends over a certain philosophy of nature. It has a psychology, however, that deals only with the earthly soul. It also has a theory of government. Finally, it rises to its highest point when it reaches the threefold aspect of art, science and religion. Yet it goes no further; it does not enter into the spiritual worlds. In the most spiritual way, men like Hegel and Fichte have described what exists in the external world; but anything that would look beyond the outer world is suppressed. Thus we see that the very element that has no counterpart in the spiritual world, namely, the life of rights, of the state, something that is entirely of this world, makes up the greatness of the thought structures that appear here. One looks at the external world as spirit but is unable to go beyond it. Yet, in the process one trains the mind, teaching it a certain discipline. Then, if one values a certain inner development, this can be accomplished, because, by schooling oneself through what can be achieved in this area by occupying the mind with the realm of ideas, one is in a sense inwardly propelled into the spiritual world. This is indeed remarkable.

I must admit to you that whenever I read writings by the Scholastics, they evoke a feeling in me that induces me to say that they can think; they know how to live in thoughts. In a certain other way, directed more to the earthly sphere, I have to say the same of Hegel, Fichte or Schelling. They know how to live in thoughts. Even in the decadent way in which Scholasticism appears in Neo-Scholasticism, I find a much more developed life of thought than is found, for example, in modern science, popular books, or journalism. There, all thinking has already evaporated and disappeared. It is simply true that the better Scholastic minds, in the present time, for example, think in more precise concepts than do our university professors of philosophy. It is somewhat surprising that when one allows these thoughts to work upon oneself, for example, when reading a Scholastic book, even a truly Scholastic-Catholic text, and allows it to affect one, using it in a sense as a kind of self-education, one's soul is driven beyond itself. Such a book works like a meditation. Through its effect, one arrives at something different that brings about enlightenment. Here, we confront a very strange fact.

Consider that if such modern Dominicans, Jesuits and priests of other orders, who immerse themselves in what remains of Scholasticism, would permit the educational effect of Scholastic thought forms to work upon them all the way, they would all come through this discipline in a relatively easy manner to a comprehension of spiritual science. If one would allow those who study Neo-Scholasticism to follow their own soul development, it would not be long before those priests of Catholic orders in particular would become adherents of spiritual science. What had to be done so that this would not happen? They were given a dogma that curtails such study, and does not allow what would develop out of the soul to come about. Even today, someone wishing to develop towards spiritual science could be given as a meditation text the Scholastic book written by a contemporary Jesuit that I once showed here.[65] Yet, as I told you, it bears the imprimatur of a certain archbishop. The enlightenment that would occur in a person, if he were completely free to devote himself to it, has been cut off.

We must be able to see through these things. For then we will realize how important it is for certain circles to prevent by all means the consequences of what would develop if free reign were given the effects of these matters in the souls. The Central European striving is, after all, aimed at lifting oneself out of the rhythmic man, where one dwells as a matter of fact, to the nerves-and-senses man, who possesses what he attains for himself in the ideal sphere. For these people, there is a special predisposition to understand earthly life as something spiritual. Hegel did this in the most all-encompassing sense.

Let us now go to Western man. Yesterday, I said that Western man, particularly as exemplified by the most brilliant minds as early as Bacon and others, followed by Bentham, John Stuart Mill, Spencer, Buckle, Thomas Reid, and the economist Adam Smith, has a special predisposition to develop the kind of thinking which can then be utilized in the economic part of the social organism.

If we consider Spencer's philosophy, for instance, we realize that this is a kind of thinking which stems completely from the nerves-and-senses man, that in all respects it is a product of the senses and nerves. It would be most appropriate for creating industrial organizations and associations. It is only out of place when employed by Spencer for philosophy. If he had used this same thinking to set up factories and social organizations, it would have been applied in its rightful place. It was out of place when he used it for philosophy.

This comes from the fact that Western man no longer

lives in the rhythmic system, but has taken a step upward, living as a matter of course in the human nerves-and-senses system. It is the nature of the Oriental to live in his metabolic system. It is the Central European's nature to live in the rhythmic system. It is Western man's nature to live in the nerves-and-senses system (see drawing). The Oriental lives in the metabolism; he strives upward, trying to attain to the rhythmic system. The Central European lives in the rhythmic system. He strives towards the nerves-and-senses system. Western man already lives in the latter. Where does he wish to ascend? He is not yet there, but he has the impulse to strive upwards beyond himself. It appears at first in a caricatured form, which I characterized for you yesterday as the denial of matter and the autosuggestion of the human being in Mrs. Eddy's Christian Science. Despite the fact that this is as yet a caricature, it is nevertheless a forerunner of what Western man must aim for. The aim must be something superhuman, by which I do not mean to imply that anyone who, instead of striving beyond the nerve-sense system, strives down into unconsciousness, and such as that, would thereby become superhuman.

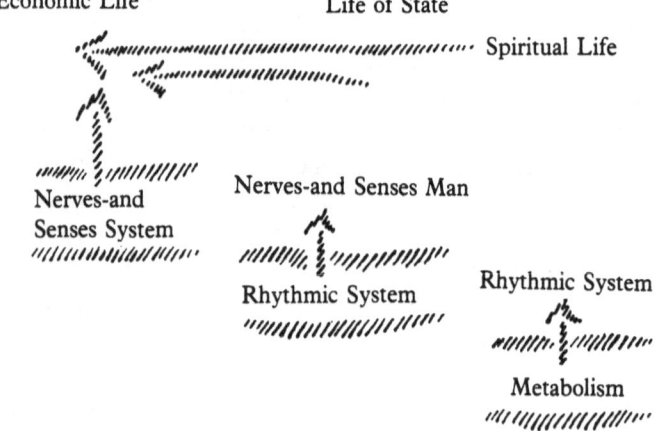

Yesterday, I concluded by saying that it is in this way that the human faculties are distributed over the world's various regions, and it is necessary for real cooperation to come about. We are in a position today where, in regard to civilization, we are completely dependent on the nerves-and-senses being of the West. I made use of a paradox, but this paradox quite clearly expresses the reality of the situation. The thoughts in Vienna and in Berlin are not the thoughts that arose from the folk spirit and then culminated in Fichte or Hegel. The spirits of Fichte and Hegel have been buried. What is written today in books and newspapers in Central Europe, in Vienna or Berlin, are not Fichte's thought forms; it is a lie when people quote Fichte today. Rather, the truth is that what reaches the public in Berlin or Vienna today is more closely related to what is being thought in Chicago or New York than to what was thought by Fichte or Hegel.

What had to happen, however, was that these three members, of which this one (in the East) was, to begin with, especially predisposed to the spiritual life, brought across the spiritual life as a tradition of its original, elementary form once existing in the Orient. There in the East the human being lived as fully within the life of the spirit itself as today he is firmly anchored here in Europe in physical life. Only the shadowy reflection of this spiritual life is found in Central Europe, and only its tradition in Western Europe. Western Europe is characterized by its own predisposition to the postmortem life, the life which is envisioned after death. I told you yesterday that in America an awareness is already in the process of developing, if only in a few sects, that man must not merely be passive about his soul life here on earth if he is to carry something through death and live on in spiritual worlds. He must acquire here through his work and actions what he wishes to carry through the gate of death. The awareness exists that the human being disintegrates if he does not provide for his immortality here, if, on earth, he does not develop a sense for ideals. This is already emerging in some Western sects, even though this ideal still appears in a distorted form.

That which is the life of the state on the other hand was striven for by what existed in the rhythmic system and could be borne upward into thoughts. This has come into evidence especially in the man of the middle (the Central European). From there, it affected the West. We are dealing with an odd phenomenon here that is only understood when one looks at its inner aspect. Strange as it may seem, something was astir in Central Europe. It goes without saying that in the rhythmic system the inclination remained for a communal human life, for a social life together in freedom. This impulse remained, to start with, deep in the unconscious realm (see drawing below). It is true, however, that impulses are present among human beings even if people are not conscious of them. Let us say, therefore, that something definite lived, to begin with unconsciously, in Central Europe in the eighteenth century; it could not rise into consciousness, but its effects were transmitted to the West. Having been received there, but not having developed inwardly as a matter of course, it turned into passion and feeling, thus into the French Revolution.

Schiller had thoughts on this. *Here* (referring to the drawing on page 12), we have the French Revolution. There is even a symbolic event attesting to the fact that Schiller pondered on what actually happened there. You know that he had the honor of being made a French citizen. He there-

West   Middle   East

Eighteenth Century

fore pondered on it all, but to begin with, it all lived in his rhythmic system. Then, through his own insight, he lifted it up into consciousness and wrote his letters concerning the aesthetic education of man. You find in these letters what one could say at that time about people living together in a truly free state. Hume then merely took this concept of the state, which Schiller had lifted up into consciousness in his *Aesthetic Letters*, and somewhat pedantically fashioned it into a system. There is something extraordinarily important in what Schiller brought out from the depths of the folk spirit in these letters on aesthetic education. Because it was something so profound, it was subsequently not comprehended when the element of the nerves-and-senses man became dominant everywhere.

I have often referred to a lonely man, living in Vienna, by the name of Heinrich Deinhardt.[66] He wrote letters upon letters about this aesthetic education of the human being, most ingenious letters. This man had the misfortune of breaking a leg as the result of a fall in the street. The leg was set, but, being undernourished, Deinhardt could not recover and died from breaking a bone. That is to say, he who already in the second half of the nineteenth century had so conscientiously interpreted Schiller's *Aesthetic Letters* died of malnutrition. And Deinhardt's letters on Schiller's aesthetic education of man are completely forgotten!

Again, these *Aesthetic Letters* by Schiller would be a good preparation for purifying and uplifting the soul so as to gain a spiritual view of the world. Schiller himself was not yet able to do this. It is always effective, however, if another person engaged in soul development takes up something originating from the one who as yet does not reach up into the spiritual world. It then has the effect of letting him see into the spiritual world. To be sure, people in Europe have revered as special remedies for the soul Ralph Waldo Trine, Marden[67] and similar superficial minds instead of Schiller, forgetting the other views that would actually lead upward into the spiritual world.

It is indeed necessary that these matters be grasped and comprehended in the whole context of life and world conditions. People have to realize how differentiated human capabilities are all over the earth. And the following must be pointed out. Up to now, no effort has been spared to publicize Schiller's riotous early works, *The Robbers, Fiesco,* or *Intrigue and Love*. People become most enthusiastic about the sentimentalities of *Mary Stuart*, the very profitable dramatic scenes of *Maid of Orleans* or the *Bride of Messina*. Today, Schiller's *Aesthetic Letters*, in which he surpasses himself in significance for all humanity—his *Robbers*, the whole of *Mary Stuart* and *Wallenstein* notwithstanding—should not only be taken up and studied, one should allow them to affect one. For today, it is up to us not just to indulge in the empty talk of philistine academics existing in regard to our classical writers such as Goethe and Schiller, but above all else to take our own stand and on our own to discover what was great about them. We go on repeating what philistine academia has said for over a century about *Wallenstein, Mary Stuart,* and so forth. Our task today is to grasp such greatness ourselves in a fundamental way, for only then can humanity progress. So, here too, we discover the necessity for a transformation, a renewal. Even what people in our schools read and hear about *Mary Stuart, Wallenstein, The Robbers,* and so forth, must be revised. In this critical age we need a complete renewal, for the times are critical indeed.

If we look over to the West, we see that with all that it can produce as the expression of mankind through the nerves-and-senses system, this West is asking for the ascent into what lies beyond human knowledge in the spiritual world. I told you yesterday that in order for the cultural life, the life of the state and the economic life to be able to assert themselves in the threefold social organism, they must work together. These three elements must work together. Let us not merely say, "Ex Oriente lux!" We can turn to the Orient, study the Bhagavad Gita, Yoga philosophy and the Vedas; we can grind away at these subjects just as we have become accustomed to grind away at others in Europe. We can start grinding away at Oriental philosophy after the other subjects have become boring to us. But we shall make no progress this way, for what was once right for the earth will not again be appropriate for the present and future; it will remain something of the past. We can admire it as something that was once right for the earth; we cannot, however, simply adopt it again in a passive manner as does the Theosophical Society, for instance. Likewise, we cannot just carry over what has been handed down to us of the European past in the old tradition. We cannot say that what is contained in the national characteristics of the Orient, of Middle Europe, can simply be renewed by us. Rather, we must ask, if we wish to achieve a realistic union of these three elements that are inherent dispositions of human nature, how can we do that? We can only do it when we realize in what way the nerves-and-senses life, which has, after all, taken hold of all of us, must pass beyond itself. It means that we must rise to something different that can come neither from the East, the Middle nor the West. It can only come through the new initiation, through the new spiritual science. It is brought about by our ascending from the most current form of thinking, trained by natural science and the nerves-and-senses being, to the science of the new initiation; acquiring from this new initiation the ways and means for bringing about cooperation between what was once the nature of the ancient Orient, later that of the Middle and now that of the West. We need a new science of initiation that can bring about a unity of these three, a living unity. In this modern age, we will not arrive at a cultural life if we do not strive for this new initiation science. We will have no proper politics, no life of the state, if we just continue in the same old way, if we do not turn to those scientific branches born of the new initiation and inquire how the politics of the future must be shaped. Neither will we achieve a new economic life, if we do not understand that form of thinking which should be applied neither to philosophy as did Spencer, nor to the life of the state as did Adam Smith, but only to the organization of the economic life. Then, however, we must also know how to integrate the latter into the two other systems. For that we need the science of initiation. We cannot progress if we cannot say to ourselves: From a comprehension of what was once the Oriental disposition, we come to the essence of the cultural, the spiritual life. By truly comprehending the disposition of the human being of the Middle, we reach the point of really understanding the nature of the life of rights, of the state. By understanding the Western nature, we gain a comprehension of what the economic life is. The three fall apart, however, if we cannot unite them in a higher unity. And we can only accomplish that when we view the three from the perspective resulting for us from the new Mysteries, which are here called the anthroposophically oriented spiritual science.

These matters must be understood, for whoever has insight into them knows that all the aspirations coming to expression today are leading towards ruin. People simply do

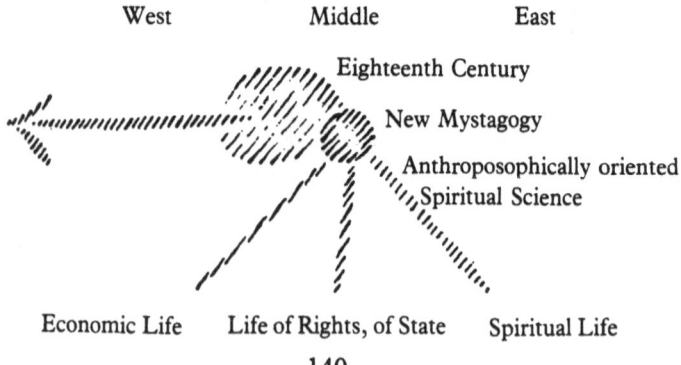

not reckon with the most important factors. Take the most radical socialists. Subjectively they may have honorable intentions for humanity, but they only count on forces of decline. They strike a wrong balance of life. We only take stock the right way when, out of spiritual science, we do not just grasp at anything arbitrarily put there, saying that this is the way it must be if humanity is to be happy, but when we ask ourselves: What will come into being when the cultural life, the life of rights and the economic life are brought into the right relationship with each other; what kind of social organism results from that? Then, such a social body will also contain its permeation with spirit. This implies the presence of a realistic economic life, not one that people dream and fantasize about, but one that can originate as the best possible one. Again, its political system will be the best possible; a cultural life will be present that will unite the prenatal life with that after death. Such a cultural life will see in the human being, dwelling here in this physical world, a being orienting himself according to his rights; a being into whom, in the cultural sphere, shines his prenatal life; a being who in the economic life cannot attain to an ideal, only to the best possible one, yet is able through initiation science in his will to transform the faculties active in the economic sphere so that they allow the life after death to shine forth. Because this is the case, anthroposophically oriented spiritual science is not just one theory among many, not something that takes its place as a party or sectarian program alongside others. Anthroposophy is something that is brought forth out of the knowledge that can be acquired when earth's and mankind's evolution are comprehended in their working together and in their totality.

In the present time, we have to admit that any other relationship to the world or to temporal reforms will lead to nothing, for what can bring progress to mankind must emerge out of the new initiation science.

Today, this must be expressed again and again in many different ways. It has been incorporated into this building; it is expressed in all the details of this structure. Looking even at its smallest segment, it can tell you about what is intended here, what is expressed in words in a variety of ways. This is what gives the whole matter here a certain uniform character. At the same time, a will comes to expression here that is intimately connected with the forces of ascent, not the declining forces of evolving humanity, something one could wish people would understand. This is what we should like to work for more and more. This is what we now wish to aim for by means of the courses[68] that will be given here this fall, in which we intend to show that the knowledge derived from anthroposophically oriented spiritual science can work in a truly fructifying manner into the individual branches of science. Then, the day will perhaps come when people will understand what is really intended here, when sufficient comprehension will exist in the world so that we can reach the point at some future date when this building, still enshrouded in mist, can be opened up. For, as long as this building cannot be opened up, there still exists something that shows a lack of understanding for what is intended here.

I shall continue with this next Friday at eight o'clock.

At eight tomorrow, our friend, Count Polzer,[69] will lecture on European politics of the last century in connection with the testament of Peter the Great. This is an interesting subject about which, hopefully, a discussion will ensue. On Friday, I shall continue with the questions, already presented, and their application to the individual human being. On Saturday, at eight o'clock, I will continue with those particular questions that relate to religious problems. Sunday at six-thirty will be the next eurythmy performance, followed by a lecture.

Lecture IX
Dornach, August 27, 1920

A hundred-fifty years ago today Hegel was born in Stuttgart, and when we recall this fact today, we should be spontaneously filled with a feeling for the tremendous change and transformation the times have undergone since the birth of this individual whose spirit was so extraordinarily characteristic of the whole of modern civilization. In a sense, Hegel does embody the essence of the Central European cultural life, which, subsequent to his influence, has changed so considerably. Having played a certain role in Central Europe, this cultural life is just about beginning to disappear from this region.

Hegel was born in Stuttgart, in Swabia; he spent his maturing years of development of his particular spiritual character in middle Germany. In the last period of his life, he was a personality of great consequence in northern Germany, where he was particularly influential in public education, but also in a number of other cultural concerns of that region. Born on August 27, 1770, having developed slowly because of a certain sluggish mentality, Hegel attended the University of Tuebingen where he studied theology. Above all else, he made the acquaintance of the much more mentally mobile and quick, young Schelling.[70] He also became acquainted with Hoelderlin,[71] who, one might say, transposed the melancholic sentiments of ancient Greece into modern times. In close relationship with these two, Hegel spent his years of study in Tuebingen. Then, like Schelling, he turned to middle Germany, to the University of Jena in Thuringia, where, again like Schelling, attracted to the personality of Johann Gottlieb Fichte, he made his first attempts at working out his own ideas of a world view. He taught at the University until 1806. In that year, while Napoleon's cannons thundered around Jena, he concluded his first sizable independent work, his *Phenomenology of the Spirit*. This work contains the attempt to re-experience in thoughts all that human consciousness can experience—from the dimmest impressions of the world to that mental clarity in which the human being experiences the world of ideas with such intensity that this ideal world itself appears to him as the very substance of spirit. One could say that this *Phenomenology of the Spirit* is something like a world tour of the spirit.

The difficult conditions in Germany at that time brought an end to Hegel's position at the University of Jena. Yet he continued to remain in middle Germany, and for the next year or so edited a political newspaper in Bamberg. Then he was principal of a secondary school in Nuremberg, until he took a position as professor at the University of Heidelberg for a few years. During his years in Nuremberg, Hegel completed his most important work, *Science of Logic*. In Heidelberg, he wrote his *Encyclopedia of the Philosophical Sciences*. Then he was called to the University of Berlin, which had been founded on the spirit of Fichte and Humboldt. There, his activity expanded in influence and authority to cover the entire educational system then being administered from Berlin, as well as other matters of cultural importance.

Hegel was a strange personality even in outward appearance when he lectured. Before him were the written pages of his manuscript, which, so it seems, were always in disarray so that he was constantly turning and searching among his pages. He was somewhat awkward in his presentation and laborious in his delivery. While he was lecturing, the thought within him worked out of deep substrata of the soul, forming itself only with great difficulty into a word, which then issued forth as if in a stuttering, disjointed manner. Yet, his lecture, which reached its audience in this way as if constantly interrupting itself, is supposed to have made an extraordinarily grand impression on those who were capable of appreciating such a personality. In other ways, too, Hegel had remarkable personal qualities. He truly entered into and familiarized himself with the whole structure of the environment in which he happened to find himself. Thus, one can observe how he actually outgrew the Swabian milieu. One can see that he retained within himself the Swabian spirit with all its special characteristic features until he went to Switzerland and Frankfurt/Main—he spent some time as a private tutor in both Switzerland and Frankfurt after graduating from the university—where he again merged relatively quickly with the life of his new surroundings.

Then he moved to Jena, where Fichte's fiery spirit operated, where, above all else, there existed something like a concentrated summation of the entire cultural essence of Central Europe—a time of which people today can scarcely form a picture. It was indeed so that when Fichte presented his expositions in the university auditorium, which, in his characteristic manner, were on a high spiritual, yet nevertheless abstract level, these discourses were continued and carried on in debates right out into the streets and squares of Jena. In very truth, a lecture by Fichte was not merely a discussion pertaining to questions of one or another kind, but an event. It was an event also in this respect, that at that time, from all around Jena, individuals in need of a world outlook came to hear Fichte speak. One who reads the correspondence, of which there is a great deal, in which people tell of hearing Fichte in Jena, will again and again come across passages testifying to Fichte's tremendous spiritual influence. Indeed, long after Fichte had died, decades later, people who had heard him in Jena still spoke of the great influence he had upon their soul life. The philosophical fire-spirit, Schelling, was stimulated by what flowed as the power of spirit into the world; the more ponderous Georg Friedrich Wilhelm Hegel was motivated as well, and joined forces with Schelling to develop Fichte's philosophy further. At the beginning of the nineteenth century, Schelling and Hegel published the *Critical Journal of Philosophy* in Jena. Its articles certainly stood on the highest levels of abstract philosophical thinking, but in such a manner that one sees how these utterances, couched in thin abstractions, concern themselves—as though welling up straight from the human heart—with those affairs of human life and the world that have always been the high points of all striving for a world concept. Following this, Hegel worked his way to a certain independence, and in 1806 wrote his *Phenomenology of the Spirit*, which, however, is actually a phenomenology of consciousness.

As I said, Hegel always stood completely within his milieu. The riddles of his surroundings worked deep within him. Just as the Swabian spirit with its depth, as found in a few select Swabians, was so strongly revealed in Hegel's youth, so was this whole spirit of philosophy, comprising in concentrated form the whole new cultural striving, that took hold of him in Jena at the beginning of the nineteenth century. It was out of this philosophical spirit that he wrote and taught, a spirit which was always nourished, and increasingly maintained, however, by an overview of the general world condition.

Out of this spirit, too, arose Hegel's *Logic*—no ordinary logic, but something entirely different. It was written in the second decade of the nineteenth century. One is moved to say that the most singular of all kinds of human striving on the highest level manifests itself in this Hegelian logic.

To Hegel, logic was something akin to a summation of what Hellenism, in a manner somewhat different from Hegel's, understood as logos or universal reason. During the profound inner experience that Hegel underwent while working out his *Phenomenology of the Spirit*, he began to feel strongly that if man works himself up to the intensive experience of the "idea," hence the ideas of the world, then this experiencing of the "idea" is no longer a mere thought experience but one of the divine cosmic element in all its truth, purity, and light-filled clarity. Something that had pulsed for centuries in the minds and souls of Central Europe came into inner soul existence at that time in Hegel. One need only recall the deep mysticism of Meister Eckhart, of Johannes Tauler. Recently, we have become acquainted with this mysticism from another side; yet it nevertheless remains profound—for the experience remains the same, after all, even if one is familiar with the deeper occult foundations of which I spoke here a few days ago.[72] One need only think of this mystical experience that became an inner revelation, as in Valentin Weigel, even in Paracelsus or in Jacob Boehme. One need only transform for oneself into the bright, light-filled clarity of universal ideas what minds such as Meister Eckhart or Johannes Tauler experienced more out of intense feeling than something abstract, what Jacob Boehme set out in images through inner experience, hence replacing the mysticism of feeling and imagery with the mysticism of ideas; then one has the experience that was Hegel's when he wrote his *Logic*. It was the soul's surrender to pure ideas, but in the conviction that these ideas are the very substance of the universe. It was a dwelling in something that Nietzsche later called the cold, icy realm of ideas. To Hegel, on the other hand, this was accompanied by the awareness that such an experience of the ideas was a dialogue with the cosmic spirit itself.

What Hegel experienced, not in a vaguely defined unity of the world, not in such vague concepts as those produced by the Pantheists, but in concrete ideas that were followed through from simple "existence" all the way to the fully saturated "idea of the organism" and the "spirit," what can be experienced to the full extent of the developed world of ideas, this Hegel summed up in his *Logic*. Thus, it is the intent in his *Logic* to present a structure of those ideas attainable for the human being, ideas which, as man experiences them, simultaneously demonstrate the certainty that they are of the same element by which the universal spirit allows reality to come into being. This is why Hegel called the contents of his *Logic* the divinity prior to the creation of the world. Yet, icy is the region in which a person finds himself who studies Hegel's *Logic*; this is because Hegel moves entirely in what the ordinary person calls the uttermost abstraction. He begins by presenting "being" as the simplest idea; then he passes over to "nothingness"; proceeds dialectically from "being" through "nothingness" to "becoming," to "existence," and on to "causality." One does not gain from this what the ordinary person wants when he wishes to be filled inwardly in his soul with divine cosmic warmth. Instead, one receives what in ordinary life would be called a sum of abstract ideas.

What is this *Logic*? When it is really contemplated, this *Logic* becomes an experience; it even turns into an experience that can give a person much information about many a secret of humanity and the world in general. One is induced to say that what is experienced through Hegel's *Logic* can really only be characterized by means of spiritual science. It is only through spiritual science that one finds words to characterize this experience. This is a remarkable discovery. Hegel's pupil, Rosenkranz,[73] who was devoted to his master, has presented us with a biography of Hegel, written not only in a kindly but also a spirited manner. In it, he uses words that are, I might say, in a certain respect significant for the events of that time. It was around the mid-forties of the nineteenth century that he said, "We are actually the grave diggers of the great philosophers." Rosenkranz then lists the great philosophers who rose from European civilization during the period near the turn of the eighteenth to the nineteenth century, and how they actually died within that same period. One experiences a melancholy feeling when reading this passage in Rosenkranz's biography of Hegel, for something very true has been expressed. As this nineteenth century advanced step by step, it became the grave digger not only of the philosophers but of philosophy itself, indeed, of the profound questions dealing with world concepts. The decay of European civilization, now approaching us with giant strides, first announced itself in the lofty regions of philosophy. The presumptuous philosophical systems of the second half of the nineteenth century are at bottom expressions of decline.

On the basis of spiritual science, on the other hand, one cannot speak as did Rosenkranz; based on spiritual science, I would say that even what is outwardly, physically dead must also come to life. For what is eternal in the human being works on eternally, on one side in supersensible worlds, but on the other side also in the earthly realm itself; and if it falls to the impulses of decline to have grave diggers, it is up to spiritual science to seek out what is eternally alive soul essence in what is dead and to place it before the world in its ever continuing life. Therefore, I would like to speak today not of the dead but of the living Hegel.

To be sure, however, living personalities of Hegel's kind also become, in a certain sense, sharp critics of what—partly from indolence of soul, partly from sheer bad will—presently forms an alliance with the powers of decadence. Therefore, from the spiritual-scientific standpoint, I must say: Yes, it is true that Hegel's logical dialectic runs its course in the cold, icy realm of what at first seem to be abstract concepts. To experience Hegel's *Logic* actually means finding oneself dwelling in a multitude of concepts, which a thoughtless person does not care for, about which the thoughtless man would say, "That does not interest me." But this conceptual world of Hegel's, this sum of apparent abstractions, these icy, cold concepts, what exactly are they? One can investigate what these concepts are, particularly through what spiritual science offers us. There is no doubt that they cannot be eternal universal reason itself, for universal reason could never have created from this sum of pure abstractions the entire multiform and, above all, warmth-pervaded world of ours. These logical concepts, these logical ideas, seem like transparent conceptual veils; indeed, Hegel himself calls his logical ideas shadow images.

Therefore, what Hegel initially experienced in this logic is, of course, something that it cannot be. It is a sum of ideas that begin with "being," pass from "nothingness" to "becoming," and so on through many such concepts, ending with the "idea bearing its own purpose within itself"—therefore, concluding with what ordinary consciousness would also still call an abstraction. It is certain then that the world could not have been created out of such ideas; nor is this logic to be viewed as the living spirit, that is, what must be grasped in supersensory perception as living spirit. Indeed, I would say, it is out of an admittedly subjective feeling that Hegel declares that the contents of this logic are the thoughts of God prior to the world's creation. Out of these thoughts, one could never in any way comprehend the rich abundance of the created world. And yet, if one allows oneself to go into these thoughts, the experience is a strong and powerful one. What exactly is it then that is contained in this logic?

Look at our building here.[74] It is intended to have as the central group in the middle of the eastern end a kind of Christ figure, with Lucifer rising above it, and below Ahriman, as though being thrust into the earth by the Representative of Humanity, who inwardly preserves complete balance of soul. The intention is to represent the full human condition in this group. In reality, man is, after all, that being who must seek the balance between what tries to rise above the human being and what draws him down into the ground—the balance between the Luciferic and the Ahrimanic nature. Physiologically, physically speaking, the Luciferic force is that element in us which brings about fever, pleurisy, which brings man into conditions of warmth that tend to dissolve him, cause him to be dissipated in the world; the Ahrimanic force brings about ossification, calcification. Speaking of the soul level, man is the entity who must seek the equilibrium, on the one hand, between rapturous mysticism—between theory, between all that strives to the insubstantial but nevertheless light-irradiated realm—and what pulls him down, on the other hand, to the pedantic, philistine, materialistic and intellectualistic sphere. Spiritually speaking, man must hold the balance between the Luciferic force always wishing to lull him to sleep, always tempting him to yield himself up to the universal all, and the Ahrimanic force that shocks him awake again and again, striking through him with a violence that does not let him sleep. One does not comprehend the nature of the human being if one cannot place it in the middle between the Luciferic and the Ahrimanic force.

Yet, the experience of the human soul at this middle point is a complicated one; the soul can only fully experience this complexity in its development in the course of time, and one must understand each of the successive stages of this development. One can say that whoever understands Hegel and the way he elaborated his *Logic* can see how, at that time, in the second decade of the nineteenth century, mankind began to calcify, to become materialistic, to densify inwardly, to become entangled in matter. In the realm of knowledge and perception, this age gives the impression of sinking down into matter. As in a picture, humanity appears to be sinking into the material element, with Hegel standing in the center, working himself out of it with all his might and snatching away from Ahriman what he has that is good, namely, the abstract logic that we need for our inner liberation, without which we will not achieve pure thinking. Hegel wrests this logic from the powers of gravity, from the terrestrial powers, presenting it in all its cold abstractness, so that it may not live in the Ahrimanic element dwelling in man, but can rise into human thinking. Yes, this Hegelian logic is wrested from the Ahrimanic powers, torn free from them and bestowed on humanity. This is what mankind needs and without which it cannot progress—which, however, had first to be rescued from Ahriman.

Thus, Hegelian logic actually remains something eternal; thus it must continue to be effective. It must ever and again be sought for. We cannot do without it. If we try to manage without it, we either fall back into the nebulous softness of "Schleiermacherei,"* or we founder in what people immediately became enmeshed in when they have approached Hegel without being able to grasp him. For there appears on the one side the image of Hegel, who lifts himself out of Ahriman's realm, who rescues from Ahriman what, as pure logic, has to be saved for mankind, actually has to be saved for human thinking. On the other side, there arises the image of Karl Marx, who also orients himself on Hegel, taking up Hegel's thinking, but is gripped by Ahriman's claws and dragged into the lowest depths of the material bog—who by Hegel's method arrives at historical materialism. Here, we cannot help but see, side by side, the upward striving spirit, snatching the logic away from Ahriman, because, with this logic, one must truly keep onself upright by means of all

---

*Note by translator: "Schleiermacherei"—an apt play on words around the name of Hegel's contemporary, F.D.E. Schleiermacher (lit. = veil maker). Steiner described his world view as ardently devotional and sincere, but introspective. See *Riddles of Philosophy*, pp. 165-168.

one's inner human soul forces, and the one who, with this logic, sinks into the Ahrimanic morass.

Hegel actually appears as a spirit that can be understood only if one tries to comprehend him with the concepts which only spiritual science can supply. This is what Hegel became through the influence brought to bear on him by Fichte's fiery words in Jena, the essence of which he then formulated in his way, during his subsequent sojourns in Bamberg, Nuremberg and Heidelberg.

Subsequently, he was transferred to northern Germany. He always experienced fully what his surroundings contained. In a humanly personal manner, his inner life awakened to what was around him. Thus he became the influential genius of the University of Berlin. Now the world experienced through him that work which he had to create out of the very middle of the modern civilized world if he was truly a spirit fully belonging to this middle. In the last few weeks, we have, after all, been characterizing the East, the Middle, and the West. We have found that it is the economic thinking that flourishes particularly in the West; in the East, spiritual thinking flourished; in the Middle, the legal, political element has chiefly raised itself to a special flowering. Fichte has written a work dealing with natural law. The most enlightened minds occupied themselves with ideas concerning human rights. It was just at the time of his move to northern Germany that Hegel gave the world his *Basic Principles of the Philosophy of Rights or Natural Rights and Science of the State in Outline*. Everything that could be termed a defamation of Hegel was due chiefly to this book, which contains the remarkable sentence: "Everything reasonable is real, and everything real is reasonable."[75]

Whoever can appreciate that it was Hegel who wrested human reason from the clutches of the Ahrimanic powers will also recognize his right to search it out, and to make it effectual throughout the world. Thus, because his field of action was the Ahrimanic which cannot lead a person upward to what lies before birth or into what is active after death, Hegel became an interpreter of spirituality, but only of the physical, earthly one; he turned into a philosopher of natural science and history. Yet he depicted what dwells in the external world in the relation of man to man and which then develops systematically as organized human life. This he summed up in his concept of "objective spirit." In the expression of rights, in morality, in the implementation of treaties and so forth, he beheld the spirit active in the social organization itself. Regarding these matters, he stood completely within not only the spatial, but also the temporal milieu. It was not yet the trend of that time, particularly in the area where Hegel lived, to worship the state as much as was the case later on. Therefore, it is incorrect to view the concept of the state appearing in Hegel's writing in the same light as must be done in regard to later times. Within his structure of the state, for example, Hegel still acknowledged free corporations, a corporate life. All the antihuman elements that made their appearance later in the Prussian realm were not yet in evidence when Hegel, one might say, deified the idea of the state in Prussia of all places; but this grew out of his attempt to see at work in the world that reason which he had wrested from Ahriman through his logic.

Thus, we cannot help but say that this is basically the tragedy that has since been enacted historically in such a shocking way. The element living in Middle Europe is indeed something we must not regard in the same way as do Western eyes, particularly since the mendacities of recent years. It is something best characterized by the fact that, even now, it gives the impression to a mind such as Oswald Spengler's that the only social salvation for the impending age of decline must come through Central Europe, not in order to counteract the decline—Spengler does not believe in such counteraction—but merely to make the decline that will take place tolerable, until, in the beginning of the next millennium, total barbarism supposedly will come into being.

One can say that in the twenties of the nineteenth century Hegel appears as the ruling spirit governing the whole realm of Prussian education; he stands there with the kind of reasonableness I have just characterized for you. It is a reasonableness that is born, as it were, out of the ice of Ahriman, but it also possesses in its spirit structure something of an inner firmness, having nothing mathematical about it, yet containing a tremendous force, an element of fine spirituality.

Now, one has to understand that what was present as the special element of Central Europe has to be characterized also from *this* aspect: that right into the ninth century its lack of culture still included the practice of blood sacrifice. This showed characteristics that have a certain value when taken up by such a spirit as Hegel's. Such a spirituality, however, is rare, it does not repeat itself. Hegel's students were basically all small minds, and the one who, in a certain respect, was a great mind, Karl Marx, quickly succumbed to the Ahrimanic powers. The element which then gained ground was the very one that precipitated the plunge into the Ahrimanic abyss.

Hegel salvaged something from what plunged into this abyss—something that must be eternal, something he could only salvage because it was saved from just *this* element. It was necessary that this be done by a person whose soul essence was of the very being of Middle Europe. This was the case with Hegel. He was Swabian by birth and by virtue of the region of his youth: middle German, Franconian and Thuringian in respect to his maturation; and he was so pronouncedly Prussian in the final period of his life that he experienced Prussia as the center of the world, with Berlin as the very center of this world center.

There is a certain inherent force in Hegelianism, truly

not a physical force but a different one, namely a spiritual force; Hegelianism contains something that must be taken up by every spiritual world view. For any spiritual science would have to become rachitic if it could not be permeated by the skeletal system of ideas which Hegel wrested from the ossifying grip of Ahriman. We need this system to become inwardly strong in a certain manner. We have need of this sober thoughtfulness if, in our spiritual endeavors, we wish to avoid the degeneracy of nebulous, cozy mysticism. We also need the force that lived in Hegel; we require the force of his creed of reason, if we do not wish to sink into what Karl Marx directly succumbed to when he tried independently to work himself into Hegel's mentality.

It would really be necessary at this point in time—which is perhaps one of the most important moments, more important even than 1914—that as many people as possible recall this significant element in Hegel. For a true recognition, especially of Hegel, could bring about a certain awakening of soul. And an awakening is needed! No one believes, no one wishes to believe, what dangers are actually at work in European civilization and its American appendage; one does not wish to believe what forces of decline prevail. In public life today, only the forces of decline are taken into account. No one wishes to perceive, to feel the uplifting forces. Let us focus on single characteristic things that just recently may have caught our attention. What thoughts are harbored, for instance, in the attitude becoming prevalent now in the civilized world in regard to the traditional spiritual life? I am not referring to *our* spiritual life, for we intend to bring a new spirit into humanity's civilization. What are the thoughts in the attitude of mind now growing and spreading in relation to the life of the spirit? You can find such thoughts in a recent article[76] written by the rector of the University of Halle for the *Hallischen Nachrichten* under the title, "Gradual Abolition of the Universities." He states:

At least this much appears certain, namely, that a government agency has actually put forward the suggestion to close down a part of the German universities. Other educational tasks are held to be more important, and it is believed that greater financial resources have to be freed for them. Since these resources are unavailable, it is thought that a number of universities should be abolished in order to found a type of civil service school where persons who have not attended a university would be educated so that they could administer the official posts allotted to them.

So, civil service training begins! In Russia it is going at full speed. And the Western world pays no attention! They will have to pay bitter attention to it, however, if an awakening of souls does not take place, if even the best minds continually turn a deaf ear to all that refers to the spirit; and, for their own amusement, certainly not for the good of this world, they continue to entertain the world with the timeworn slogans of liberalism, conservatism, pacificism, and so on.

And particularly morality among our intellectuals is fast going downhill. Here is a small indication of it. But first, I must mention that when Ernst Haeckel retired from his professorship at Jena, he himself chose as his successor his pupil Plate,[77] who had recently arrived from Berlin. He installed him, so to speak, for Haeckel's voice really carried weight at the University of Jena at the time of his retirement. He installed Plate in all the responsible posts he had held: His professorship, his administration of the Zoological Institute and the Phyletic Museum, established for Haeckel himself on the occasion of his sixtieth birthday[78] by the Haeckel Foundation that had come into existence. It was from all this that Haeckel withdrew, installing in his place his pupil Plate. Now I would like to read you a news item[79] of a few days ago:

> One year ago, eight days after Haeckel's death, an obituary notice in the *Berliner Tageblatt* by Dr. Adolf Heilborn made

the first mention of the martyrdom inflicted on Haeckel during the last ten years of his life, as a result of the conduct of Professor Ludwig Plate. On April 1, 1909, Haeckel had relinquished the chair of zoology at Jena, which he had occupied for forty-eight years, and the directorship of the Zoological Institute and Phyletic Museum to his former pupil Ludwig Plate, for which the latter expressed his heartiest thanks to "his highly honored Excellency." Upon settling down in his new positions, one of Plate's first official acts was to demand that Haeckel clear out his workroom in the Zoological Institute without delay. When Haeckel protested,[80] Plate's explanation was: "Since April 1, I have been sole director of the Phyletic Museum, and you are to comply without question to all my directions." This prelude and the further developments of the conflict were related in simple words by Heilborn who was Haeckel's pupil and friend, with the result that Professor Ludwig Plate brought an action of libel against him at the District Court in Jena. Following this, Dr. Heilborn made public all the relevant facts in a small brochure, *The Lear-Tragedy of Ernst Haeckel* (Hoffman & Campe, Hamburg/Berlin 1920), based on Haeckel's unpublished letters and notes, and on official documents. Heilborn could make use of a turn of phrase that a witty advocate once used before the court: "I move for the condemnation of my respected opponent on the same grounds which he himself has brought forward." Nothing weighed more against Plate than his own remarks. From Haeckel, who had made endowments to the University of over a million marks, who had donated his large library and collections representing fifty-five years of work to it, Plate demanded the return of a number of allegedly missing books, and at another time the return of a considerable number of cardboard boxes. Furthermore, Plate stated the following: "This grave injustice which has been done to me can never be erased; however, in recognition of his great services to science and because he is my former teacher, I shall forgive him."—and "No one will hold it against me that after all these experiences I have broken off all personal contact with Haeckel.

So much for Plate versus Haeckel. I am reminded of a lecture once given by Ottokar Lorenz,[81] one of the better historians of earlier times. I did not agree with its content, but one expression appealed to me that he used right at the beginning. At a Schiller jubilee, Ottokar Lorenz had to lecture on "Schiller as a Historian." As I said, I did not agree with the content, but he said:

> Indeed, from the standpoint of present-day science, there is actually nothing more to be said about Schiller as a historian. If I nevertheless do say something more, it will be on behalf of the High Senate and my honored colleagues.

The High Senate and the colleagues were all sitting there. Now follows what we could call a special declaration by the High Senate and the colleagues. For he says:

"In the academic world of Jena, Plate stood quite alone."

—I question whether he stood by himself when he came into the lecture hall!—

> The anatomist Schwalbe once wrote: "It is unbelievable . . . how Plate behaved. I am amazed that the students in Jena did not react. It would be a really good deed if they could make it too hot for him in Jena."

Thus write the professors, the "honored colleagues," who thoroughly deplore that the students did not manage to torment Plate enough to make him leave Jena. These honored colleagues who write like this—in private letters, of course—have, however, carefully avoided being unfriendly to Professor Plate when he enters the lecture hall.

> Heinrich Heine once said that Lessing's opponents, due to their association with him, were preserved, like an insect in amber, from vanishing without a trace. Now it would be discourteous to apply this comparison to living persons, however well it would fit in a scientific context. We will therefore con-

tent ourselves with Heilborn's remark to the effect that nothing will remain of Plate's name and work except the sinister remembrance of the martyrdom that he inflicted on Haeckel.

One could cite a great many similar examples of academic morality, of the morality of the present-day intelligentsia. What comes to light thereby is that today we have to do not merely with the struggle of this or that world-view versus another; we are dealing today with the struggle of truth against the lie, and in this conflict it is the lie that directs its weapons against the truth. Today, truth's struggle against falsehood, which is extending its grip further and further on mankind, is more important than any dispute over other concepts.

It was perhaps thought to be exaggerated when, in a recent lecture, I said that the people of Europe are asleep. They will have to experience bitterly—I mentioned this in a different context—how the most extreme effect of the Western world concept is spreading in Bolshevism across all of Asia, and will be taken up by the people of Asia with the same fervor with which they received their sacred Brahman at one time. This will indeed happen, and modern civilization will have to face up to it. And one feels the deepest pain on seeing the sleeping souls in Europe, who fail so completely to evoke in their minds that real earnestness which is what matters today.

A few days after I had expressed this here, I came across the following news item:

> Some days ago, I had the opportunity to take a look at a 10,000 ruble note in possession of a representative of the Soviet Republic. What astonished me was not so much its high denomination; rather, what struck me was that in the center the bank note bore a finely and clearly drawn swastika.

This symbol, which a Hindu or an ancient Egyptian once looked upon when he spoke of his sacred Brahman, is seen today on a 10,000 ruble note! In the strongholds of politics, people know how to influence human souls. One knows what the victorious advance of the swastika signifies, the sign which a great number of people in Central Europe are already wearing today—again based on other underlying reasons—one knows what it means. Yet one is unwilling to listen to something that seeks to interpret the secrets of today's historical developments out of the most important symptoms.

This interpretation, however, can proceed only out of what can come to light through spiritual science. One must take a good look at what is presently going on. One must focus on the tendency to devastation in regard to the established cultural life, the tendency that is seeking to transform even the vestiges of this old cultural life into schools for civil servants and bureaucratic machinery, and that has morally sunk down to a low point such as I described to you in regard to Herr Plate, who is Haeckel's closest pupil, the favorite pupil of that inwardly decent, good man, Haeckel! Haeckel did not do things like that; the Ahrimanic, materialistic culture does.

In this age—in which one knows how to proceed if one goes about it consciously—one should recall great minds such as Hegel, born 150 years ago in Stuttgart, who in an inner struggle of soul and spirit wrested from the Ahrimanic powers those concepts and ideas which are needed to acquire sufficient inner spiritual steadfastness for ascending the ladder into the spiritual world; but who also offers much else of inner spiritual discipline. Truly, through the way in which his ideas can be alive now, Hegel should be treasured on the part of spiritual science; and because of what can live of him today, let us commemorate him today, on this, his 150th birthday.

He died of cholera on November 14, 1831, in Berlin, on the anniversary of the death of Leibnitz, the great European philosopher. What he has left behind, has, to begin with, either been misunderstood in the outer world, or been misrepresented by his students, or else has been dragged down directly into the Ahrimanic sphere, as in Marxism. With the help of spiritual science, the soil must be found in which the eternally enduring force that was born 150 years ago in Stuttgart in Georg Friedrich Hegel—a force containing the best extract of European spiritual life, which exerted its influence throughout sixty years in Middle Europe—can grow. It must not be buried; it must be awakened to life in spiritual science, a life such as we now truly need in this intellectual, moral and economic decline.

Lecture X
Dornach, August 28, 1920

I have often had to mention here that the science of initiation is required for the forces that are to bring about a reconstruction of declining civilization; that it is necessary to know what can be gained from beyond the threshold of the supersensible world. One can say that the spiritual evolution of humanity has proceeded from a knowledge and corresponding attitude, feeling and will that were drawn from beyond this threshold. Everything that is discovered when we go back to mankind's primordial treasures of wisdom becomes intelligible when we can trace this original wisdom to the revelations derived from mystery knowledge; when we can assume that, to begin with, sources of knowledge, of feeling and will, were accessible to humanity in its earth evolution that are not accessible by means of the purely human forces known to people today. As evolution progressed, human beings increasingly had to depend on what can be derived from the human being himself. This then is essentially the content of the forces that have been active during recent centuries in the development of civilization.

These forces that have emerged out of man himself up to now have produced a condition of civilization which, if left to its own devices, would inevitably lead to its own downfall. The majority of people today do not believe this as yet. They continue to talk and act automatically in the same old way, rejecting what is drawn from the same spiritual sources from which the ancient mystery wisdom was drawn, but now in a new way, directly through the forces of man himself. We must go quite concretely into what can be disclosed to present-day humanity as a sort of basis for all that is needed in the immediate future in the way of natural science; a knowledge that comprises human ethics, moral philosophy, but also social will. We must therefore go into certain matters that have been discussed here in the past few weeks from any number of viewpoints; today, I shall refer to them again from yet a different point of view.

When we are awake, we are, in the first place, surrounded by the outer sense world, by what produces the impressions made on our eyes, ears, organs of warmth, and on our senses as a whole. The external sense world is spread out around us, and the inner life of most people mainly consists of a further elaboration of the outer impressions. From the other side of the threshold this outer world presents an appearance that differs from the one it exhibits on this side. You know, of course, what humanity has come to in these last centuries by confining itself basically to viewing the world from this side of the threshold. To put it in a word, I would say that mankind has reached the point of looking at itself, so to speak. What man himself beholds we call the threefold man, the head man, the rhythmic man and the limb and metabolic man. Here, we shall indicate diagrammatically the tapestry that spreads round about us (see sketch on p. 3), which in the main constitutes the content of the sensory world. From this side of the threshold people now speculate on what is behind this sense tapestry. They say that behind it molecules, atoms and substances perform all sorts of dances. They give these dances any number of names, but they are convinced that when the human being looks out through his eyes, listens to the outside through his ears, in short, perceives outwardly through his senses, that some sort of material world lies behind it.

From the other side of the threshold, no such world of substance is disclosed. If a person penetrates only a little

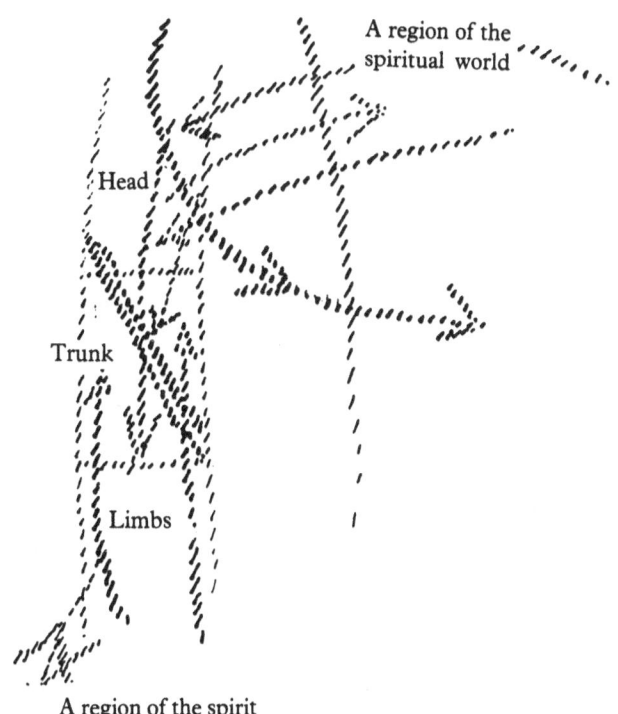

A region of the spirit

way into the region beyond the threshold, it is immediately obvious that a certain region of the spiritual world lies behind the tapestry of the senses; meaning, we are essentially dealing with a world of spirit which is located behind this sensory world.

When we take into consideration that the human being consists of the ego, the astral, etheric, and physical bodies, we have to say that when man is awake, meaning, when he is immersed in his organism with his ego and astral body, he has no share in the spirit region behind the tapestry of the senses. In sleep, on the other hand, having drawn his ego and astral body out of his physical organism, man dwells within this (upper) region of the spirit world with his ego and astral body. From the time he falls asleep until he awakens, man participates in the region lying, as it were, behind nature in a spirit-nature world. One could also say that it is the world to which man belongs for this period; a certain part of the spiritual realm is in fact allotted to him for this state of sleep.

Now man also has insight into himself only to a certain degree. He can brood about himself to some extent and then, referring to his soul nature, he speaks of thoughts, feelings and will impulses, but in most instances in a very vague manner. From this inner nature, which remains quite undefined to him, he draws the thoughts that represent memories, but he does not see behind his inner being. Thus, we can say that just as a sort of barrier stands between ourselves and a certain region of the external world, so, too, a barrier can be drawn through which the gaze, turned inward, does not penetrate. If the human being would, however, penetrate into this region that lies in a sense on yonder side of the mirror which reflects his memories, he would not discover what many mystics, affected by illusions, believe. For they assume that all one has to do is brood over one's inner being and the loftiest spiritual insight can be attained. Instead, man discovers there the mysteries of his organization, the secrets of the wondrous structure expressed in the human organism. Were man really to penetrate the barrier, he would not behold the images of a Mechthild of Magdeburg, Meister Eckhardt or St. Theresa; he would perceive the human organization, something that would appear thoroughly prosaic to certain illusion-prone mystics, but does not seem prosaic to one who possesses the right feeling for the actual mystery of the universe. One is indeed justified in saying that far more wonderful than the images of St. Theresa, Mechthild of Magdeburg, or Johannes Tauler; far more remarkable than these reminiscences forged by the reflections that exist as memories are those saturated with impulses of sensations radiating up from liver, stomach, spleen, and so on; far more wonderful than all that—yes, more remarkable, too, than what has been depicted in archetypal pictures of mankind's evolution through myths, legends and such like—is what establishes itself in the prosaic organs of the human interior. Strange as this sounds, the truth must be grasped at this point. What establishes itself there is, first of all, actual earthly substance, the element, in fact, that constitutes earthly matter. We do not find earthly matter in the outer world; it is found within the human skin. Again, this whole inner structure of man's organs is none other than something that is being pressed in a sense out of another spirit region. It is a spirit region that in a manner of speaking sweats out of itself what is present as organs in the human organism. When man looks into his inner being upon penetrating the tapestry of memories customarily radiating towards him, this organic structure is first discovered, although mystically embellished on occasion. Just as he can penetrate from beyond the threshold through the tapestry of the outer senses, when he looks through this memory tapestry, he then beholds behind this organic structure the other region of the spirit to which he belongs from the time he falls asleep until he awakens. It is a spirit region that man pays no attention to, but it is the one that bestows on him the forces expressed in his limbs.

When we contemplate our senses, we find that forces dwell in them that are mainly those lying behind the tapestry of the senses. Yet they penetrate us through the openings of our senses (see sketch) unbeknown to us, when we observe the world purely from this side of the threshold.

In our organs, too, forces are present that come from that spiritual region (Steiner here referred to the previous diagram), and the forces we possess in our arms and legs are really those that come from that other region of the spirit.

Thus, the moment man is observed from the other side of the threshold, he is perceived as the confluence of two spirit domains. What confronts us when we contemplate the human being here in the earthly world is basically only an apparent unity. In fact, man is not a unity at all. He is the confluence of the spiritually active forces from the two regions I have indicated to you. The forces that live in our eyes or in our ears, for example, are of quite another origin than those that develop when we put one foot before the other, or move our arms. One cannot harbor such a concept without realizing that man is embedded, as it were, in the whole cosmos, that owing to his senses he belongs to one particular spirit region of the cosmos and through his limbs to another. Only what lives approximately in the middle—the rhythmic man, the system of the lungs and the heart and all that is connected with it—is actually of earthly origin; it is woven, as it were, out of a kind of world in the middle. Thus, man himself is a threefold being. Without understanding this threefoldness, we cannot comprehend man. I said that this is how the human being appears when we view him from beyond the threshold. We learn to see him as a member of the whole cosmos. One becomes aware through spiritual science how man lives in the whole cosmos and is fashioned out of it. One is then no longer ignorant of the truth that must be perceived, namely, that man's task is not merely comprised of what he accomplishes here on earth; he has tasks to fulfill in the whole of cosmic evolution. He represents an essential factor, to be reckoned with in the whole spiritual cosmic evolution.

Thus, one can say that spiritual science opens our eyes to what man represents as a member of the cosmos. Compared to this, just picture how liliputian the ideas appear that people today think up concerning the human being. Nowadays matters have reached the point where a person will only accept as knowledge something derived from this side of the threshold. He only looks at what is revealed to him between awakening and falling asleep, between birth and death. Moreover, he would like to construe all the tasks that the human being can accomplish here on earth from the concepts and ideas derived from this liliputian comprehension of man. We make no progress this way. We move closer and closer towards total decline precisely because our intellectuals will not venture to construe the tasks in this world by utilizing ideas other than those gained from waking life, from what lies between birth and death. What man accomplishes, however, is of an essentially much vaster scope. This can only be understood when the insights gained by ordinary observation of life are illumined and fructified with those that can be known by means of viewing the world from beyond the threshold. There can be absolutely no improvement in the development of civilization in the world if we do not accept what can be attained for human knowledge, feeling and will from beyond the threshold.

One is moved to say that it is especially painful when one finds that programs concerning life are drawn up today out of all the truncated knowledge, curtailed on all sides, which has been amassed by humanity in the last three to four hundred years. One is really in a strange position in regard to these programs. Religious denominations exist today which, at least textually, trace their faith to earlier ages, to times when ancient mystery knowledge was still alive. Their creed is no longer understood in these religious groups. It is only textual tradition, everything else has been squeezed out like a dry lemon. It is in fact no longer there, though in a certain sense one or the other person can penetrate to an understanding of it, particularly if he presses forward to what is usually prohibited by his church. Then a person can acquire a good deal from the traditional knowledge of the confessions. For instance, if, independent of what is prescribed for him, a Catholic reflects upon the Trinity and the Incarnation, he can arrive at significant insights. Indeed, it would be more sensible in many respects to reflect upon the Trinity or the Creed than to patronize all the movements that emerge today and forge a new creed and knowledge out of the modern truncated torso of learning. For what mankind has accumulated in recent centuries and utilizes today in order to launch into movements that introduce apparent improvements in the world is far short of what has remained from antiquity in tradition, even though it has been deformed by the confessions. It is lamentable to see how all sorts of scholastic or women's movements, fabricated out of the truncated knowledge of the last few centuries, believe that they can stir the world, whereas they only talk around the real questions.

It must be said that all this rests on a certain invincible pride of modern humanity, an arrogance that will learn absolutely nothing. If a person has grown up in a movement, in some party, he generally feels that this party has not yet reached just that particular insight which he, based on his viewpoint in life, has attained on his own, and so he sets about reforming it. It is the regrettable fact of the present day that so much immature nonsense appears as reformatory ideas. Truly fruitful things can only be accomplished if these movements that hope to shake the world will allow the influx of all that can be investigated beyond the threshold of the sense world. For, you see, there is a certain domain of the spirit out there beyond the tapestry of the sensory world. What purpose does it serve? Just think, this spirit region is the very world we are in when we are awake, albeit not consciously, but in reality we are in it with our whole organism; for, as we stand, as we walk, we are within this world, we just do not see it. We continually move through this world, we are in it; we accomplish our actions in it. And when men engage in politics in it, for example, in Bolshevism, then what Bolshevists do not perceive strikes back at mankind.

The Bolshevists only wish to construct a world out of what they see, but they are not in the world that they see—they are in the world that lies beyond the tapestry of the sense world. When women's movements appear today and make all sorts of demands, they do this based on what they see, but they make these demands for the world that they do not perceive. It therefore always backfires out of the world we are in, which in reality is there, but is not present in the demands that are raised, because people stand firm against receiving anything from the spiritual world.

This world we live in, this region, naturally has its significance in the great universe. To what purpose then is it there? You see, the world we live in between death and a new birth is a different world from the one existing here behind the sense tapestry. The world we enter between death and a new birth is another domain of the spiritual world. It is mainly the spiritual region where those beings dwell whom we refer to when speaking of the hierarchies of the Angeloi, Archangeloi, and so on. Yet this world of the nine hierarchies can only subsist when, through the physical human being—and it can only happen through him—it enters into a certain mutual intercourse with the world that I have described here as the spirit region beyond the domain of the senses.

When you live in a house and wish to have contact with the outer world without actually stepping outside, you must look out of the window. When the gods of the nine hierarchies wish to communicate with this world, they must do so through man. They cannot do it directly, they must do it *through* man. It is a region of the world that can be contemplated by the gods only by means of human beings. Man must enter the physical world from the world he inhabits between death and rebirth in order to bring about a reciprocal intercourse for the gods with the world evolving here (see sketch below). And for what purpose does this world, developing beyond the sense tapestry, exist? If this world were not there, the physical world would disperse in all directions. It is the world that would be reduced to dust, for it is the world in which only forces of antipathy hold sway. The world beyond the sense tapestry (circle) holds this physical world together. In the physical world, the tendency exists to expand and spread out constantly; this world (circle) holds it together.

The gods, too, however, only come into contact with this centripetally working world through the human being. The reason man has entered the cosmos is so that the world of the gods can come into a relationship, into a perceptive relation and intercourse, with this centripetal world.

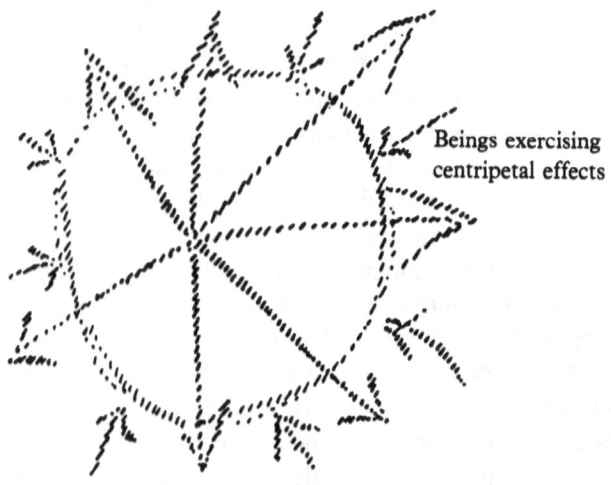
Beings exercising centripetal effects

Viewed from beyond the threshold, this centripetal world is cold and icy. To experience it is to be affected by something rigidifying, calcifying; yet it is filled with wisdom. It is woven, as it were, out of wisdom-filled thoughts, but it is cold, rigid, evoking chills. This cold, rigid world of forces holds the other (physical) world together. The human being is not organized so that he can sense this centripetal world directly. The person who enters the realm beyond the threshold feels this chill, this cold contraction. This coldness is the sign that one is actually entering with one's ego and astral body into the world which man enters each night, but without consciousness, not experiencing it. It is a sign that you enter consciously when you come into a world that makes you freeze, pervades you luminously with infinitely intensive wisdom, yet makes you freeze. Without this experience of freezing and stiffening to begin with, you cannot sense yourself on the other side of the threshold with your ego and astral body.

This is an experience that can be had and it is, in fact, one that can be gained only through actual experience. Indeed, in accordance with the explanations that you find in my books—*Knowledge of the Higher Worlds* and *Occult Science*, which are sufficient to have these experiences if they are consistently pursued—the region beyond the threshold has to be entered. For it is a region that is as real as the sense realm.

However, if one is familiar with it, when one comprehends that this region (beyond the sensory realm) exists—for one cannot truly understand the physical world without knowledge of the other one—then one realizes something else, namely, why one does go about in it. True, is it not, one cannot go about perpetually freezing and feeling chilled; this is why a boundary has been set up for his ordinary consciousness. One would really pass bad nights if one were consciously to experience the time between falling asleep and waking up. Then why does one go about in it—for, after all, one also goes about in the same world when one is awake—why does one? Man brings into this world of centripetal forces cosmic forces that dwell within his inner being. When we grasp clearly in our mind's eye what it is that lives as forces in man's inner being—we shall speak of it in more detail in the next lecture—it is an element that we can call love, warmth, warmth of soul; the human being carries this soul warmth into the cold domain. This is preeminently his cosmic task. He is the source of warmth for this sphere. If I may so express myself, inasmuch as the gods have created man—to put the matter trivially—they have created the opening for just this region that must hold together for them the world that would otherwise disperse in dust.

This is only one example. Tomorrow we shall hear of others, and particularly those that have to do with the social field so we may realize what mission men's social life on earth has for the whole cosmos. However, this is just *one* example of how, from beyond the threshold, man is seen to have a task that is not exhausted by what is normally viewed as his task within this (physical) world, but how he has a cosmic mission, how he exists for something, so to speak, that lies within the scope of the great universal plan of the divine spirits. And just as one must realize that man's existence is in fact there in order for something to take place in the universe, so must one be able to see that in everything, even in regard to the most minute achievements of humanity, man is a member of the cosmos. One must realize that everything he does signifies something that surpasses what he can first perceive with his consciousness, and that all he does signifies something in relation to the whole cosmos. By expanding ordinary, small human perceptions, they can be transformed into cosmic world perceptions. This is of primary importance in spiritual science, and it is what humanity needs today.

In the last three to four centuries, the whole of civilized mankind has fallen in a way out of its celestial sphere. It has occupied itself merely with what happens from birth to death and between waking up and falling asleep. The whole of modern life is composed only of this. *This* life, however, is doomed to death; this life is a gradually dying life. Place into it as many socialistic theories as you like as well as their metamorphoses into so-called actions; they will only hasten the decline. Bring any number of women's movements into this life and do not allow them to be fructified by a new spiritual science, and it will be less and less possible to attain what is actually instinctively desired by means of such feminist movements and the like.

What has to be fructified today must always be grasped at the right end. Oswald Spengler, who wrote a book about the decline of the West, has calculated correctly from actual scientific hypotheses that the decline of the West must definitely take place—that is, if one can only take into consideration the means at Spengler's disposal. In some measure, Oswald Spengler is right. This decline will certainly be forthcoming if an impulse does not come from spiritual science. Of course, he does not admit to such an impulse and therefore, from his standpoint, he is quite correct to write only of the West's decline. Out of this feeling of decline, Spengler—this theorist of decline—can, nevertheless, make many significant statements. He makes quite pertinent remarks at one point, for instance, about recent philistine, middle-class philosophies, mysticisms, or whatever one wishes to call them, such as vegetarianism, the manner in which discussions about food are ordinarily carried on, especially in those philistine magazines that are usually displayed in vegetarian restaurants. It is a commonplace philistine philosophy, the most philistine imaginable. But why is that? Is it so in the absolute sense? Yes, what is discussed there is naturally philistine in the absolute sense; for during the last three or four centuries people did not perceive the spirit concealed behind these things. People do not talk of the spirit today. Vegetarianism, anti-alcoholism and other fine subjects are all debated from the standpoint of pure materialism. The spirit concealed behind them is not seen. Thus, the (negative) things have actually triumphed. Philistinism has arisen because the people who would like to begin to be spiritual are often really the worst materialists. They absorb the concepts of other materialists and, in some fashion, frame a spiritual system from them.

Now, in this regard, even theoretical constructions are extraordinarily interesting. As most of you know, a certain Leadbeater is active in the Theosophical Society. This Leadbeater has written all sorts of books, and a great number of people were particularly charmed when he wrote something like an occult chemistry; I even met scholars who were most delighted by this occult chemistry. What really happened? This Mr. Leadbeater has become acquainted with the materialistic chemistry of the present with its molecules and atoms. This materialistic chemistry of today with its molecules and atoms describes oxygen, hydrogen, nitrogen, iron oxide, sodium acetate, and so on, building them up from these molecules and atoms. Out of such atoms, Leadbeater builds up the spiritual worlds, the spirits and the angels. He creates a spiritualism out of materialism. I have seen people who went about nearly enchanted when, among many things, the so-called "permanent atom" once swam around like a drop of fat on the soup of the Theosophical Society—such drops of fat sometimes did swim about, didn't they? This permanent atom—a remarkable thing! The human being dies; returns to earth again. What is it that has here endured? Of course, people could not imagine that the human organism is constituted of forces. It would be an actual impossibility for them to picture how the human limb system organizes itself from one life to the next, how the head is structured out of the previous incarnation. For in regard to the head and the limbs, these people only conceive of something grossly material which is naturally placed into the grave. They cannot imagine that forces are contained within, and that one is actually referring to these forces when speaking in this way. After all, something must pass over from one life into the next! There is *one* atom among the millions and billions of atoms; this one atom passes through the spiritual world, then the atoms of the subsequent organism group themselves around this one atom, the permanent atom. It was the delight of theosophical folk to see how this drop of fat, the permanent atom, floated on the water soup of the Theosophical Society—the spiritual water soup, that is.

Truly, these matters were only mentioned in order to show how everything at the present, even something wishing to strive for the spirit, is corroded by the materialistic conceptions of the last three to four centuries; to stress how one must leave these ideas behind in order to arrive at any kind of constructive new direction. It is, however, as I pointed out yesterday: At the present time, there exist forces that are absolutely unwilling to allow anything to arise that can aid humanity in an upward reorganization.

You may ask: Then does humanity desire its downfall? One really cannot assume that people wish the downfall of the whole of civilization. Yet, observation shows that they do, for they continue to live automatically in the old established manner. I will explain to you why they wish that. I need only indicate a single phenomenon and this will give you an explanation. Have you never seen insects flying about in a room where a light was burning and saw how they dived into the flame? Consider such a phenomenon, and then you will have a picture of the mood of modern humanity. One must simply take the phenomena of nature for what they are—symptoms of the activities of forces in the universe. We shall speak more about these things tomorrow as we seek to find the bridge to a certain form of social thinking.

Lecture XI
Dornach, August 29, 1920

It was my aim in yesterday's lecture to evoke an idea of man's position in the universe. If he is considered from the viewpoint attained beyond the threshold that lies between the world of the senses and the supersensible worlds, then man's being is understood to be an integral member of the cosmos. Yesterday, I first sought to show how man stands externally in the cosmos, as it were, by indicating that there exists a spiritual world behind the tapestry spread out about us containing all the sense impressions. I stressed that this spiritual realm is a chilly, cold world. We are within this domain unconsciously as you know, between falling asleep and waking, but in reality we then dwell in it without experiencing its actual character. We then mediate the spiritual world's intercourse with this domain by carrying warmth-bestowing love into it. This then is *one* region of the spirit. As I pointed out yesterday, however, the spiritual region that is our actual environment is a different one; it is the one that lies below that mirror that reflects the memories within us. It is this domain of the spirit that gives rise to the forming of our limb organism and all that belongs to it; it is to this spirit region that the ordinary mystic strives. He does not find it because it can only be disclosed if man penetrates the secrets of the physical and etheric organisms and discovers what it is that forms and molds this organism and permeates it with movement. This spiritual region differs essentially from the spirit domain described in connection with the external world. It need not first be warmed by man; it gives the impression of warmth. It is a region endowed with forces opposite of those in the other domain. Concerning the latter, I said that it is equipped with centripetal forces that hold the spiritual cosmos together. This other region, the source of the forces that move our limbs, is permeated with the opposite, namely, centrifugal forces. These are active perpetually, expanding the spiritual universe far and wide as it were. They are the centrifugal forces, but you must not picture them as physical forces. They are spiritual beings. Here, in a sense, we look into the constitution of the universe. We relate what constitutes the universe to what is within ourselves. We trace the forces that live in our eyes, our ears, in short, in our whole sensory apparatus, and we recognize them as the forces that hold the world together. We find in ourselves the forces through which we move our arms and legs, by means of which a number of other things occur in our limb organism. We pronounce them to be forces that if left to themselves would disperse the universe in all directions. We as human beings are set within this nexus of forces. Within it is found a world of the most diverse beings, those beings with whom the nine hierarchies, of whom we have spoken on many occasions, come into relation through the human being, who is the intermediary between worlds of gods. One would like to put it like this: The gods encounter each other through the human being.

Thus, one looks into the universe and beholds the human being in a certain respect as the mediator between divine worlds. One wishes that the awareness of this would penetrate human souls, for only such an awareness could overcome the egoistic elements of traditional religions. Indeed, these old religious elements are to a large extent founded entirely on egoism. In existing denominations, sermons are preached to appeal to people's egoistic instincts of immortality and the like. In the traditional religions, the egoistic instincts are addressed. One need only have a feeling for how people speculate on these instincts. Spiritual science aims at presenting man in such a way that he becomes conscious of the role he plays in the universe. He arrives at the realization that through him a world of centripetal forces and a world of centrifugal forces are connected; in fact, they meet one another only in man himself (see drawing below).

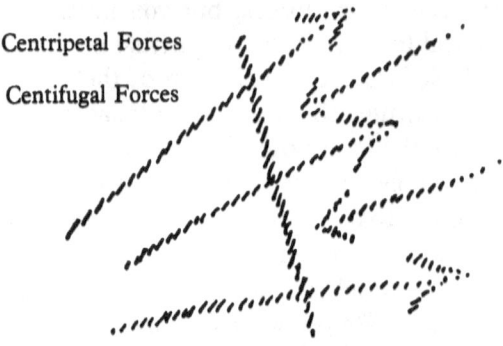

If what I have just said does not remain a colorless theory but passes over into man's whole nature of feeling and perception, then he feels himself standing in the universe and says, "I am here for the sake of cosmic evolution; through me passes the stream of cosmic events." This feeling of being an integral part of the universe must permeate the consciousness of the present and of the immediate future. Think how this feeling contrasts with another that has been brought to the surface of human development by the civilization of the last three to four hundred years. Have these last centuries arrived on their own at anything like such an awareness of the human being? Indeed not; science has in no way reflected on what the human being is and signifies in the cosmos. Attention was directed to the various types of animals. People learned to recognize how one animal form evolved from others and concluded that man is the highest of the animal forms. Man was added on to the lower animals, so to speak, as the highest animal. People learned to know man in his animality; they did not speak at all about the essential being of man. From now on, a reversal must take place in the souls of mankind. The human being must again become aware that he represents a channel for divine forces, that in a way he is the stage on which hierarchies encounter each other so that they may work together in the universe. Man should also know that when he has a low opinion of himself, acts basely and degrades his awareness of humanity, he will not be a mediator between the higher and the lower worlds. Man must learn to think of himself as a being that belongs to the cosmos. Divine beings who serve the centrifugal motive powers and divine beings serving the centripetal powers meet each other in man.

Where do they find their balance? The centripetal forces work principally through the human head; the centrifugal ones work primarily through the limb system. The middle man, the rhythmic man, is the one who is supposed to bring about the balance, the consonance and harmony between the centripetal and centrifugal cosmic forces. Consider what that means! It implies that when the human being develops a certain mood of soul, an inner attitude, which, as we have seen from a variety of aspects, can only come about in him through spiritual science, he gives a certain nuance to his whole inner experience, and it takes its course in a certain manner. This is expressed even in his very organism, the rhythms of heart and breathing. This means, in other words, that the manner in which man breathes and his heart beats has significance not only within the human being but within the whole cosmos. In the human heartbeat we have the combined activity of different worlds of gods or spirits. The ancient saying that man is a temple of the divine emerges anew from the modern knowledge of initiation science.

Therefore, what arises from these insights of initiation

science will have to bear a different character from what the traditional religions can bring to man. They reckon with his egoism. And the world conception that can come about through spiritual science—on what does that count? It reckons with man's responsibility in regard to the world; it appeals primarily to his sense of responsibility. It exalts the human being by showing him his position as an essential member of the whole universe.

This attainment of a certain consciousness of humanity is what is so urgently required. For what is the reason that mankind has fallen into such chaos today, the chaos into which, all over our civilized world, the social order has partly disintegrated already, and in part threatens to disintegrate? The reason is that the human being has forgotten his position in the cosmos; he wishes to know nothing of it. A person who does sense his link with the cosmos will realize that world evolution cannot be depicted as proceeding merely from causes outside man. He will know that it is primarily the forces in man himself that have caused the earth's origin and that will bring about its end, carrying it over into other metamorphoses of universal formation. It is in the human being that we above all must seek for what we should know and feel, and through which we are intended to shape our will.

What is the nature of the forces that work chiefly in the human head and are related to the centripetal, compressing forces of the cosmos? They are the forces that are the oldest in our universe. Recall my description in *Occult Science* where I depicted the ancient Saturn evolution, and had to indicate that the human sense life emerged out of it. Behind our sense tapestry lies what has remained behind of this Saturn evolution as the cold, frosty world that has developed from the initial condition of warmth, into which we today must carry warmth. What lies behind the tapestry of the senses is, as it were, the oldest of worlds. We enter it unconsciously from the moment we fall asleep until we awaken; though, actually, we move about in it all the time. This world bestows on us everything connected with our senses. Shaping the senses in a way from within outwards, the centripetal forces work into our senses, into our eyes, ears, and from there into our physical brain, into which we think. Inasmuch as we go through the world as thinking beings, we actually pass through it with that human property that is fashioned for us out of this environment; that is to say, with the oldest forces that have already reached disintegration. We must never forget that these are the forces that have already arrived at dissolution.

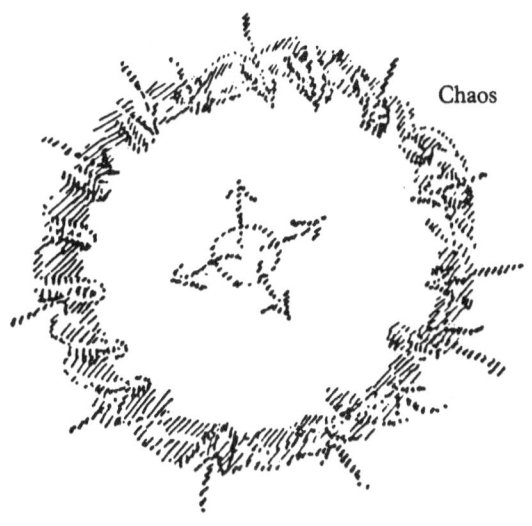
Chaos

It is really like this: If one makes a diagram of the universe as it draws apart into distant space, yet is held together centripetally at this boundary, we discover the oldest forces of the universe (see sketch above). In a certain sense, they disintegrate. And our comprehension, our human intellect, arises from these disintegrating forces that are passing over into death and have turned into chaos.

It was modern humanity's destiny that since the last three to four hundred years this intellect had to be especially developed. This intellect, however, arises, so to speak, out of the dying chaos remaining from the ancient Saturn evolution. Right into the present, into the social life, people have been trying to introduce reforms based on these very forces. These forces, however, are those that exert their normal effect just when they are destructive. We could not think if we did not have them. We could not develop our intellect without them. We destroy the social order if we try to permeate it with what results out of this, our intellect.

Any activity of thought must call upon the intellect, the intellect that arises from chaos. We must not, however, apply to social reforms something that emerges out of chaos. In Eastern Europe, we see the extreme offshoots of European intellectualism appearing in social reforms. What has arisen in Eastern Europe will spread across Asia, Europe, and the West unless, while there is still time, not once again an intellectual counteraction, but a different action is brought about that we shall consider right away. We need these forces for our spiritual life, our free cultural life. We need them because what is to be produced by our intellect can only arise from the chaos. But these forces are not usable if they are joined with the forces active in the social life. Here, the same intelligence that is useful and productive in the narrowly defined life of the mind is harmful. The element that brings about inventions and creates gifted poems must arise out of the chaos, the mature material aspect of the human organism, but it must not be believed that it can bestow social impulses to man's external life. It is important for mankind to begin now to have clear insight into these matters. This will not be the case as long as people continue to reject any consideration of spiritual science. Nonetheless, what bestows greatness on the actual life of the spirit has to arise from this chaos. Mental life must emerge out of the chaotic substrata of man's individuality.

This links the question of education with that of general culture. For anything of this nature that is to be given to humanity must arise from the chaos that man brings with him when he descends through birth from higher worlds. He brings the disintegrating organism of the brain. From this chaotic brain organism arises the element that can constitute the life of the spirit. At the opposite end of mankind's organization, the forces must develop that can underlie social ideas.

There, however, I am touching on something still quite incomprehensible to modern humanity's dreadful prejudices. Modern people believe that they think only with the head. This is nonsense; man thinks, feels and wills not only with the head but with his whole being. Arms and legs are just as much organs of the soul as is the head. It is one of the worst prejudices that the soul life was apportioned organically in a one-sided way to the nervous system. Only the intellectual life is apportioned to the nervous system. Hence, it is from the centrifugal forces, the fresh organic forces that do not represent the chaos but dwell particularly in man's limb organization and in all that belongs to it, that we must develop that which can result in social impulses, above all those of outer life and particularly the third member of the social organism, namely, the economic life. Here we are dealing with the youngest developments. In the head organization underlying the mind and spirit we deal with the oldest formations. In everything forming the basis of the economic organization we confront the youngest developments, those that are the bearers of the human will. In man of today, they normally rest entirely in the unconscious; they must, however, be drawn up into consciousness through initiation science, the science of the Mysteries. And how can they be drawn up? I do not need to describe to you how the actual free spiritual life has to come about. It begins with the education of the child; from the child's individuality it draws out what was sent down by the gods from the spiritual worlds when the child entered through birth into physical existence. There, we work out of the chaos, out of the dark, misty depths, in order to lead the human talents and gifts out of the spirit, through the chaos of matter, into physical existence.

It is a different matter when we must call upon the youngest member of man's organization, of which the human being is completely unaware in normal consciousness. There initiation science must draw everything out of unconscious depths. How does this take place? Well, social thinking is different from thinking out of the spirit. In the case of spiritual thinking, everything is based on the development of the individuality. In the case of social thinking, one can, for instance, figure out statistically how many persons among a thousand twenty-year-olds will reach age sixty. The necessary figures are easily obtained by taking a thousand twenty-year-olds from a certain region; of these, so many will reach age thirty after ten years; ten years hence, a certain number will reach age forty; and so on for age fifty and sixty. A certain type of calculation, the theory of probabilities, relies on what can thus be deduced from the numerical course of the development of groups of people. And in the matter of social institutions, one can rely upon this calculation. The insurance systems are based on these figures. If I insure my life when I am twenty, I have to pay at the rate arrived at by someone having calculated how many persons among one thousand twenty-year-olds will reach sixty, meaning how much one still has to pay at sixty. By considering this matter from the social standpoint, from that of the group, it works; otherwise all insurance companies would be bankrupted. They rely upon such groupings of facts in humanity's development.

Does this calculation have any value for the individual? Does it tell me at twenty how much longer I will probably live? Nobody will say to himself, "This means that I shall live only so many more years." The probable length of life according to which I insure my life is different from the one I count on as an individuality. We are dealing with two quite different spheres of thinking and forming judgments. One has to consider the human being in quite a different way when trying to insure him, hence wishing to make some social arrangements, than when one thinks as an individual human being about one's own life.

What should be done if we wish to arrive at social arrangements in general, particularly those of an economic nature? We must engage in statistics along the same lines as these insurance statistics; we must compile results. From this, we never arrive at the wisdom that arises from man's inner being, the chaos; instead, we obtain something that can be expressed in numbers. Just look around at what people have come to, especially those devoted to Western science. You find statistics everywhere; based on statistics, decisions are made on how much duty should be paid for this or that article, how much is needed for one thing or another. The calculation is quite similar to that used for insurance. When we focus on the individual element that stands creatively in the spiritual life, we are subject to forming a quite different judgment than if we turn to what becomes established socially in groups of people. What becomes socially established, however, in human groups and can thus be calculated is connected with the centrifugal forces, the youngest forces of man's organization that have not yet reached consciousness. Therefore, their content must be concluded from statistics.

Those who have a particular kind of enthusiasm, a cynical enthusiasm like Nietzsche[82] had, for all that springs from man's inner chaotic being and works itself out of it, attribute value to this alone, and despise everything of a group order. Nietzsche had a tremendous scorn for anything of a group nature in the world. This is the reason why, particularly in his early years, he considered the whole development of humanity in such a manner that only the single chosen individuals had value in his view. He regarded world history as being merely the path whereby the others, the insignificant ones, provided a sort of circuitous route for a few outstanding individuals. This was the foundation of Nietzsche's first world conception. He wished to focus solely on the few geniuses evident in human evolution. As for the rest, Nietzsche said that the devil or statistics could have them. They were more or less the same thing to him. What is connected, however, with the economic structure and judgment which deal with the centrifugal, the youngest forces of humanity's organization, is, and has to be, founded on statistics today.

Nevertheless, nothing really sound and wholesome can result from statistics. Trotsky and Lenin[83] have acquired their principal tenets from such statistics. In the purely economic thinking of the West, statistics play a major role. Yet, the whole of statistics has no direct value. Try sometime to compile statistics. You will not get much from them, however ingeniously you go about it. Indeed, it must be admitted that what goes on by means of statistics as sociology is a pretty bad thing. Nothing much results or has resulted from it. Basically, some people classify the figures one way, others group them a different way; accordingly, the most diverse counsels are advocated.

What is the reason for this? The reason is that the forces to which all this relates, the centrifugal forces, are indeed the youngest forces in the human being, and have in no way risen into the realms of consciousness. Man is still childishly lost in this region. We therefore have to say that if one wishes to establish social science and impulses upon what exists in the normal, modern consciousness of humanity, nothing constructive would result. There will be no clear insight into what is necessary until men admit that modern science and consciousness are impotent in shaping a social judgment in the form which is necessary today. For what is required? It is necessary to know that an individual can get nowhere with figures; only associations can do something with numbers—groups of people who make use of these experiences, each complementary to the other. Yet, despite this, such associations will still accomplish nothing special unless they have forces of direction, and what kind must they be? They must be those arising from imaginative perception, from initiation science. There will have to be those who are initiated in a certain sense, who will guide the experiences of associations into the right direction, particularly in the economic life.

Where will spiritual scientific directive forces first be required, if the needs of mankind in the present and near future are correctly understood? They will be needed precisely in the domain of the economic life. There, associations must be formed. The results that associations compile with their figures must be given their guidelines from the effects that can be gained solely from inner experience in the higher worlds. The life of the spirit, the life of geniuses, must be drawn from the chaos of the natural human organization by means of education. The basis of the economic life must be given its guidelines from initiation science. Initiation science must regulate whatever is collected by the different associations from various professional, industrial or agricultural circles, and so on. It is precisely the economic realm that makes the influence of the spiritual life mandatory, particularly in economics. There will be no advancement without it. For, in the sphere of economics, everything will remain instinctive if it is not brought to consciousness by being developed in the manner I have stated. Therefore, one should really say, "First of all, get a broom and out with everything that negates the spirit in the economic life!" On that depends the future welfare of mankind.

Away with everything that rejects the spirit in the economic life—there above all! There, it is the most compelling; otherwise, economic chaos will result and with it the general chaos of civilization; and this, I might say, is becoming evident clearly and plainly enough.

People's way of thinking during this catastrophic, world-historical moment has been strange. Since 1914, they have seen the advent of a world catastrophe. What have been their thoughts? They felt that if only peace would come within a year, all would be in order again. When peace did not come, they said, "If only it comes next year everything will be all right!"—and so on. Then came a peace that was actually only the starting point for greater conflicts. Now people continue to sleep. They do not see that the forces of decline accumulate and grow stronger from month to month. They do not wish to see it. And why not? Because they do not want to accept the spirit; they do not wish to have what alone can help to restore the world. It is of no use to believe today that compromises can be made with anything carried over from the past. That does not work. The world is asking to be built up anew; from new sources it must have new forces. What must be brought to bear as initiation science—from which forces could originate such as those I have characterized—it is this that is newly trying to come into the world. Initiation science must be accepted because without it the measures intended to lead to an ascent will deteriorate without fail, and there will be no progress.

What is needed is that a strong awareness of these things is established particularly in those people who will shoulder the greatest responsibility in the near future—I have already spoken of these facts here—namely, the Anglo-American world. The nations of Central and Eastern Europe are struck down. Inasmuch as their power and, above all, their influence are increasing, the English and American people have the definite responsibility to turn towards the life of the spirit.

This was the reason it was of such great importance that the representative center of our spiritual movement stood on neutral ground during the catastrophic years. Dornach offered a neutral ground on which those from all nations who wished to come could meet one another, where what was rooted in the soil of spiritual science itself placed no obstacle in the way of anybody. What stands here now was placed here, I might say, out of Central Europe. Truly, those were certainly not the worst forces of Central Europe which, in a material respect as well, established what stands here now. It stands here as if asking, "Does the world confront this with understanding?" Central Europe cannot be asked whether the world has an understanding for it. It is crushed to the ground, nearing its spiritual and economic devaluation, but that it had values may be evident from the fact that it could place this building here. This structure* now stands here as a question to man's comprehension for it. It is indeed an international question, a question directed to the world: Will this building stand here unfinished one day, as conditions now appear to suggest? Will it be unfinished, with only that part constructed that was built by Central Europe and added to by neutral regions? Or will the Anglo-American world bring understanding to this question that is directed to the future of humanity? One should experience this question as a deeply significant one. For either one will say "yes" to the spirit, and then the ways and means will be found to finish what otherwise must remain incomplete; or one will say "no" to the spirit, and then an unfinished building will stand here as a sign that one has no wish to understand the forces of ascent. Then, however, one will have given a negative reply to the question of whether one wishes to take the progress of humanity seriously.

---

*Note by translator: Reference to the First Goetheanum.

Lecture XII
Dornach, September 3, 1920

In our spiritual-scientific endeavors, it is important to acquaint ourselves gradually from the most diverse points of view with what we are supposed to understand. One can say that, particularly in regard to spiritual-scientific subjects, the world expects an uncomplicated, facile approach towards conviction; however, this is not easily provided. For as far as spiritual-scientific facts are concerned, it is actually necessary to attain our conviction in a gradually evolving manner. To begin with, this conviction is still weak. One becomes acquainted with the same things from ever changing new viewpoints; thus, conviction increasingly gains in strength. This is the one premise from which I should like to start today. The other will relate to various matters that I have discussed here for weeks; it will relate to what has been said concerning the differentiation of humanity throughout the civilized world.[84] Let me indicate briefly a few of the most salient facts that are of some importance to our considerations in the next three days.

I have pointed out in what sense the Orient is the source of humanity's essential spiritual life. I then indicated that in the central areas, in Greece, Middle Europe and the Roman Empire—what must be discussed covers vast periods of time—there primarily exists the predisposition for developing the legal, political concepts. The West is notably predisposed to contribute economic concepts to the totality of human civilization. It has already been mentioned that when we look across to the Orient, we find that the life of its civilization is basically decadent today. In order to evaluate properly what the Orient really signifies for the whole of human civilization, we have to turn back to more ancient periods of time. Among the historically accessible documents which are proof of the Orient's essential nature, the Vedas, the Vedanta philosophy, stand out above all; they and others are in turn evidence, however, of what was present in the Orient in still more ancient epochs. They indicate how a cultural life was born out of a primeval, wholly spiritual disposition of Oriental humanity. Subsequently, for the Orient too, ensued the times of obscuration of this spiritual life. Yet, a person who is able to contemplate in the right way what is happening in the Orient at present—although it is a mere caricature of what was formerly there—even today will still note the aftereffect of the ancient spiritual life in the decadent phenomena.

During a somewhat later period, the essentially legalistic, political thinking developed throughout the central regions of the earth. It evolved in ancient Greece and Rome, later on in the regions spread over Europe from the Middle Ages onward. The Orient originally possessed no actual political thinking, particularly not what we today define as juridical thinking. This is not in contradiction to the existence of codes of law such as Hammurabi's and others. For if you study the contents of these codes, you recognize from the whole tone and attitude that you are dealing with something quite different from the mode of thinking defined in the Occident as juridical. It is only in recent times that an actually economic form of thinking has developed in the West. As I have already explained, even science as it is practiced now is assuming those forms that really belong to the economic life.

As far as the Oriental spiritual life is concerned, it is interesting to observe how everything that the Occident has possessed up to now is basically also a legacy of the Oriental spiritual life, although in metamorphosed forms. Some time ago, I pointed out here how considerably this spiritual life of the Orient has been transformed in Europe. We are confronted by the fact that the capacities that held sway in the Orient have yielded up a perception of the immortal human soul, but in such a manner that this immortality was intrinsically bound up with prenatal existence before birth. The soul perception of the Oriental mind had a view, above all else, of preexistent life, of the soul's life between birth and death preceding this earthly existence. Everything else followed in consequence of this in a manner of speaking. From this view resulted the mighty relationships, only dimly glimpsed by the Westerner to this day, that one might call the karmic relationships, which subsequently left a reflection, albeit only a faint one, in the Greek concept of destiny. What is it, really, that passed over, that flowed across into the Occidental version of those concepts, even those with which an attempt was made to understand the Mystery of Golgotha? It was something that was strongly tinged by legalistic thinking. There is a radical contrast between contemplating the path of the soul in the sense of the Oriental world conception as descending from a spiritual world into the physical realm, noting how the karmic relationships are viewed there from wide perspectives, and considering the juridical idea of holding court over the soul that, in the Occident, has invaded these Oriental concepts. We need only recall Michelangelo's magnificent painting in the Vatican, in the Sistine Chapel, where the World Judge, like a cosmic magistrate, adjudicates upon good and evil men. This is the Oriental world view translated into Occidental legalism; this is in no way the original Eastern world conception. This legalistic thinking lies entirely outside Oriental perception. Indeed, the more advanced the concept of the spirit became in Central Europe, the more it culminated in the Roman legalistic element.

Hence, in the central regions, we are dealing primarily

with the element predisposed for the juridical and political thinking. Civilization is, however, not only differentiated over the earth in this manner but in yet another way. If we study the accomplishments of the East, if we consider the special nuance of Oriental soul life, in particular where it is at its greatest, we find that this soul life is most eminently atavistic and instinctive, notwithstanding the fact that its fruits are primarily cultural; and all of mankind has continued to sustain itself on them. This spiritual life emerges out of unconscious imaginations that are, however, already muted by a certain ray of consciousness. Nevertheless, it contains much that is unconscious and instinctive.

The spiritual life produced by humanity up until now is indeed brought forth in a way that points to the highest spheres of which the human soul can partake, but the lofty heights of these spheres were reached in a sort of instinctive flight. It does not suffice to retrace the concepts or images produced by the Orient. Rather, it is necessary to focus on the singular kind of spiritual and soul life, by means of which, especially in its flowering time, the Oriental arrived at these conceptions. To be sure, we only gain an idea of this distinctive soul quality that I have already characterized by relating it with the life of the metabolism, if we want to have a feeling for the whole original soul structure contained in the Vedas and other texts. We simply must not overlook the fact that the Orient has reached its decadence today; for example, we should in no way confuse the mystic, nebulous manner which, despite his greatness, distinguishes Rabindranath Tagore,[85] from the true essence of Oriental soul life. For, although Rabindranath Tagore possesses what has been handed down to this day of the ancient Eastern soul life, he permeates it with all manner of modern, Western European affectations and is, above all, an affected individual.

Spiritual science must indeed lay hold of these matters, step by step, and in such a way that we do not merely accept some rigidly set up concepts, but really envision the unique soul nuance involved here. Thus, we find in the Orient an instinctive cultural life, permeated through and through with the trend for the legalistic and political soul life developing in the central regions. There, we come to the development of the half instinctive, the half conscious. It is most interesting to examine how a purely juridical thinking is produced from the souls of people, say, like Fichte, Goethe, Schelling or Hegel. It is purely juridical, but it is partly instinctive, partly a fully conscious thinking; something that is, for example, the special charm of Hegel's mode of thinking. A completely conscious element only appears in the Western soul, where consciousness develops out of the instincts themselves. The conscious element is still instinctive in the Western soul, but instinctively the conscious emerges in Western economic thinking. Here, for the first time, mankind is called upon to attain to a conscious penetration of even public, social affairs.

Now we come across something quite strange. One might actually recommend that those to whom it matters for one reason or another should now try to understand the configuration of civilized humanity's thinking by becoming acquainted with the attempts of the English thinkers to arrive at a mode of social thinking, say, the attempts of Spencer, Bentham, particularly Huxley, and so on. These thinkers are indeed all rooted in the same atmosphere of thought in which Darwin was rooted; they all really think as Darwin thought, except that they try, as does Huxley, to develop a social view out of their scientific way of thinking. A strange feeling pervades us when we delve into the attempts by Huxley[86] to achieve a social thinking, for instance, about the state, about the legal aspects of human relationships. It gives one a strange feeling. Let us suppose the following: Someone wishes to acquire a sense, a feeling for what I have here in mind, and to that end reads Hegel's book on natural rights,[87] on political sciences, Fichte's philosophy of rights,[88] or something else by a minor Middle European mind; afterwards, he reads, possibly, Huxley's attempts to advance from scientific to political thinking. He would experience something like the following. He would say to himself, "I read Hegel and Fichte; the concepts here are fully developed, they have strong contours and are precisely drawn. Now I read Huxley or Spencer, and I find the concepts primitive; it as though one had just begun to contemplate these questions. Confronted by such things, it does not do to say, "Well, the one was perfect, the other imperfect." This does not suffice at all when one confronts realities.

Let me present to you a parallel taken from an entirely different realm. It can happen that one lectures on some spiritual-scientific subject, say, the former embodiment of the earth, the Moon embodiment. A variety of facts are set forth. Someone reads or listens to this lecture who is clairvoyant in a quite atavistic manner. It could be an individual who is outwardly illogical, who in practical life is unable to put five words together in logical sequence, who is inept in everything and therefore of no use in ordinary life. Such a person listens to what is being related about the configuration of some Moon era. Now, this same person who is quite dull and blundering in outer life and unable to count up to five properly, yet who is atavistically clairvoyant, can take in what he has heard, enlarge upon it, develop it further and discover additional facts not mentioned earlier. The things that such a person then adds can be infused with extraordinarily penetrating logic, a logic that arouses admiration, while, in everyday life, this person is clumsy and illogical. This is entirely possible, for if someone is atavistically clairvoyant, it is not *his* ego that joins his images together in a logical manner, although he can discover the images by himself. The images are joined by various spiritual beings dwelling within him. We become acquainted with *their* logic, not his.

This is why we cannot simply say that one view is on a higher, the other on a lower level; in every case we have to go into the specific character of the matter. This is true here too. The views of Fichte, Hegel and other less illustrious minds are half instinctive, only partly fully conscious ones. What arises, on the other hand, in the West as primitive economic thinking is indeed fully conscious. The concepts such as those thought out by Huxley, Spencer and others are impertinently conscious, but conceived in a primitive way. What had appeared in former times in instinctive or half instinctive form emerges here consciously but in quite an elementary way. I shall illustrate this by means of a concrete example.

Huxley tells himself that if we observe nature—he naturally looks at it from the Darwinian standpoint—we find the struggle for survival. Every creature fights ruthlessly for self-preservation, and the whole animal kingdom's struggle is waged so that the naturally strong survive by annihilating the weak. This theory has penetrated into Huxley's flesh and blood. This, however, cannot be continued on into humanity. Freedom such as we must seek in human social life is nonexistent in nature, for there can be no freedom—thinks Huxley—in a realm where every creature must either assert itself ruthlessly or perish. There can be no equality where the fittest must always eliminate the less fit. Now Huxley turns from the natural realm to the social sphere and is compelled to conclude that, indeed, this is true, but in the social realm goodness should prevail, freedom should reign. Something should come to pass that as yet cannot be found in nature.

It is again the great chasm that I have characterized from so many points of view. Once, Huxley very aptly calls man "the splendid rebel," who, in order to establish a human kingdom, rebels against all that prevails in nature. Something therefore ensues here that is not yet found in nature. Now again, Huxley actually thinks along scientific lines. He is compelled to search for natural forces in man that constitute the social life and rebel against nature herself. He looks in man for something concrete that serves as the basis for the human social community. The other forces of the kingdoms of nature cannot establish this social community; in nature, the struggle for survival holds sway, and there is nothing that could hold humanity together in a social structure. Nonetheless, as far as Huxley is concerned, there is nothing but this natural cohesion. Hence, this "splendid rebel" must in turn have natural forces which, although they are forces of nature, rebel against the natural forces in general. Now, Huxley finds two natural forces that are at the same time the basic forces of the social life. The first one is actually worked out wrongly, for it is not yet capable of establishing a social life, only family egoism. It is what Huxley calls the family attraction, something that is active within blood relationships. The second force he lists that could form a sort of natural foundation for the social life is something that he calls "the human instinct for mimicry," the human talent for imitation.

Now, there is something that appears in the human being in the sense referred to by Huxley, namely, the faculty of imitation. It means that one person follows what the other does. This is the reason the individual pursues not merely his own directions, but society as a whole, the social life, runs along the same lines, as it were, because one person imitates the other. This is as far as Huxley goes. It is very interesting, because you know that in describing the human being we list the following: The element of imitation from the first to the seventh year; from the seventh to the fourteenth year, the element of authority; the one of independent judgment from the fourteenth to the twenty-first year. All three, of course, participate in the social development. Huxley, however, stops short at the first; he is only laboring to emerge from the primitive level. He has taken hold of nothing but the force that is active in the human being only until his seventh year. We are confronted with nothing less than the fact that if the social community as envisioned by Huxley were actually to exist, it would have to consist entirely of children; human beings would have to remain children perpetually. Thus, in envisioning the social life, Western society has, in fact, only advanced to the stage applicable to children. The social science striven for in full consciousness has progressed no further than this. That is most interesting.

Here, you can detect the primitive aspect in connection with a particular element. The West works its way out of the scientific-economic thinking and attains something in a conscious manner that has been reached in the central regions in a half conscious, half instinctive way on a higher level. We can actually follow up these things in detail and they can thus become most interesting. All matters brought to light by spiritual science can invariably be followed up by means of details. It only requires a sufficiently large number of people to develop enough diligence to pursue all details of spiritual-scientific matters.

Is it not actually rubbed into us in this instance that something else must be present that cooperates in the social development of existence? For, certainly, social structures cannot be established in which only forces of imitation hold sway. Otherwise, they could only contain children; human beings would have to remain children forever, if the social life would originate only through mutual imitation. In order to arrive at something that can throw light on the primitive attempts, and can also bring together East, Middle and West, we must proceed from initiation science. This means that we have to link the train of thought that we tried to connect with the above to what initiation science can offer to humanity, so that mankind may be capable of developing a social life truly structured in conformity with the spirit.

People fail to observe how the environment of the human being is pervaded with quite clearly differentiated forces. Modern science has reached the point where it states that we are surrounded by air, for we inhale and exhale it; but there is something that is even more obvious in our life than "the air around us," something that people fail to notice. Take the following simple fact that no one today takes into consideration, yet is something that could be understood by anybody. An animal kingdom is spread out around our human kingdom. This animal kingdom includes creatures of every imaginable form. Let us picture to ourselves this whole manifold animal kingdom around us. In the case of a table, everybody knows that there are forces present that gave this table its shape. In regard to the animal kingdom surrounding us, we ought, naturally, to assume the same, namely, that just as air is present, so, in the environment, the forces are contained that bestow form upon the creatures of the animal kingdom. We all dwell within the same realm. The dog, the horse, the oxen and donkey do not move about in a different world from the one which we also inhabit. And the forces that bestow the donkey shape on the donkey affect us human beings too; yet—forgive me for speaking so bluntly—we do not acquire the form of a donkey. There are also elephants in our environment, but we do not assume the shape of elephants. Yet all the forces fashioning these shapes surround us everywhere. Why is it that we do not take on the forms of, say, a donkey or an elephant? We possess other forces that counteract them. We would indeed acquire these shapes if we did not have these other opposing forces. It is a fact that if we as human beings confront a donkey, our etheric body constantly has the tendency to assume the shape of a donkey. We restrain our etheric body from doing so only because we have a physical body possessing a solid form. Again, if we face an elephant, our etheric body endeavors to assume the elephant shape and is prevented from doing so only because of the physical body's solid shape. Whether it be elephant, stag-beetle or dirt-beetle, the etheric body tries to assume the shapes of any and all creatures. Potentially, all the forms are present in our etheric body, and we comprehend these forms only when we retrace them inwardly, as it were. Our physical body merely prevents us from turning into all these shapes. Therefore, we can say that we carry the entire animal kingdom within our etheric body. We are human only in our physical body. In our etheric body, we bear with us the whole animal kingdom.

Again, there flows all around us the same complex of forces that creates the plant forms. Just as our etheric body is predisposed to assume all animal shapes, our astral body is inclined to reproduce all the plant forms. Here it is already more pleasant to make comparisons, for, while the etheric body is imbued with the tendency to become a donkey when it sees one, the astral body wishes merely to become the thistle on which the donkey feeds. But this astral body is definitely ensouled with the tendency to accommodate itself to those forces that find their external expression in the plant forms. Thus we may say that the astral body reacts to the complex of forces that shapes the plant kingdom.

The mineral kingdom is again a force complex that develops the various shapes of this specific realm. This acts within our ego. It is quite evident in the case of the ego, for you only think in terms of the mineral realm. After all, it has been reiterated time and again that the intellect can only grasp the inanimate. Hence, what is contained in the human ego understands the lifeless. Consequently, our ego dwells in the complex of forces that creates the mineral kingdom. The physical body, as such, lives in none of these realms; it has, as you know, a realm of its own. In my *Occult Science, an Outline*, the mineral, plant and animal kingdoms are dealt with separately; this signifies that the physical body possesses a domain of its own. The animal kingdom, on the other hand, is actually found in the etheric body; as far as this viewpoint is concerned, the plant kingdom is found in the astral body, and the mineral kingdom in the ego. From my various books, however, you are familiar with something else. You know that during earthly life these various bodies are worked upon. I have described how the ego, the astral body, the etheric body and even the physical body are worked on. I initially outlined it there, I might say, from the human, the humanistic intention. Now let us try to depict it from another point of view.

Take the mineral concepts that the human being acquires. He experiences the external world, after all, by experiencing it in mineral concepts and forms. Only enlightened minds like Goethe work their way up to the pictorial forms, to the morphology of plants, to metamorphosis. Here, the shapes are transformed. The ordinary view, still prevailing today, on the other hand, only dwells in the solid, mineral forms. If, now, the ego works on these forms and develops them, what is the result? Then, the result is the conscious cultural life, one of the domains of the threefold social organism. The ego creates the cultural life while working inwardly upon itself. All cultural life is, in fact, inner formative development of the ego. What the ego acquires from the mineral realm and in turn transforms into art, religion, science, and so forth, that is the cultural sphere, the transformed mineral kingdom, the spiritual realm.

What results from the tendency of the astral body, residing in the subconscious depths of most human beings, to assume every plant form possible? When you transform this tendency indwelling the astral body, when it radiates up into consciousness in half instinctive, half conscious form, what comes about then? The domain of rights, of the state, comes about.

Now, if you comprehend what holds sway in the relationships between human beings, namely, what is now, within external life, transformed from man's experiences of animality in the ether body, then you arrive at the third domain of the threefold social organism. Were we to stop at the etheric body as it comes to us from birth, we would only have the tendency in this etheric body to turn now into a donkey, now into an oxen, now into a cow, now into a butterfly. We would reproduce the entire animal kingdom. As human beings we do not merely do this, however, we also transform the ether body. We accomplish this within the social life by living together with others. When we face a donkey, our etheric body wishes to become a donkey. When we confront another human being, we certainly cannot say without uttering a real insult that now, too, we wish to turn into a donkey. This is not possible, at least not in ordinary life; here we must change in another way. I should like to say that, here, the transformation becomes visible; here, those forces come into play that are effective in the economic life. These are the forces that assert themselves when a human being confronts his fellowman in brotherliness. In this way, in the brotherly confrontation, those forces are active that represent the work on the etheric body; thus, through the work on this body, the third realm, the economic sphere, comes into being.

Animal Kingdom:	Etheric Body	Economic Realm
Plant Kingdom:	Astral Body	Realm of Rights, of State
Mineral Kingdom:	Ego	Cultural, Spiritual Realm

Thus, just as man is connected on the one side with the animal kingdom through his etheric body, he is related on the other side in the external environment with the economic sphere of the social organism. We could say that if man is viewed inwardly, spiritually, from the physical body towards

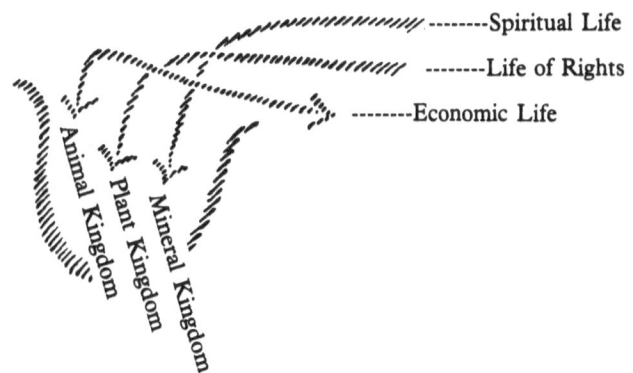

the etheric, we find the animal kingdom within man. Outwardly, in his surroundings, we find the economic life.

When we penetrate into the human being and search out what he represents by virtue of his astral body, we find the plant kingdom. Outwardly, in the social configuration, the life of rights corresponds to the plant kingdom. Again, penetrating the human being, we discover the mineral kingdom corresponding to the ego. Outside, in the environment, corresponding to the mineral kingdom, we have the cultural life. Thus, through his constitution, man is linked to the three kingdoms of nature. By working on his whole being, he becomes a social being.

You see that we can never arrive at a comprehension of the social life if we are not in a position to ascend to the etheric body, astral body and ego. For we do not understand man's relationship to the social order if we don't ascend like that. If one proceeds merely from natural science, one stops short at the "human instinct for mimicry," the faculty of imitation; one cannot progress. In thoughts, one makes the whole world puerile, for it is the child that still retains most of the natural forces. If one wishes to advance further, one needs the insight into initiation science. We need the insight into the fact that the human being is bound up with his etheric body through the animal kingdom, with the astral body through the plant world, and with the ego through the mineral realm. We need to know that owing to his observation of the mineral world man attains to his cultural life; that due to the transformation of the deep instincts harbored by him and owing to his kinship with the surrounding plant world he attains to the life of rights, of the state. We realize that these deep instincts correspond to the sphere of rights and the state. This is why, at first, the life of the state contains so much of the instinctive element if it is not infused with the cultural element of jurisprudence. Finally, we have the economic sphere which basically represents the metamorphosis of those inner experiences gained in the etheric body.

Now, these experiences are not brought to the surface from within by the science of initiation, for Huxley is not motivated in any sense by initiation science to explore the connection between man and the economic life. He observes the exterior, the conditions economically present outside. The whole complex of relations between the economic sphere, the etheric body and the animal kingdom is unclear to him. He looks at what is outwardly present. Consequently, he can certainly not advance beyond the most primitive, elementary level, the faculty of imitation.

From this we realize that if people would wish to continue extracting social thinking from modern science, they would remain caught up in absurdities and something quite dreadful would have to ensue. Over the whole earth, a social life would have to arise that would bring about the most primitive conditions; it would lead humanity back to a puerile social life. Gradually, untruth and lying would become a matter of course simply because people could not do otherwise even if they wanted to. They would be thirty, forty, fifty or even older, yet they would have to behave like children, if, with their consciousness, they only wanted to comprehend what is derived from science. People would only be able to develop the instincts of imitation. Even today we frequently have the feeling that only these instincts of imitation are being developed. We watch the appearance, somewhere, of yet another reform movement of a radical nature. It really only contains the instincts of imitation derived from some university philistine. Much of what, today, looks most illustrious when given the polish derived from the customary falsehoods would appear very different in the light of initiation science. Modern comprehension of the world, however, is limited to what can be seen in the light of the concept of imitation unless one is willing to advance from ordinary, official science to the science of initiation, the science that draws its substance from the inner impulses of existence.

Thus I have tried to show you how the aspects that are lacking in the present, the very aspects through which it becomes evident where the present age must remain stuck because of its inability to penetrate reality, can be fructified and illuminated by the science of initiation.

Lecture XIII
Dornach, September 4, 1920

Yesterday, I tried from a certain angle to point out the need for a structural organization of the social order. At the same time I drew attention to the fact that what in spiritual science may be termed presentation of proof consists in recognizing that these facts under discussion are supported from the most varied aspects; finally, that the degree of conviction increases in proportion to the amount of such support.

I should like to repeat briefly what has been brought forward. We are familiar with the constitution of the human being; we know that he is composed of physical body, etheric body, astral body, and what we call the ego. We are also aware, however, that this constitution of man is something that is, so to speak, in a state of flux. You can follow my descriptions in my books, *Theosophy* and *Occult Science*, and you will learn from them that physical, etheric, astral body and finally also the ego are not really something static. Instead, you will find that the purpose of human evolution consists in the very fact that man, throughout his repeated lives on earth, works upon these members of his organization. Thus, after a certain time, after a certain number of incarnations, he is born in such a way that it is possible to say that he normally consists, as it were, of physical body, etheric body, astral body and ego. Then, however, he first begins to work on his ego, continuing this work through a number of incarnations. When the ego has been strengthened, having completed a certain amount of work on itself, this work then passes over to the astral body. Again, when, with the help of the ego and through its own efforts, the astral body has in this manner completed inner work upon itself, then this activity passes over to the etheric body and finally to the physical body. Here, however, we already enter the realm of the distant future. For you know that the human being essentially retains his outer form throughout the incarnations that we trace in the first place. You also know from my *Occult Science* that this human form has undergone fundamental changes in the course of time and will also continue to do so in the future. These changes, these metamorphoses, are imposed upon it by the activity of the more refined members of the human organism, the astral and etheric bodies, in their work of perfecting the physical body. Ultimately, in distant future times, man's physical body, too, will assume different forms.

Now, this work that the human being performs upon the members of his organism is connected with the human environment, just as man is similarly connected since his primal beginning with his natural environment through his individual members.

We must indeed be clear about one thing. Let us take the physical body of man. It stands as a unique phenomenon within the natural order. In a way, it is lifted out of this natural order. If we are sufficiently observant of the strong differentiation existing between the human being and the various species of the animal kingdom, we cannot help but say that the human being should not simply be placed at the end of the animal kingdom as the evolution theorists would have it. He is not only a composite of all animal forms in the entire animal kingdom; he is also a composite at a higher stage. Therefore, we can class this physical body of man with nothing but itself. In all that surrounds us, in all our natural environment, we are unable to find anything that could be placed in the same category with the physical body of the human being. This human physical body, then, stands by itself (see outline on next page).

Proceeding inward, we now advance to the etheric body.

Here we reach man's next and already mobile component. In a way that some of you may feel is peculiar, I have already described to you the extent of the etheric body's mobility. It has the tendency to confront the animal world in a certain way, having a particular affinity with this realm. I have said that when we confront an elephant, a donkey, a calf, or other animal shapes, our etheric body has the inner tendency to imitate the given form, to become similar to it. It is prevented from carrying this out entirely, but it has the inner tendency to assume these animal forms. It has a special kinship with them. Due to the forces concentrated in the physical body, the etheric body is prevented from realizing these tendencies, but it strives to do so. One of the first experiences of initiation is the emergence of this inner tension and urge in regard to the animal world, of wishing to become like the animals. Thus we can say that concerning his physical body the human being is *not* related to the animal world, but his etheric body displays a quite decided kinship with that world.

We now advance to the astral body. Here we come across a similar inner relationship to the plant world. When the astral body faces the plant kingdom, it has the tendency to become plantlike, that is, to become like the particular plant it confronts. I said to you yesterday, rather as an aid for your memory, that if we stand in front of a donkey that is eating thistles, our etheric body desires to resemble the donkey and the astral body the thistle. This is a fact. In this way, we are related to the kingdoms of nature surrounding us. With our astral body, we are related to the plant world.

Physical Body	
Etheric Body:	Animal World
Astral Body:	Plant World
Ego:	Mineral World

As I have said, in regard to our ego we are related to the mineral world. That seems natural, for it is something inaccessible to immediate consciousness, something that we can also establish most easily in regard to ordinary consciousness. In fact, we owe the entire content of our consciousness to this kinship with the mineral world. We form the content of our consciousness essentially out of the mineral realm. I have told you that it is due to the fact that man's ego in its present condition is organized in the direction of the mineral world that we are unable through our scientific efforts to advance to an apprehension of the plant world, let alone the animal world. We are unable to lay hold of the living and continue to argue back and forth whether the living can be comprehended or not. Only people who, like *Goethe*, proceed from a different manner of perception can acquire an awareness of the fact that the living can, in a certain way, be entered into. In the same manner as ordinary consciousness merely traces man's kinship to the mineral world, initiation, of course, offers the possibility of tracing inwardly what takes place in the astral body in regard to the plant world, or in the etheric body regarding the animal world.

I also told you that the human being works on his ego. Throughout his repeated earth lives he develops his ego. He thus transforms the content born out of the mineral kingdom. He creates from it his science, his art, and his religion. Everything that in this way appears as the content of culture and civilization is, basically speaking, transformed mineral kingdom.

Imagine, for example, that you are looking at a Greek statue. There is, of course, no life in it. All that is circumscribed by the mineral, however, such as form and structure, has been attained by you because of your transformation—and here it is an artistic transformation—of the images and sensations you have been able to receive directly into your consciousness from the mineral kingdom.

So it is with the other contents of culture. In every cultural content, insofar as it consists of art, science and religion, is expressed what the ego has achieved as work upon itself, naturally in cooperation with other humans, and what is, essentially, transformed content derived from the mineral kingdom. Whoever pursues these matters without prejudice will find that in the activity of the ego he is dealing with a transformed content won from the mineral kingdom.

By strictly defining what lives in man's social environment, we discover the following. Everything brought into being because the ego transforms the content gained from the mineral realm and forms it into a cultural life (which then exists in our midst as art, as literature, science, religious denominations or the contents of their creeds, in fact all that is essentially comprehended by means of the ego's self-transformation) defines quite clearly what we call the cultural realm of the threefold social organism. Here you have, then, the possibility of strictly defining the spiritual or cultural domain of the threefold social organism. Such a spiritual domain would not exist at all were the ego not to transform its own being so that it can work artistically, religiously and scientifically on what is derived from the mineral kingdom.

We transform our astral body, too, though not in the same conscious manner in which we transform our ego. If we survey the content of our culture, we find its most conscious component parts to be those from the spiritual domain just characterized. Only half conscious are the concepts that regulate the life between man and man (although here they have come into existence most poignantly) and comprise the life of rights and all that pertains to the sphere of rights—namely, the relationships between man and man. Anyone who cannot comprehend the difference between a concept belonging to the religious, scientific or artistic sphere with one pertaining to the sphere of rights, of the state, is without doubt not a good psychologist or observer of the soul. In a very different way do we regulate the relations, the dim awareness between people: What is my duty to the other person? What are his rights and what are mine? All these questions playing between man and man issue from a much dimmer consciousness than that which deals with science, religion and art. The realm of interplay between man and man, where matters cannot be decided by individuals as in science, art or religion, which can be determined only by human social life, by agreement and reciprocal understanding, is the realm that comprises the life of jurisprudence or the state, the sphere of rights of the threefold social organism.

We experience with an even duller consciousness a third domain that comes into existence because we transform our etheric body. This is a domain of which we acquire an awareness in a most indirect manner through all kinds of vague dietetic rules and so forth. It is a domain which we experience almost in a state of sleep and which sends its effects into full consciousness to such a slight degree that not even the relations between people can throw light on it. The domain of rights can be illuminated by the mutual agreement between people, and it constitutes a certain ideal of our social order that in the sphere of rights we have introduced full democracy where all people of legal age are equal and can secure their rights through mutual understanding. The dullness of consciousness which has as its content the transformation of the astral body suffices for the individual when he is sustained by an understanding with his fellowman. The human being must grasp science on his own; religion he must generate for himself; art he must bring forth from the wellspring of his individual being, the innermost fountain of his personality. These must proceed from the most wide awake, clearest consciousness. Here, he must rely entirely upon himself, upon his individuality. One even considers it somewhat abnormal that associations have recently cropped up from time to time in the arts. As a rule, they usually consisted only of two people, as when playwrights collaborate. Occasionally one reads in theater programs, "Popular Comedy by X. Y. and U. Z." In most instances, however, as those familiar with this field know, it is not a proper association of two. As a rule, some elderly gentleman who in his youth had written plays, but whose talent, if such it can be called, has since evaporated, enters into an agreement with an as yet unknown young man, lets him write the drama, makes a few corrections, and has now added his name to it. Thus, the young playwright, too, has slid into the limelight. In this manner, "associations" have come about in this area, but anybody senses that this is something abnormal, for what actually belongs to the spiritual sphere must also belong entirely to the personality of an individual. By comparison, with regard to the settlement of rights, the human being is able to manage if, as an individual personality, he has the support of another individual. This, however, does not suffice in reference to a sphere into which consciousness does not really penetrate. In the etheric body where etheric processes run their course, it is not enough if man as an individual confronts another individual. Where man as an individual confronts mankind as a whole, it is necessary to form associations; it is necessary that judgments or decisions be formulated by individuals in association, hence, that individuals pool their experiences. Deeds and accomplishments then must spring from associations, not from individual personalities. Here we are referred to a life where the individual person can do nothing by himself, where he can accomplish something only when he is part of an association, and where the association enters into reciprocal relationships with another association. In short, we are directed to what really takes place within the human social community in this duller consciousness—the economic sphere of the social organism.

Thus we can say that if we look in a backward direction

at what the human being represents today, in the direction of nature, we find him grounded with his etheric body in the animal world, with his astral body in the plant world, with his ego in the mineral world. He does, however, transform these existing component members of his. He transforms his etheric body; as a consequence of this, the economic sphere arises around him in the life of the human community, the economic life in which, in turn, he is grounded with his etheric body in the outer world, in the social organism. With his astral body, man is anchored in the rights sphere of the social organism; with his ego he is grounded in its cultural sphere. Thus, as human beings, we stand linked together with the three kingdoms of nature on the one side; on the other side, we are linked with the social life in accordance with the three members of the social order: the spiritual, the rights, and the economic.

Physical Body		
Etheric Body:	Animal World	Economic Sphere
Astral Body:	Plant World	Rights Sphere
Ego:	Mineral World	Cultural Sphere

We must now proceed from the basis of a completely clear manner of conception in order to deepen still further this whole insight we have thus gained. Let us keep well in mind that the social order in its structural organization is brought about by the metamorphosis of our etheric body, astral body and ego that we carry out in successive earth lives. Looking at it in this way, we find, as it were, what man contributes on his own to the emergence of the social life by means of the structure of his organism. The social life, in turn, reacts upon the human being. Up to now we have considered the will aspect of the social life. We observed how it comes into existence, how it flows out of the configuration of human nature. Keep in mind that it is present in reality when it has flown out! So, the economic sphere flows out of the etheric body or out of the transformation of the latter; the rights sphere arises from the astral body; the spiritual or cultural sphere from the transformation of the ego. Now, these three spheres, having thus issued forth, are then realities and in turn react upon the human being. First, he produces them out of his own being; then they react upon him.

You see, we must also take into consideration this second form of human interaction. We can say of it that it is more from the aspect of cognition. What we have considered so far, namely, the manner in which the human being brings about the threefold social organism, was more from the will aspect. Now we turn more to the cognitive side, and consider what kind of impressions arise when man's environment reacts in turn on him. Then, observation shows that the spiritual sphere reacts upon the human physical body, although only to a very slight degree in the present incarnation. To be sure, it can to some extent be noted that the human being, as he develops within a certain relationship to his environment, adopts something from his environment insofar as it is the cultural sphere. If a person grows up in an artistic atmosphere, one who is sensitive to this will note it in his physiognomy. A prosaic environment will, likewise, be noticeable. However, this is only a matter of a most delicate nuance of life. For the most part, we can say that in regard to the way it is formed in *this* earth life, man's physical body does not exhibit a strong influence from the spiritual environment. All the stronger is this influence in regard to the following earth lives. It is true that in our subsequent incarnations our physiognomy will bear the marked result of our spiritual environment in this life. The way we look today, the kind of physiognomy we now possess, is essentially due to the influence of the spiritual environment in which we spent our previous earth life. If one has a feeling for this—although this is possible, I might say, only in a certain general sense—one can, indeed, see in the face of a person the sort of environment in which he lived in previous earth lives. Certain discrepancies also arise from matters such as these which, at times, confront us quite emphatically in human life.

Imagine, let us say, that in regard to his former incarnation a person descends from a cultured family; he now grows up in an uncultured family. His face then bears that subtle nuance of life that I spoke of before, although, perhaps to a trifling degree. Perhaps, in his face, he strongly reveals what he brought over from his former earth life. Often, it is only in this context that one understands how it is possible that a crude fellow can sometimes have quite delicate features. The things in human life are related, indeed, in decidedly complicated ways.

Now we can say: Yes, but the human being does not take along his physical body into his next earth incarnation; after all, he discards it. This is true of the physical substance, but I should like to repeat what I said some time ago (drawing). What you actually behold as the physical body in its form is not the physical organism of man; it is the *form* (see drawing). Into this form, matter is merely inserted. It is absorbed by the form. The form is something absolutely spiritual, and I refer to this form when I speak of the effect of the spiritual sphere upon the physical body. What is discarded are only the material particles that are built into the form. The form man possesses is not laid aside; on the contrary, it sends it effects into the next life, especially what is developed through the agility and nimbleness of the limbs, hands and arms, feet and legs. This comes to expression in the shape of the head in the next incarnation.

The physical organism, then, decidedly bears its traces into the next earth life, carrying them into it in accordance with the provision of the cultural sphere that surrounds it in this life.

The rights sphere, on the other hand, reacts upon the etheric body (see drawing below). After death, while the physical body—its material substance, not the form—is delivered over to the earth, the etheric body is surrendered to the cosmos and dissolves into it. What is present and active as forces in it, however, is borne across into the next earth life, or at least affects it. Actually, however, through spiritual science we can know empirically that it does so only to a very slight degree. Whereas the form of the physical body powerfully transmits its effect into the next earth incarnation and, along with it, all that it has gained from the cultural sphere surrounding the physical body, what now comes from the rights sphere in the etheric body works, first of all, upon the cosmos. This is a most important discovery made by the science of initiation.

We live in this world. Because of the way and manner in

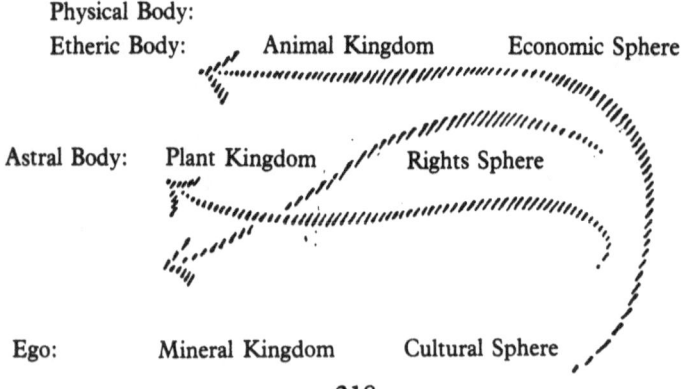

which we have been placed into the social context of the world, we have a certain state of mind. We confront those with whom we come into contact in life with certain rights' concepts or concepts and sensations resembling the feelings of rights. This gives our soul a certain configuration. Simply speaking, let us say that I have a certain relationship to ten people in life. The one I love, the other I hate, I am indifferent to the third, I am dependent on the fourth, the fifth is dependent on me, and so on. In the most diverse ways, then, my rights and duties concerning these ten persons are outlined. All this crystallizes into a certain soul state in me, but not only in a superficial manner, for the emotional fiber of my soul is conditioned by it. This position within the social order from the viewpoint of the rights sphere brings about a certain configuration of my etheric body, which is transmitted to the cosmos upon my death. After this body separates from me, what vibrates in my etheric body here (on earth) continues to vibrate in the cosmos, causing further reverberations.

Unfortunately, such things pass entirely unnoticed by what today is called science. Consequently, this science has no consciousness of the more intimate relationships between human life and cosmic life. The course taken by wind and weather today, hence the manner in which the rhythm of our external climate develops, is essentially the continuation of rhythms brought about by the life of rights in the social organism of past ages.

The human being stands indeed in a certain relationship to outer reality, even the reality of nature. It is important to realize that what develops all around us as the sphere of rights is not something merely abstract, man-made, arising and again disappearing; instead, what is at first a thought content, having its being initially in the realm of rights, lives in a subsequent age of earth existence in the atmosphere, in the vibrations, in the entire configuration, and in the movements of the atmosphere.

If man understands this properly, it gives him a sense of his connection with the entire life of the earth. Only this allows him to realize how significant it is whether he develops one or another kind of political life, a good or bad life of rights. All things physical, in fact, derive originally from something given order or disorder by spirit. Spiritual science, therefore, must insist that the human being has a fully alive, conscious evolutionary connection with the cosmos.

What is it like today? In our present era of decadence we have reached the point where we apprehend nature with abstract concepts. We construct a natural science that is actually devoid of all that lives in the human being, a natural science offering a content that fundamentally is not the content of human life; and what the human being experiences within himself stands in no relationship to what is occurring outside him. This is one side of the picture.

On the other side, the human being, though completely separated, as it were, from this knowledge of nature that he develops, is supposed to advance to a sort of awareness of God, or to a consciousness of his relationship to God. Both these views will have nothing to do with each other, really cannot have anything to do with each other because of the manner in which they have evolved to the present day. Spiritual science, on the contrary, shows in concrete detail how the human being is not only connected with the whole world, but how he himself cooperates with it. Out of what arises we can interpret the way man has lived in previous earth lives. In earlier incarnations, we founded legal systems. Now we live again. We have a certain kind of weather, wind and so forth, seasons with this or that configuration. Now we experience externally, in the atmosphere, what once upon a time we set up as the order of justice. Here, man in his consciousness grows into what surrounds him as his environment. We no longer talk here abstractly and in general of man's having a consciousness of God within him, of forming a unity with the surrounding world; here we learn to recognize in detail how this unity is constituted, how the human being is joined with the entire universe.

Just think, what would we know of the human being if we had no idea that it is the blood of his head that flows through his legs, if, therefore, insofar as it is enclosed within the skin, we did not consider the entire circulation processes in the organism? In the same way that we cannot consider the head by itself, for instance, ignoring the connection to the remaining organism, we must not consider the human being in one earth life by itself; instead, we have to focus on the cycle of metamorphosis. What at one time is a social system of rights conceived by the mind will become an order of nature at another, albeit distant, future time. With the help of spiritual science one can see how the thought-out political order of one age is connected with the atmospheric order of nature of another time.

If these views evolve in such a manner that man's sense of participation in the world, his feeling of oneness with it, is thereby intensified, then indeed will that indispensable reconciliation take place between science and religion that is absolutely necessary to the upbuilding of our social life.

Just as the rights sphere acts upon the etheric body and the cultural sphere upon the physical body, so does the economic sphere act upon the astral body, and we may say that it is just upon this innermost principle of human nature that the economic sphere acts. You must distinguish the following: The economic sphere originates from the etheric body, but when, in turn, it reacts upon the human being, it reacts upon the astral body. The reaction is unlike that which proceeds from the human being. It is impossible merely to construe these matters schematically, for they must be derived empirically from observation. Because the economic sphere acts upon the astral body, brotherliness that should exist in the economic sphere is borne through the portal of death, for the human being takes along his astral body for a certain time. What is thus established by virtue of brotherliness in the human soul is carried through death into the spiritual world, and there continues to be effective as such. Thus, what has already been discussed by me from other points of view appears again from this particular aspect.

The economic sphere (that is to say, the manner and method by which, in associations, we form the basis for our economic decisions and actions together with our fellow men) reacts on man's astral body and shapes it. It is, in fact, this formation of the astral body, attained because of brotherliness in the economic sphere, which the human being carries through death. As an idealist or perhaps even a mystic, one ought not to hold the economic sphere in particularly low esteem, for it is just in this sphere that we can develop brotherhood, as has often been pointed out. The spiritual element that is brought into the apparently material life is the very aspect acquired by the human being for his higher realm. What we establish in the cultural or spiritual sphere we draw from the mineral kingdom; it is something that we basically carry within our predispositions that we bring with us through birth. What we implant in the economic sphere, on the other hand, is something so strongly united with the soul that we bear it with us through the portal of death.

Physical Body			
Etheric Body	Animal Kingdom	Economic Sphere	Astral Body
Astral Body	Plant Kingdom	Rights Sphere	Etheric Body
Ego	Mineral Kingdom	*Cultural Sphere*	*Physical Body*
		Considered from Will Aspect	Considered from Cognitional Aspect

The facts are such that we must say, yes, people believe themselves to be idealists, or mystics, and feel obliged to disdain materialism, but no one becomes an idealist by disdain of materialism. Rather, he is an idealist if he knows how to spiritualize matter. What counts is not that we confront the economic life in false abnegation, that we scorn and slight it, but that we shape the economic life so that it bears the impression of the spirit everywhere, that this economic member of the social organism becomes a sphere molded and impregnated with the spirit by man. This is what is essentially decisive for the future.

And on a small scale, as I have already mentioned, this does make itself felt through the fact that people believe they are idealistic and spiritual if they deny the spirit any material tribute and think: It is not necessary really to offer this or that sacrifice to the spirit. The spiritual is, after all, spiritual—so they say—one must esteem it highly, not drag it into the dust by giving money, of all things, as an offering for it! By that token a proper idealist would be one who says to himself, "Oh, I revere the spirit, but I keep my wallet closed and do nothing for the care of the spiritual life!" One despises matter, despises above all the worst, the most Ahrimanic form of matter, closing one's purse tightly so as to make sure that nothing can escape to sustain the life of the spirit. These are facts that in some degree are connected with the state of mind so easily arising in idealists and mystics. Matter is scorned rather than spiritualized. Where does this contempt for matter come from? It arises because today's idealists and mystics are frequently the greatest materialists, because they are so controlled by matter that they can resist it in no other way than by dreaming themselves into a contempt of it. Their contempt, however, is only imagined. They despise matter, because they themselves cannot cope with it. They are too deeply immersed in it.

We must be clearly aware that certain feelings and attitudes exist in our time that are really only masks. Many a person parading around as a mystic today is just a materialist, as I have had occasion to explain from other aspects in the last few weeks. From what I have tried to bring close to you today, it becomes apparent, above all else, how, through spiritual science, the feeling of solidarity between the human being and the world can awaken and become more and more intense. In our present time this is necessary!

Actually, man has been able to arrive at a certain point in his evolution because he did not have to contribute anything to it. In the course of earth's evolution, we have proceeded from the beginning of earthly existence itself. In the beginning of earth evolution divine spiritual beings provided for us; they incorporated into the earth's organization the soil, the climate, finally even the cultural life. You know that there were great teachers in the mystery centers whose teachers were in turn the gods themselves. Thus, nothing human had been stored up; instead, the divine had been taken over. The gods had provided for mankind everything that was at hand in good order. This has essentially vanished in our time; I have shown you this in the most varied connections. The catastrophic character of our age is connected with this dissipation of the primeval, divine content and the creation of a new content by human beings on their own. They then create this new content not merely for human life in the cultural, political and economic sphere, but also for what issues forth from these domains into the life of nature; and the future of the earth must be man's own creation, his own concern.

In regard to humanity's present mentality, therefore, the views of a person like *Spengler* are quite correct, unless men awaken that inner fountain which can give rise not only to creative impulses for the activities of the cultural, political and economic spheres, but which must act creatively out of these spheres for all of earth life, including the life of nature itself. For civilization will not only pass over into barbarism, as Spengler has already proven scientifically, but the whole earth will approach its doom, will never reach its goal. If only people would imbue themselves with this awareness that the future events of earth evolution depend on humanity itself! For then, out of this feeling, the powerful impulse could emerge that we need today in order to lead the obviously declining order of the world again into an ascending direction, in order to challenge the drowsy souls who refuse to see what is actually happening, in order to transform these sleepy souls into awakened ones. We need an alert humanity today. Only a watchful mankind can survey what occurs around it and know the tasks placed upon it by the course of human evolution, in regard to which present mankind is being confronted with severe tests.

Lecture XIV
Dornach, September 5, 1920

In order to comprehend a number of things that have to be mentioned in connection with previously presented matters, it is necessary to recall several facts. We have seen how we are connected with our environment, with the other realms of existence. We have seen how our etheric body is directed toward the animal kingdom, the astral body toward the plant kingdom and the ego toward the mineral kingdom. We have seen how, as a result of the work which the ego performs upon itself together with others within the social order, there arises what we know as the cultural development of mankind in art, religion and science. I said yesterday that these soul contents—art, religion and science—are basically nothing else than what comes about through the work of the human ego upon itself. Thus we have here one of the examples showing the connection of the human being with social life. Art, religion and science are really, in the widest extent, the contents of the actual spirit realm of the social organism.

Then we have what comes into existence through the transformation of the astral body. As a matter of course, this transformation must be essentially more subconscious at the present stage of human evolution than what is accomplished in the spiritual realm of art, religion and science; and what grows out of the metamorphosis of the astral body is essentially what we have to designate as the rights sphere within the social organism. Then, even more subconsciously, we have what results from the transformation of the etheric body because of our living in union with our fellowmen. All that springs from this, all that men do through the transmutation of their ether body, belongs to the economic sphere of the social organism. Here then we have the connections, the relationships of the human being to what is outside him. Yesterday, too, we saw the significance of such relationships that the human being has to the life of the social order outside him. For, as we have seen, he thus actually prepares the basic natural foundation for his next life on earth. He works in a certain measure at the creation of earthly existence itself. It would indeed be desirable for as many people as possible to grasp the extraordinary importance and relevance of the present moment of human evolution.

It can be said that until this world-historical hour the evolution of humanity has, in general, rested on the providential care of the forces standing above man in the higher hierarchies. As we know, mankind achieved a certain development of the ether body during the old Indian cultural period, a certain development of the astral body during the Egypto-Chaldean time, and a development of the intellectual soul in the Greco-Latin time. Now humanity is on the point of lifting the consciousness soul from the depths of soul existence. But since the germ of what is to come must always be present in the preceding evolutionary stages, what is to be the content of the next cultural epoch—the unfoldment of the spirit-self—is already proclaiming itself; however, this development of the spirit-self must of necessity proceed from man himself.

We have passed through various earth lives. When we speak of the men of the primeval Indian time, of the ancient Persian, the Egypto-Caldean and the Greco-Latin times, we are, in fact, speaking of ourselves; for we lived under quite different conditions in those ancient times. We lived in surroundings of animal, plant or mineral nature prepared for us at the instigation of our divine progenitors, who were the humanity on the Moon, the Sun and Saturn and who, in the pre-stages of the earth, experienced what we are experiencing today. What constitutes content upon an earlier planetary evolution remains as form for the succeeding one. We lived on what was bequeathed to us by the gods, the beings of the higher hierarchies. Now we have reached the point where the earth would dry up and wither, if man, in a sense, did not spin out a new thread of life from himself.

Just think how all this was really prepared for us. Naturally, we have a spiritual life within our social life. The people of the Occident are proud of this social life; they are proud of their art, religion and science. Human beings must distinguish, however, between the Mystery of Golgotha as a fact, and the manner in which it has been heretofore understood through concepts obtained from religion, art and science. We have comprehended the Christ according to the standard of what we possessed as spiritual content in our souls. Here in the Occident we have established something like a continuation of the old spirituality. When anyone is able objectively to enter upon the nature of the actual spiritual life of Europe and its American extension, he finds that in the end it is all an Oriental heritage. It is nothing else. Certainly, we have changed any number of things. As I have already pointed out in these lectures, the quite different world view of the Orient which, once upon a time, could magnificently grasp the causative connections between the successive earth lives of the human being, but which later in the Greek concept of the cosmos had become a shadow of itself in the *fatum*, in destiny—all that turned finally through the Latin Roman element into something juristic. I have indicated how this is felt when we look at Michelangelo's painting in the Sistine Chapel where Christ appears in the role of World Judge, a cosmic jurist, deciding between good and evil human beings. The world concept had become juristic. This was not so in the Oriental world view.

Then there was added what results from economic thinking. Bacon was one who actually proceeded entirely from economic thought, and all of Europe allowed itself to be taught by him. What we possess in our sciences, and what today constitutes the popular view of the world permeating all European circles, is the result of this Western economic thinking which, as I have indicated, simply did not stop with the economic sphere, but has entered the higher domains, the rights domain and even the cultural domain. If individuals like Huxley and Spencer had employed their thinking to bring order into economic relationships, they would then be in the right place. They are out of place when employing their particular kind of thinking for the purpose of creating science. Yet the whole world has imitated them.

We can therefore say that what we possess of actual spirituality is fundamentally only an obsolete legacy of the ancient Orient. Later, legalistic, political thinking began in Greece and Rome. It would simply be nonsense to believe that this could have existed in the ancient structure of the Oriental state. The dignified patriarchal structures, of which the early Chinese constitution was a reflection, were not state formations in the sense that the European understands them. What we now possess as the rights structure did not yet exist in Orientalism. It entered into Occidental culture, faintly at first, by way of Greek thinking, and then quite strongly by way of Latin thinking. Thus we must say that our entire spiritual life basically still has a character which was inherited from what the Oriental possessed. Bear in mind, however, how I had to present this emergence of the Oriental spiritual life. It arose out of man's metabolism —out of the inner impulses of metabolism—in the Vedas, in the magnificent poetry of the Orient. It must be sought as a new outgrowth of the metabolism, just as blossom and fruit issue from the tree. Anyone who can look upon the inner relationships as they are in reality knows how to look upon the blossoms and fruit of the tree; he will observe how the sap rises up from the earth, ascends in the trunk, shoots out into the branches, turns green within the leaves, becomes varicolored in the blossoms and achieves ripeness in the fruit. This is what presents itself to our eyes. If we then note the result in our metabolic processes of what is drawn up with the substance coming from the earth and taken up into ourselves, how it is digested and burned up, how it passes over into the blood, is refined and etherized within the body, we see that it sprouts, flourishes and ripens just like the vegetative process that turns to blossoms, fruits and trees. It only changes into something else by sprouting, flourishing and ripening through the human organs; it turns into the poetic fruit of the Vedas, it becomes the philosophic fruit of the Vedanta philosophy. In the Orient, the spiritual life was considered a fruit of the earth, of the metabolism that courses through the human being, just as one looked upon the process coursing through the verdant, fruit-bearing tree. What appears in the Vedas and in Oriental poetry is intimately bound up with the essence of the earth. It is the flower of the earth. It is nonsense when men of today make our earth into a lifeless product, as geology does, for instance. For not only what arises from the earth in flower and fruit belongs to her, but also what has arisen like a philosophical fruit in the primordial epochs of mankind in the Vedas and the Vedanta philosophy. Whoever wishes to see nothing but stones come into existence in or upon the earth, whoever sees her only as tillable soil, whoever views the earth as nothing but mineral substance, does not know the earth. For to her belongs also what she has borne in times past as blossom and fruit through the body of man.

Then the other age arrived, the age in which man had already emancipated himself from the earth. He was no longer connected with the earth, but only with the climate and atmosphere, in which he brought to expression his rhythmic system rather than his metabolic system. It was the age in which the mighty spiritual intuitions of antiquity were no longer manifest, but in which man's concepts of rights developed.

In the more recent age, particularly since Bacon, the human being has begun to withdraw completely into himself, to divorce himself from the earth, and to manifest what lives only within himself as mere intellect within the economic thinking of the Western world. Thus, what evolves through the human being is differentiated over the earth.

All these are matters to which we must pay attention at present. If we would pay attention to these things, we must certainly bring our soul to an inward awakening. We must seek to comprehend what spiritual science can give us. We must confess to ourselves that the time is past when, after having worked hard all week, we can simply sit down and listen to an abstract sermon about the connection of the human being with a divine world order. Those times are over; that is antiquated.

It is the duty of modern humanity to comprehend quite concretely how man's essential being is itself linked with the cosmos, how its existence is bound up with the cosmos. Only as a consequence of this comprehension will the human being understand the necessity of dividing the social life into the spiritual sphere—which is basically only a heritage from the Orient grown more and more lifeless, for our spiritual life today is dead—and the other two spheres. The old Oriental of primeval times could never have grasped what is meant when we say that we do not understand life. Today we say that we do not understand life, for we live only in the dead mineral realm, even though we do so with our ego, which the Oriental did not yet do. Precisely here, life must enter. After all, what do we mean when we strive as human beings to accord a special place and emphasis to the spiritual sphere within the social organism? What is it, after all, that we desire here?

As long as the spiritual or cultural sphere is bound up with the wholly differently constituted rights or state structure—or worse, with the economic life—so long will the single human individuality be unable to contribute to the spiritual life what this spiritual life should contain. Let us understand one another on this particular point! With the thinking habits of the present it is not an easy task to understand just what matters here. In what follows I shall attempt to make comprehensible just what needs to be grasped in this respect.

Consider, for instance, the case where the state enacts its school laws. These school laws are put through either from a despotic, tyrannical point of view or from a democratic one. How are they made? Let us put the matter quite simply. Picture to yourself three people sitting together. When three people sit down together they are "terribly clever" in an abstract sense. Three people who get together really know everything about all things; it is not much better when 360 people come together as a party—they usually know everything about all things. One knows exactly how to set up paragraph one: how religion should be taught; paragraph two: how German or any other language should be taught; paragraph three: how arithmetic should be taught; paragraph four: how geography should be taught. Wonderful paragraphs can be worked out that should represent an ideal condition for the educational system. Then all this can be made into rules and regulations, and then put into effect. It is quite immaterial whether it is done by three or three hundred people, it will always be very clever, for people are very clever when they construct something in abstractions. Then it becomes law. It is something else, however, when, for instance, someone confronts a class of fifty real children.

They have quite definite characters; they are not the wax we pretend they are, when, with great cleverness, we formulate paragraphs one, two and so forth. Children can be molded only as far as their special peculiarities and abilities allow.

In addition, something else enters the picture. The teacher himself confronts the class with *his* particular capabilities. They, too, are limited. And one with experience knows that rules can be *this* good in an abstract sense (referring to larger form in drawing); the clever teacher, however, can only apply them *this* well (referring to the smaller form). In abstractions, everything can be figured out. In reality, however, it is a question of dealing with reality. In the educational system that is part of the spiritual sphere, the state as such can accomplish nothing but abstractions. These can be quite wonderful and outstandingly good, but leave the state out of it! Take it out of the educational system, which is a part of the spiritual sphere! Make the educational system dependent on the teachers themselves who are available at a particular time. Then it will be a reality; then it will not become a lie but something that is in accordance with the particular age. That is what is meant by working toward realities. Something else, however, takes its place: Paragraphs one, two, three, ten, fifty are all dead, and the way in which they are observed is actually something absolutely irrational. What lives through the body of teachers and comes into existence in the living collaboration among real teachers is alive. Here you have the point where life enters into what is derived from the dead mineral. A higher sphere is reached. We bring life, illuminated life, into the spiritual sphere by resting it upon human individualities, not upon paragraphs one, two, and so on. We infuse life into the spiritual sphere; out of an ether body we permeate the spiritual sphere around us with what is derived from the living human being. In your own attitude of mind, what is otherwise dead, inanimate, a machinelike thought, turns into a living being. The spiritual sphere spreads out as something inwardly alive over the entire earth. That is what must be understood inwardly. One must feel how life streams out of an undreamed-of soul depth into the independent life of the spirit, and how we actually vivify this self-reliant spiritual life by founding it upon the human individuality.

You see from this that what we draw forth from spiritual science for everyday life has to do most intensely with realities. One could really despair when one sees how little actual energy and enthusiasm is generated in humanity for this vivification of the spiritual sphere. One feels as though humanity were imbued by the same attitude of mind as is a person who desires to see only stillborn children brought into the world, and who does not wish the spark of life to enter the body that otherwise would come into the world dead. This is how one feels about modern mankind. Humanity sits upon a dead culture, as if stuck with pitch to comfortable seats, not willing to rise to the enthusiasm of vivifying the spiritual life. Enthusiasm is what we need above all else, for this spiritual life will not be revitalized out of its dead traditions.

Next is the rights sphere. I said that it is born out of instincts, out of half conscious instincts. This rights sphere was still something semiconscious, glimmering up into consciousness, when born out of Greek life, more particularly, out of the Latin-Roman life, and was then elaborated upon further. Now it is to be placed independently on its own democratic basis. What has developed under the impulse of the rights sphere up to now? The legal paragraphs came into being in which the individual has such a small share that I must say there has been hardly anything that has left such a bitter taste in my mouth as when I had dealings with a lawyer. This has happened repeatedly in my life. One goes to somebody who is a representative of the law, a man learned in the law. One is concerned with a specific case. One watches this lawyer go to some filing cabinet. He takes out a bundle of briefs. With much effort, he fits together what he is reading at the moment; he himself is quite detached from the matter at hand. One wishes to know how this case fits into the framework of the law. He goes to his library, takes out a certain law book, leafs through it at length, but nothing results because in reality he is entirely unacquainted with the subject. Nothing at all of a living, human connection is present in such a proceeding.

A matter of litigation once caused considerable correspondence between a lawyer and myself; I do not wish to relate the whole affair. In the end, it turned out that it was necessary to refer also to a book on international law. The case had been going on for nearly two and a half years when the good man told me that he did not have a book on international law, and I would have to procure it myself. He said, "You will have to supply me with the necessary data anyway, if I am to give you further advice!" Now, those who know me are aware that I am certainly not boastful in such matters. I am certainly not conceited, either. I obtained the book on international law, and within two hours it was clear to me just how the case stood. One need only look into matters with a healthy mind and one finds that what otherwise might be protracted over two years can be accomplished in two hours. This is how far removed the human element has come from what really exists as the system of rights, which has become entangled in what is derived from the three members in the social organism. We must return to a life that experiences what holds sway in rights in the same way we experience the external sense objects. We must be connected in a living manner with what exists as the rights body.

The true meaning of democracy is for the dead paragraphs to be humanized, and for our feelings to participate in what otherwise lies buried in the dead paragraphs. Just as life enters the spiritual sphere through what can be born out of spiritual science, so also will feeling enter into the rights sphere through what is being willed by spiritual science. What lives from man to man will then be felt.

We proceed to the third sphere—the economic sphere. We know that this takes place very much in the subconscious; that based on what he has to deal with an individual today is simply not in a position to penetrate with full consciousness into what is at hand in the economic sphere. Associations must be formed in which the experience of the one supplements the experience of another. Out of associations, out of group formations, the decisions must subsequently be made. Whereas each one of us must individually create out of ourselves what is commensurate with our talents in the spiritual sphere, what is active in the economic sphere must result from a group decision. From such group judgment, governing reason will then emerge and hold sway in the economic life.

1. spiritual life: life   etheric body
2. rights sphere: feeling   astral body
3. economic sphere   reason   ego

Reason will reign in the economic sphere. This means that we contribute what we have evolved in ourselves as a gift from the gods. We contribute what we have evolved as our etheric element, what we have developed in regard to feeling as astral body, and what we have evolved as reason for our ego. All this we bring to the outer world. In the economic sphere we need not yet make the contribution as individuals; therefore we do so through associations and groups. But what we have developed individually in the ego—reason—becomes something that permeates the whole economic sphere if we aim at associations in the proper manner. Hence, we carry the impulses existing in our ether body out into the social order, into the spiritual life, by enlivening the spiritual life. We carry into the rights sphere what pulsates in our astral body as feeling, and we bear into the economic sphere what lives in our ego as reason. As human beings, we have attained three things in the cosmic order: etheric body, astral body, and ego. We leave the world again with the etheric body, astral body, and ego. We yield it up to the world. We fashion the world order out of ourselves. Why should it be otherwise? Among the lower animals much is exemplified for us by the spider that spins out of herself what must come to pass. Man must indeed become a world creator, and must form out of himself what will constitute his environment in the future. We bear the future in us. I have discussed this from the most varied points of view.

Of what use is all the philosophical talk about the reality of the world? We should inform ourselves about the reality of the world by looking at the realities of the future. What is to be real in the future is borne today within us as ideality. Let us fashion the world so that it will be real. This must not live in us merely as theory; it must be a feeling in us, an innermost life impulse. Then we shall simultaneously have a cognitive relationship and a religious relationship to our environment. Out of this innermost impulse, art, too, will become something quite different in the future. It will turn into something that unites with immediate life. Our very existence will have to shape itself artistically. Without that, we will inevitably drift into the philistinism of a Lenin, a Trotsky, or a Lunatsharsky.[89] It is only the spirit created by man out of himself that can save us from this morass; and if the life of rights is not to succumb to utter desolation, we must permeate it with feeling, and we must permeate the economic life with reason.

There was a man who looked back at the way and means the world developed and he said, "All that is real is rational, and all that is rational is real." He, however, looked back to what the world had become through the old gods; he did not look to the future. It was Hegel, of whom I spoke here on August 27th, his 150th birthday. Today, we are at a point where the world is irrational, and where man must make it rational once more. We must realize this, and this knowledge must pass into thinking, feeling and will. There is only one social reform: People must realize what part mankind must play in the shaping of the world order.

This is what we ought to repeat to ourselves each morning and night so that we will understand anew what nonsense it is to speak of the eternity and preservation of matter. Everything surrounding us as substance will pass away. What dwells in us as ideals will replace the vacuums brought about by the destruction of matter. The ideals that live within us for the time being will occupy the empty spaces as future reality.

In this way the human being must feel a bond with the world order. In a new way he must experience Christ's words, "Heaven and earth will pass away, but my words will not pass away."[90] One who understands this utterance knows that it is a genuinely Christian saying. For Christianity starts from the destructibility of matter and external energy, whereas the recent natural scientific world outlook mocks Christianity by promulgating the conservation of matter and energy. Indeed, heaven and earth—meaning all matter—will pass away and all energy cease to be, but what forms within the soul of man and dwells in the word will be the world of the future. That is Christianity.

This newly understood Christianity must eradicate the anti-Christian attitude of the modern materialistic world outlook, which fantasizes about the conservation of things transitory—matter and energy. Things have gone so far that the tenets of Christianity, namely, eternity of the spirit and the avowal of the transitory nature of matter, are considered sheer insanity as compared to the firmly established phantasm of the conservation of matter and energy. It has gone so far that we lie when we still allege to be Christians, while we lend a hand to the dissemination of an anti-Christian world outlook. One who holds fast to modern natural science's basic views on matter would only be honest if he could recant Christianity. Above all, in reality, representatives of Christian confessions, ministers and pastors, who make their compromises with modern natural science, are inwardly quite certainly the worst enemies of Christianity. There is no other way but to begin to see these matters clearly and honestly. We must definitely speak about these things more and more in full earnestness. Without this, there will be no progress. All talk of reforms of which any number of organizations and reform movements chatter today is mere fantasy; it is only grist to the mill of those who bring about the decline. The only hope for renewal can come from grasping the living spirit, the living spirit that has to find its source in the creative human being and which, in turn, becomes the foundation for the reality of the future, not just of some ideal future, but that of the cosmic future.

In all truth, not until modern humanity accepts this metamorphosis of modern thinking with the same ardor with which world outlooks were once accepted in former times, not until then will decline transform itself into ascending progress. One wishes that what is thus being stated would not only be comprehended conveniently by concepts; one wishes that it would be grasped by the feelings and that it would pulse through the will. For, unless it is sensed and felt, unless it pulses through the will, all talk of emerging from this catastrophic age remains so much talk into the wind. Most people are unaware of the terrible way in which we are sailing into the decline that now is taking hold already of the physical environment. The physical, however, is always the consequence of the spiritual. The physical of the future will be the consequence of the spiritual we harbor in our souls today. The physical of the present is caused by the spiritual of the past, and the most recent physical conditions are brought about by the most recent past spiritual activities of mankind.

When we hear today that out of about 600 school children in Berlin an average of much more than one hundred do not have shoes and socks at present and no hope of getting them; when we are told that many more than a hundred and fifty of these 600 children have parents who cannot even purchase rations for them and who no longer receive a warm breakfast before going to school; that in the course of the last school year over a hundred of these children died of tuberculosis—just add this up for yourselves!—then, my dear friends, you have material occurrences. These physical occurrences are the external expression of the spirituality that has been nurtured in mankind during the past few centuries. One must ask today: Do people wish to go on cultivating social movements, women's movements and any number of other reforms while continuing the thoughts that have borne such fruit? Or are they willing to create and draw from a new source? This question should place itself in shining letters before our souls as we experience and feel the point in time at which we now stand.

Lecture XV
Dornach, September 10, 1920

If we make a survey of what takes place in the civilized world today, of what is present in it, we actually find—indeed, we may say this after the many explanations which have already been given—that civilization is increasingly falling into ruin. If we understand what spiritual science can tell us about the secrets of the universe, we must realize quite clearly that everything that takes place outside in the physical world has its source in the spiritual world. The causes for what takes place at any time in the historical development of mankind also lie in the spiritual world. Another truth, which cannot be called to mind too frequently, is that in the present moment of time, humanity's condition requires each individual to contribute something toward the reconstruction of culture from his own inner being. We no longer live in an age in which it suffices to believe that the gods will help. In the present time, the gods do not count on human beings recognizing them and their intentions, and much that a short time ago was not yet left to mankind is left to men's decisions today.

Such a truth must be grasped in all its gravity, and basically by each one individually. To do this it will be necessary, above all, to understand a number of things that we have outgrown. Gradually, in the course of the materialistic age, one might say that the human being has reached the point of grasping everything from a certain absolute standpoint, a standpoint, moreover, that differs according to the human being's age. When a person is twenty-five years old today, he feels called upon to judge everything. He believes that it is possible to have a final opinion about everything without undergoing any kind of development. Perhaps when he reaches the age of fifty, he may look down with a certain sense of superiority upon his faculty of judgment twenty-five years ago. At age twenty-five, however, he will in no way feel drawn as a result of his upbringing to seek and reckon with the more mature judgment of a man of fifty.

Among the causes underlying our present chaos, the one just outlined is by no means the least important; instead, it is one of the most significant, though admittedly one that had to exercise its influence upon the whole evolution of mankind. Only by man's feeling completely emancipated in a certain sense from the whole world context; by adopting an absolute standpoint not only personally in the life between birth and death, but at any given moment of this life; by assuming the standpoint that he is able to judge everything in a sovereign manner; only because this illusion was added to the many other illusions of life—and in the merely physical world everything is in a sense illusion—the course of human development will gradually lead the single human being toward freedom.

We should bear in mind, however, the great difference between our present epoch, which sets out from this standpoint, and the past epochs in which entirely different life impulses lay at the foundation of human existence. We must pay heed to the life impulses of former times, which in turn are intended to become those of the future, to which all efforts in the present should be directed again. Indeed, such earlier life impulses must be observed. They only disappeared slowly and gradually in the course of human evolution, and we underestimate the whole tempo of modern spiritual development if we do not perceive the speed with which, in a few centuries, materialistic impulses have melted away a tremendous amount of the spirituality that once existed.

In order to gain some starting points for a real study of the present, which we shall pursue tomorrow, let's turn our minds back to, say, the best period of ancient Egyptian life. Naturally, in the life of ancient Egypt or ancient Chaldea, there certainly existed social institutions in the outer world as well. These social structures were inaugurated and implemented by certain human beings. However, these individuals did not make judgments by pursuing thoughts in their wise heads on how to come up with the best social arrangements, or by following their opinions on what might be right for the communal life of people. Instead, they turned to the initiation centers. In actual fact, the sage who was initiated into the mysteries of the universe in these centers was the actual leading advisor of the highest social rulers, who, depending on their rank and maturity, were in large part themselves initiates into the cosmic secrets. When one was supposed to make provisions concerning the affairs of the social order, one did not consult the clever human brain—in the literal sense of the word—but one consulted those who were capable of interpreting the heavenly signs. For one knew that when a stone falls to the ground this is connected with the forces of the earth; when it rains that has to do with the forces of the air—the atmosphere. If, on the other hand, human destinies should be fulfilled that are supposed to interact with each other, this has nothing to do with any natural laws that can be figured out in the above manner. It has to do with those laws that could be traced in the cosmos by means of what makes the course of the stars evident. So, the course of the stars was read in the same way we read the time of day from a clock. We do not say, "One hand of my clock is down here on the right, the other is on the left." Rather, we say, "We know that this position indicates that the sun has set so many hours ago, and so forth." Likewise, these individuals who could read the course of the stars said to themselves, "This or that constellation of the stars signifies to us one or the other intention on the part of those divine spiritual beings who guide and direct everything we may call human destiny." One beheld the intentions of those accompanying spiritual beings of the cosmos by looking up to the course of the stars. One was clearly aware that not everything that man has to know reveals itself here on earth; indeed, the most important things he has to be aware of, the forces that work in his social life, reveal themselves in manifestations observable in the cosmos outside the earthly sphere. One knew that the concerns of humanity here on earth cannot be managed unless one investigates the intentions of the gods in the realm outside earth. Therefore, everything that was to be accomplished here within the social order was connected with the sphere outside the earth.

Where do we find any inclination today to investigate these great signs visible in the cosmos outside the earth, when here or there the belief arises again that some reform movement should be introduced? A far more important symptom than materialism, than anything which has arisen in the form of natural scientific materialism, is the fact that man no longer consults the cosmos outside the earth in regard to his earthly concerns. One does not become spiritual by setting up theories concerning the human being or anything in the universe; one will only become spiritual if one understands how to connect humanity's earthly concerns with the cosmos outside the earth.

In that case, however, one has to be convinced, above all, that the affairs of this world do not allow themselves to be arranged according to the judgments acquired by mere natural scientific education. Then, one has to be able to introduce into the whole civilizing education the capacity to connect the sphere transcending the earth with earthly concerns once more. Then, it was necessary, above all, to discern more clearly how this capacity was lost in the course of human evolution, and how we gradually arrived at the point of wanting to judge everything only from an earthly standpoint. Let us consider something that is now prevalent in the world, a component of social agitation.

You have all heard of the effort appearing everywhere to introduce compulsory labor—to require a person to work by means of some social order based on the legal decrees of this social order—no longer to appeal merely to what obliges man to work, namely, hunger and other motivations, but in fact to establish compulsory labor legally.

We see how, on one side, this compulsory labor is demanded by socialistic agitation. We note how, in Soviet Russia, this compulsory labor has already led to a downright rigid form, with human life taking on the aspect of life in the barracks. We also find that radical socialists enthusiastically uphold compulsory labor. We see also how the sleeping souls of the present receive news such as this, how government officials here or there have even determined to introduce compulsory labor. One reads this like any other news item, and does not pay it much attention. One rises in the morning as one usually does, eats breakfast, has lunch, goes into the country for the summer holidays, returns again and, in spite of the fact that the most important and fundamental events are taking place in the world, one behaves as one has always been accustomed to behave. Yet, mankind should not insist on clinging to old habits. Mankind should take seriously what it is that matters today, namely, having to relearn about all conditions of life. Even when we see that the demand for compulsory labor is being opposed, what are the viewpoints from which these matters are attacked? We have to admit that the opponents are as a rule not much brighter than those who advance these demands. For the most part, they will ask, "Well, can a person still find joy in his work?"—or something like that. All the reasons cited for and against the above are worth more or less the same, because they arise from the same judgments that are limited only to what takes place here between birth and death; they do not originate from a sufficient insight into life. When the spiritual scientist comes and says, "Go ahead and introduce compulsory labor, but in ten years you will have terrible results, for suicides will increase at an alarming rate," people will view such a statement as fantasy. They will not recognize that this conclusion is derived from an inner knowledge of the relationships existing in the universe. They will not be willing to study spiritual science and to discover the basis from which one can find such a judgment justified. Instead, people will go on living as usual—some getting up in the morning, breakfasting and lunching, traveling into the country for the summer and more of the same, others sleeping away their time in some other manner, refusing to take these questions seriously. Still others will found clubs, social associations, women's associations, and so forth—things that are admittedly quite nice—but when such efforts are not connected to the actual cosmic order, they lead nowhere. Our age is much too conceited to abandon absolute standpoints which assume that, at any age, one definitely has a conclusive judgment about all things.

During these days and in the last few weeks I explained the way in which the various branches of the threefold social organism have originated in the different territories of earth evolution. I said that, fundamentally speaking, all our spiritual life is only a transformation of what originated a long time ago in the Orient. But when we look into what was described on numerous occasions in the past few weeks from one aspect, and investigate it in regard to the standpoints which I have indicated just now, we find that, insofar as it referred to human destiny, all this knowledge of the Orient was deciphered from the course of the stars, from what exists outside the earth, and the Greek concept of destiny was the last ramification of such extraterrestrial wisdom.

Then came the knowledge arising from the Middle region.

As we indicated, this was a more juristic knowledge; it was something that man drew more out of his own being. It was not linked with observations of the cosmos outside the earth. I told you that the higher-world outlook of the Occident has been permeated with a juristic element, how the events that run their course in humanity's development were placed under juristic concepts. Punishment is meted out by a cosmic judge just as the human judge hands down a penalty for some external misdeed. It was a juristic view, a juristic manner of conception, that permeated the entirely different form of the Oriental conceptions concerning the spiritual world.

This view of the spiritual world was connected with the fact that in the initiation centers those who were found to be sufficiently mature were initiated into the nature of that which was sent down to earth from invisible realms by what was revealed in the visible. Then, the events that were to take place on earth were guided according to the intentions of initiation. Naturally, in the case of such a knowledge it is necessary to take into consideration more than the singular standpoint of any given age, by which one believes oneself able to make an absolute judgment on all sorts of matters. From the viewpoint of initiation, the whole evolution of man must be considered, also what the human being brings into earthly existence through birth, and what can reveal itself to him when, in earthly life, he beholds a revelation of the supersensible existence.

In recent times, something that was basically a science of the heavens has become permeated with a juristic element. This celestial science itself and its fate must be considered a little now. The sacred knowledge of the Orient was something that was cultivated in its purest form in the initiation centers perhaps 10,000 years ago in the Orient. Later on, although no longer in such pure form, it was cultivated in Egypt in a still relatively pure manner. Having become popularized in a certain sense, it was used by swindlers and conjurers on the streets of the later imperial Rome, although transformed into visible magic tricks. This is, after all, the course of world events; something that is sacred in one epoch can turn into the most unholy thing in a later age. While the highest Oriental knowledge belonged to the streets in the later imperial Roman time, juristic thinking was developing out of Romanism itself on the basis of the late Egyptianism, and subsequently dominated the world. In the ages that followed, but only slowly and gradually, what had once been brought down from the stars as human wisdom in the Orient grew dim and finally died out. For, even in the thirteenth century, Thomas Aquinas[91] still said, "Human destiny, all of destiny occurring in the sublunar world, is guided by the Intelligences of the stars. It is, however, by no means something inevitable for man." So this Catholic-Christian church father of the thirteenth century does not refer to stars, to planets, merely as physical planets; instead, he speaks of the Intelligences that dwell in these planets who are the actual rulers of what should be called human destiny. What had once arisen in the Orient was really still present in the twelfth, thirteenth, fourteenth centuries, although in its last ramifications, as an aspect of the Christian Catholic Church. It is simply a terrible misrepresentation of the present Catholic Church to withhold these matters from the faithful, so that the church can declare it a heresy, for example, to assume that the individual stars and planets are ensouled and permeated with spirit. By doing this, the Church not only denies Christianity; it even denies its last teachers who still had a more direct connection with the sources of the spiritual life than does the present age in any sense. Therefore, one must point out that it was not so very long ago that the conception was completely abandoned which still pictured the world as permeated with spirit. If people would teach the truth today concerning what still held sway in the spiritual life of the eleventh, twelfth, thirteenth, fourteenth and fifteenth centuries; if, following preconceived opinions, they would not distort what prevailed in those times, then even this would still have a fructifying effect for a spiritualization of the present world-view. The materialism, the natural scientific materialism, or the materialism of the mystics or theosophists, particularly the materialism of the Catholic Church, could not exist. For what is contained in the dogmas of the Roman Catholic Church originated from the purest spiritual science; and this pure spiritual science beheld the spirit everywhere in the universe.

All that was beheld as spirit in the universe by the eye of the soul has been discarded. The universe became pervaded with materialism. For that reason, naturally, nothing remains except words of faith. For example, behind the Trinity, the doctrine of the Father, Son and Holy Spirit, stand the most profound mysteries. On the other hand, there is nothing contained any longer in what is taught today as the dogma of the Trinity. On one side, there is the doctrine, the belief of the religious denominations, on the other side, natural science devoid of spirit. Neither can save humanity from the misery into which it has fallen. In order to render rescue possible, it is necessary that a sufficiently large number of people rouse themselves inwardly. For, particularly in the present epoch, the possibility exists in man's inner being to pick up those threads of a soul-spiritual kind which, if their power is inwardly experienced in the proper way, lead to an understanding of what can be gathered from spiritual science for an illumination of the life of nature as well as the social life. One should not wish to retain at all costs the bad habits of one's inner life, however they have developed during the past few centuries. These bad habits are based on the opinion that if one can keep quiet and be passive, the gods will eventually enter into one, reveal everything within, and mystical depth will be illuminated by an inner light, and so forth. The present age is not suited for that. It demands an inner activity of soul and spirit from the human being; it demands that man turn and look at what is trying to reveal itself within. Then, he will find under all circumstances what wishes to reveal itself within, but he must be willing to unfold such inner spiritual activity. One must not believe, however, that much can be gained by some inner pseudomystical doings; above all else, one has to trace the spirit in the external things of the world.

I have called your attention to what happened, for example, in the East, in Asia. Once upon a time, so I told you, conditions in Asia were of a kind that the human being felt his heart expand, felt his soul grow warm, when, guided by the thought of the sacred Brahman, he directed his glance to the mighty external symbol of the swastika, the hooked cross. It made his inner life unfold. This inner mood of soul meant a great deal to him. Today, when an Oriental receives an ordinary Russian 2,000 ruble note—which is not worth much, for small change will no longer do for buying anything, only thousand ruble notes—he sees on it the beautifully printed swastika. Those thousand-year-old feelings that once upon a time inwardly beheld the sacred Brahman when the eye was directed to the swastika are certainly stirring. Today, the same emotional qualities arise on seeing the 2,000 ruble note.

Do you believe that one has a spiritual view of the world if one does not look at something like that and say to oneself, "Those are the Ahrimanic powers who are at work here; herein lies a super-earthly intelligence, even though it is an Ahrimanic intelligence?" Do you believe that it suffices merely to say, "Oh, that is the external material world! We direct our glance heavenward to spiritual things; we don't pay any attention to things for which people only have words?" If you seek for the spirit, you must look for it even where it turns up in the mighty aberrations of external world evolution itself, for there you can find the starting point for other aspects.

It is the tragedy of modern civilization that people believe that only human forces are at work everywhere, forces which arise between birth and death. Actually, our world is permeated all over by supersensible forces, spiritual powers which manifest themselves in the various events that take place. If one wishes to do something, if one tries to realize intentions so that this or that result may come about, one needs to look to those benign spiritual powers capable of working against other spiritual powers; and the spiritual powers that can oppose the others have to be born in man through his own inner activity.

In regard to all this, however, one actually does need to look up into the spiritual world. This is something that is most inconvenient to many people. This is why the great majority of people in the world find even talk of initiation science unpleasant. For there is one thing that initiation science must make clear, under all circumstances, to the human being. Man is organized, in the first place, in the direction of his intellect. Certainly, there are other aspects to his organization such as digestion, metabolism, heartbeat, breathing, and physiological processes. He bears instincts within, hence, soul entities, and so forth. In addition, he bears within him what is termed intelligence, and the present age is especially proud of this intelligence. But where does our intelligence come from? Materialism believes that our intelligence is derived from those processes that occur below in the liver, in the heart; they then become more refined and turn into the processes within the brain. These processes in the brain are just a little different from those that take place in the liver or the stomach, but these same processes produce thinking. We know that this is not so. Those processes that run their course in the brain just as those in the liver or the stomach would cause no thinking at all. Up in the brain something takes place; out of the constructive processes destructive ones are constantly developed.

Here, not only upbuilding, but disintegrating processes are at work; matter is forever falling out into nothingness. Thus, we are not dealing with an upbuilding in the brain. Any constructive process only serves to nourish the brain, not to produce thinking. If you wish to focus on those brain processes that have something to do with thinking, and you wish to compare them to the remaining organism, you must not compare them to the constructive processes, the processes of growth, but to the processes of elimination. The brain is constantly involved in elimination, and, as I said, the processes of destruction, of disintegration, of death, are the accompanying phenomena of intelligence. If our brain were incapable of elimination, we would be unable to think. If our brain would only contain upbuilding processes, we would exist in a dull, instinctive condition; at most, we could attain to quite dim dreams. We arrive at light-filled clear thinking precisely because the brain secretes and eliminates substances. Thinking only functions parallel to processes of elimination. It is only because the human organization eliminates what is useless to it that thinking establishes itself out of the spiritual world.

Now take the thinking that has developed especially since the middle of the fifteenth century, the thinking of which modern man is so proud. It comes into being because we destroy our brain, because we bring about in it processes of disintegration, of elimination. Suppose that you are Trotsky or Lenin, traveling to Russia—transported there on orders of Ludendorff[92] in a sealed railway carriage and escorted by Dr. Helphand[93] (it was such a train, going from Switzerland through Central Europe, which brought Lenin accompanied by people like Dr. Helphand to Russia under Ludendorff's protection)—suppose you are such a person and you believe that out of the processes representing intelligence—the only processes from which natural scientific thinking of the past few centuries has emerged—the social order could be developed. What kind of a social order will that turn out to be? It will be a reproduction of what takes place within the brain during the thinking processes. Do not think that what we develop without is different from what we develop within, if the only processes employed are thinking processes! If you try to establish a social order with them, it will be something destructive, just as thinking processes in the brain cause destruction—exactly the same thing. Thinking, applied to reality, destroys. One can gain insight into such matters only when one looks into the deeper secrets of the being of man and the whole world. This is why humanity needs to pay attention to these things if any sort of valid judgment concerning public affairs is to be rendered. It does no good at all today to base discussions about any social concerns on the suppositions of the past few centuries, for they no longer hold water. It is important here to realize that completely different processes must come to pass in the human spiritual life; again, the science of initiation must step in and draw from spiritual resources what can never be gleaned from mere sources of human intelligence. A social science of the present can only emerge as a consequence of spiritual science. This can and must be grasped from its very foundation.

This is what is in fact important for modern man, namely, that he does not attain a relationship with spiritual science merely in some superficial manner, but that he learns to recognize how completely spiritual science is linked to human destiny for the future.

In order that a person can gauge something like this, a feeling must develop in the human being for what is asserting itself with profound earnestness out of the spiritual resources. For such a feeling to come about, however, much must be eliminated, above all else the generally prevailing frivolity. Recently, in a lecture that I gave for local teachers, I indicated a symptom in which such frivolity appears today. One of our friends in London made efforts to arrange a gathering of a number of artists here in August. It was for the purpose of their becoming acquainted with our building and forming a sort of center from which the impulse could go out that is now so necessary if the building is ever to be completed. An English journalist was informed, not one from an ordinary daily paper but from a magazine that calls itself "Architect," in other words, a publication that wishes to be taken more seriously. The journalist was even given a description in writing of what was intended. This fellow was so flippant and frivolous, however, that he wrote, "A visit to Dornach is anticipated by such and such persons. Dr. Steiner himself has promised to acquaint the visitors with what is going on there, and it is believed that ten days will suffice for this excursion. Of this time, four days will be spent on travel, and during the remaining six days, the visitors will be able to recuperate from the shock they will have experienced following their first impression of Dornach." So, this frivolous character has no idea what he is supposed to write about, and for his penny-a-line, is only capable of making a stupid joke so that his readers can accordingly continue to maintain a frivolous mood.

Things have gone so far that the general mood of people is spoiled from the very outset, spoiled by this kind of journalist; there is no longer any question of anything being accomplished. The only thing such journalists can do is seize the opportunity to make some stupid, frivolous joke. No progress will be made if the earnestness with which such matters should be discussed is not understood. One will get no further if such matters are considered to be insignificant; if, from a certain jaded standpoint, one says, for example, "Oh, one cannot take such a journalist so seriously!" From a certain point of view, one certainly need not give much credit to such penny-a-lining, but it must be evaluated according to what effect is has in the world.

These matters are indeed serious and of such a nature that they induce us again and again to say, "This building here is intended to be a landmark for what should take place for the sake of mankind's ascent!" To be sure, from certain quarters, no effort has been spared to make the building what it is now. Destiny, too, contributed its necessary share. It is, after all, true that at the outset this building was erected here chiefly as the result of efforts made by the Central European countries. But when Central Europe's financial resources began to touch rock bottom, the neutral countries were ready in a most significant, commendable manner to do something for this building. Those from Central Europe who were able to do something for the building spared no effort throughout the time of the war psychosis, stirred up by hate and opposition, to maintain this site in such a manner that people from every part of the world, from all nationalities, could gather together here. This building was saved and maintained throughout all the years of chauvinism; nobody was denied the opportunity here to encounter others in a spirit of friendship, no matter what part of the world he came from. All this, however, demonstrates the impossibility of completing this building by relying on the earlier resources; it shows the necessity for efforts by those countries that are in a financially favorable position, for they are at the beginning of a period where they are not encumbered by financial disaster and are certainly in a position to do something for the building. One would hope that a message like the following will not one day spread through the world: A landmark for the dawning spiritual life was to be erected. Those people who were swept away by the cataclysmic world events and then perished left behind as a last legacy as much as they could accomplish. Those, on the other hand, who were not swept away, who could have begun the new life, did not realize what those who were doomed left for them.

Lecture XVI
Dornach, September 11, 1920

Quite a number of lectures have now been given by me on the changes that must necessarily take place in our whole civilization. First and foremost, what was said in this connection was expressed in such a way as to appeal to the will of men. We now live in a cycle of humanity's evolution in which people have to discover inner activity in order to contribute their share towards the necessary change. For human soul substance will have to stream into external life, into the objectivity of external life, and human beings themselves will have to bring about what should appear. In the present cycle of human development it is no longer possible to wait passively for divine powers, far removed from man, to step in and to do something for human evolution, without the participation of man himself.

The essential thing is to be in a position to understand such things by observing the individual phenomena of social life and the life of nature, but today, certain phenomena of social life shall be our topic. I would like to start with a quite definite fact. Let us suppose that someone announces himself; he may, for example, send his business card with the name "Edmund Miller" printed on it. Yet, on seeing this card with the name "Edmund Miller," it would be foolish to assume that a miller was coming, a man who grinds corn. For the person announcing himself by this name may be a contractor, or a professor, or a court advisor, and so on. It would not be justified in such a case to deduce anything from the name "Miller." Initially, it would perhaps be better to form no thoughts whatever, but just to wait and see what kind of a person conceals himself behind the name. Or, through certain other circumstances, we may already know something about the actual person, the real living entity concealed behind this name, "Miller."

It is clear to us in this case that it would be quite wrong to infer from his name anything about the character of the approaching individual. If a person named "Smith" announces himself we would not think that he is a smith. This shows that in regard to those words we consider proper names, we feel the need to discover, by means of something that is not inferred from the name, what or whom we are dealing with.

Well, in this respect, even proper names have undergone a certain history. A person bearing the name Smith today no longer has anything to do with a real smith; a person called Miller has nothing to do with a miller. Yet these names originally arose at a time when name-giving such as is customary today did not exist, when people in a village would remark, "The smith said,—the miller said this or did that,"—or, "I saw the miller,"—and referred to the actual smith or miller. One who has lived in villages knows that people frequently do not refer to each other by proper names but say instead that they saw the smith, or the mason, or somebody else. Therefore, the name itself originally caused people to infer from the words what lay behind them.

All words, the whole language, will undergo the same development in the course of evolution from the fifth to the sixth post-Atlantean epoch that proper names have undergone, a development which in their case we can clearly survey. Nevertheless, human beings today are still almost completely caught up in the whole of language; we basically acquire all our knowledge out of language. In actual fact, the general attitude towards nearly the whole compass of language is to infer the things from their words. Now, it is convenient to do so, but human evolution follows a different course, and in regard to such things we must have the same attitude that we adopt in regard to natural phenomena. They contain objective necessity. Objective necessity also exists where the causality of nature holds sway in the sphere of life, something that is experienced by many people with abstract superficiality. It happens frequently—I have often pointed this out—that people will say, "I never intended to do or say this; I meant it quite differently; I had this or that intention with regard to this matter." But regardless of how pronounced the child's intention is not to get burned, when it reaches into fire, it will burn itself. Concerning the things of life, intentions that do not delve into life are not decisive; at most, only those intentions that do delve into life, or, certainly, facts, and the relationships of these facts that follow natural laws, are decisive.

People must become used to this way of thinking; based on spiritual science, this is, above all, necessary in the most eminent sense. And one must also get used to the thought: "As pleasant as it might be if one could just take words as they are, it is nevertheless a fact that the objective course and laws of human evolution point in a different direction." They indicate that man's whole conception, his whole soul life, is becoming emancipated from words. Words are gradually becoming mere gestures that simply indicate the being or thing in question, no longer designating and explaining anything fully. If spiritual-scientific descriptions are to be taken seriously, for example, then something must come about for which people are often annoyed with me, namely, that one can no longer use words in the manner that words and sentences are customarily used at present. For if one sets forth spiritual-scientific facts, one is above all presenting facts of the future; something is represented that in future time will have to become the possession of mankind. In a certain sense, one has to anticipate something that is supposed to occur in the future. What is to happen in the future must be received into one's will. Therefore, one is obliged to give spiritual-scientific descriptions in such a way that even the words point like gestures to the essential reality lying behind them. Since our ideas today concerning the reconstruction of the social order will have to be born out of spiritual science, as I explained yesterday, it is necessary that, particularly in matters of social reconstruction, we speak from the above-mentioned viewpoint. This is precisely what people did not at all wish to comprehend, for instance, in my book, *Towards Social Renewal*.[13] They absolutely wanted matters presented to them in the old style, matters that cannot be described in the old style since they are part of the future. And basically, what one is being faced with here can best be made evident by the fact that almost all the questions that, up to now, have been connected by one side or another to the expositions in *Towards Social Renewal* always proceed totally out of the old manner of thinking. No attempt is made to find one's way into the transformed new way of thinking.

Thus we may say that, particularly in the descriptions of social relationships of the future, it must become evident that we have to develop an emancipated soul life that no longer clings merely to words. One who follows my descriptions in the various fields of spiritual science, including the recent ones into the field of social life, will find that I am always at pains to describe a matter from many different sides. As a rule, I use two sentences instead of one, because the first sentence indicates the matter from one side, the other one from the other side. This is then supposed to call forth a desire in the listener or reader to approach the matter by transcending the words and sentences, as it were. This is what must be mentioned in reference to human soul life as far as the transformation of the meaning of human language is concerned. This is an important matter. It is important for the reason that the greatest part of what occurs today in regard to confusion of one's manner of thinking and conceptions comes about for no other reason than the fact that the objective laws and impulses of human evolution already demand that we free ourselves from language. Because of their easy-going habits of thinking, however, human beings do not wish to give up clinging to language. When such a phenomenon is clearly understood, it leads to a deeper insight into the whole course of human development. Indeed, from this transformation of our language or languages, we can actually build a bridge to profound spiritual facts. Naturally, this is more the case in one language than in another. But this is then a matter of the specific treatment of a language, of the meaning of words in a language in the individualized differentiated regions of human civilization, as I have pointed out.

We now live in the fifth post-Atlantean epoch of human civilization and are approaching the sixth condition of development. These evolutionary conditions are not of such a nature that a clear line could be drawn between one and the other epochs; instead, one epoch, bearing its own peculiarities, passes over into the next; and long before it arises, the future one casts its shadows—one could also say its lights—into the present. One must take hold of these lights if one wishes to participate in the evolution of humanity with one's soul.

Let us try and connect what might be termed the "suprahistorical" fact, namely, that we are supposed to work our way towards the sixth post-Atlantean epoch, with another fact known to all of us. It is this: With his spirit-soul entity, the human being descends out of a spiritual world to earthly incarnation through birth or conception. On earth, he then experiences the life between birth and death; then, he passes through the gate of death, and in so doing bears his soul-spiritual being once again into that environment of life which is definitely of a spiritual and soul nature.

Now we must clearly understand—and the significance of this for the art of education, for example, has also been outlined here recently—that we bring down from the spiritual world, at least in the form of effects, what we have experienced in this spiritual world. When we move in ordinary life from one locality to another, we take with us not only our clothes but also our soul-spiritual belongings. In like manner, one brings along into this world through conception and birth the consequences and effects of what has been undergone in the spiritual world. In the period that mankind has presently lived through, concerning which we know that it began around the middle of the fifteenth century A.D., man, through his spirit-soul entity, brought along forces of the soul life devoid of images, forces containing no pictures. It is for this reason that, above all, the intellectual life has arisen and has flourished. During this period, prior to descending through conception and birth into physical existence, the human being was endowed in a sense with something lacking in capacities, lacking in images. This explains the slight inclination mankind had for developing original creations of fantasy since the middle of the fifteenth century. Human fantasy is, in truth, only a terrestrial reflection of super-earthly imagination. The Renaissance does not contradict this, for just the fact that one had to resort to a "renaissance," not a "naissance," clearly shows that original forces of imagination were not present, only a fantasy that required fructification from earlier periods. In short, the fact is that the human soul was permeated in a certain sense with forces that are devoid of images.

Now begins the age—and in many respects, this is the real reason for the stormy character of our times—in which the souls who descend through conception and birth into earthly life bring along for themselves images from the spiritual world. When pictures are brought along out of spiritual existence into physical life, and if salvation is to arise for the human being and his social life, they must under all circumstances be united with the astral body, whereas the element lacking images only unites with the ego. It is predominantly the unfolding of the ego which has blossomed in humanity since the fifteenth century.

Now, however, the time is beginning when man has to feel: Within me there live pictures from my prenatal existence; during my earthly life, I have to make them come alive. I cannot accomplish this merely with my ego; I must work deeper into myself, and this must reach as far as my astral body.

Now, it is generally true that humanity resists the images indwelling in the astral body, images experienced prior to conception. In a way, human beings repel what is supposed to find its way out of the depths of their being into the astral body. The dry, prosaic attitude of the present time is one of its fundamental characteristics, and there are many broadly based movements that oppose an education whose concern it would be that the forces arising from the soul and trying to make themselves felt in the astral body will actually assert themselves. There are insipid, dry people who would really like to exclude any education by means of fairy tales, legends and anything illuminated by imagination. In our Waldorf School system, we have made it our priority that the lessons and instruction of the children entering primary education will proceed from pictorial descriptions, from the life-filled presentation of images, from elements taken from legends and fairy tales. Even what the children are initially supposed to learn about the nature and processes of the animal kingdom, the plant and the mineral kingdoms, is not supposed to be expressed in a dry, matter-of-fact manner; it is supposed to be clothed in imaginative, legendary, fairy tale-like elements. For what is seated deep within the child's soul are the imaginations that have been received in the spiritual world. They seek to come to the surface. The teacher or the educator adopts the right attitude towards the child if he confronts the child with pictures. By placing images before the child's soul, there flash up from its soul those images, or, strictly speaking, those forces of pictorialized representation which have been received before birth or, let us say, prior to conception.

If these forces are suppressed, if the dry, prosaic person guides the education of the child today, he confronts the child from earliest childhood with something that is actually not at all related to the child, namely, the letters of the alphabet. For our present letters have nothing to do anymore with the letters of earlier pictorial scripts. They are really something that is alien to the child; a letter should first be drawn out of a picture, as we try to do it in the Waldorf School. The child is confronted today with something devoid of a pictorial element; the young person, on the other hand, possesses forces in his body—naturally, I am referring to the soul when I am now speaking of "body," for after all, we also speak of the "astral body"—forces seated in his body that will burst out elsewhere if they are not brought to the surface in pictorial representation. What will be the result of modern mistaken education? These forces do not become lost; they spread out, gain existential ground, and invade the thoughts, feelings and impulses of the will after all. And what kind of people will come into being from that? They will be rebels, revolutionaries, dissatisfied people; people who do not know what they want, because they want something that one cannot know. This is because they want something that is incompatible with any possible social order; something that they only picture to themselves, that should have entered their fantasy but did not; instead, it entered into their agitated social activities.

Therefore, we can say that people who, in an occult sense, do not have honest intentions in regard to their fellowmen, do not have the courage to admit to themselves: "If the world is in a state of revolt today, it is really heaven that is revolting." It means the heaven that is held back in the souls of men, which then comes to the fore, not in its own form, but in its opposite—in strife and bloodshed instead of imaginations. No wonder that the individuals who destroy the social fabric actually have the feeling that they are doing good. For what do they sense in themselves? They feel heaven within themselves; only it assumes the form of a caricature in their soul.

This is how serious the truths are that we must comprehend today! To acknowledge the truths that matter today should be no child's play; such acknowledgment should be pervaded by the greatest earnestness. In general, it is no light task today to describe such things, for, in the first place, people do not care for them; secondly, they cling to words. Indeed, one who states that heaven is revolting in human souls is naturally taken literally by his words; people do not notice how he is trying to show that additional facts must be known, whereby the word "heaven" is related to something more than they are in the habit of connecting with the term. This is the same as not thinking of a miller who grinds corn when a "Mr. Miller" announces himself. The emancipation from language is definitely required in individual concrete cases if, in the sense that the laws of human evolution demand it, we wish truly to make progress.

Here, we see how something that comes from the life before birth pushes into the social life. One who is familiar with these relationships knows that he has to recognize something that is actually heavenly in what appears on earth in a caricature. This is in regard to the social questions, but there is something else in addition.

During the age of intellectualism, which has developed

predominantly since the middle of the fifteenth century, human beings have obtained very little from their life of sleep in the form of imaginations for their waking life. Even those who have somewhat more lively dreams tend to interpret them quite rationally and intellectually. In this direction, theosophists, for example, are rational and intellectual. I could not begin to describe in a small volume, only in a big one, how many people have come to me in the course of time and wished to have rational explanations for their dreams! What is important here is that even those imaginations that express themselves in dreams point to a deeper spiritual life. I have often said that the outward appearance of the dream does not matter at all; that has already emancipated itself from the actual content. The content which we receive and then interpret in words of a language, from which, in turn, we actually have to emancipate ourselves as well, is not the true course of the dream; it really has very little to do with the true course of the dream. The dream's content is represented in its dramatic sequence, in the way one image follows another, the way complications arise and are resolved; one can experience the same spiritual content in a number of different ways as a dream. One person comes and describes how he climbed a mountain; he ascended quite easily up to a certain point, then, he suddenly stood before an abyss and could not proceed. Another person relates that he was walking along a path; everything around him filled him with joy. Suddenly, when he reached a certain point in the road, a man with a dagger came up to him and killed him. Here we have two completely different dream images. Yet the process concealed behind them may be exactly the same. It can express itself in one instance in the climb up the mountain and the feeling of confronting an abyss; in another instance, it can be expressed in a cheerful walk down a path until one confronts a person who intends to kill one. The content of the images is not important; it is the dramatic sequence of experiencing something that offers resistance. It is the dynamics behind the images that matters. The course taken by the forces can envelop itself in any number of images, indeed in hundreds of pictures!

We can only understand the spiritual world when we know that what appears in the physical world in the form of dreams, or what clothes itself in images from the spiritual world in such a manner that it resembles the physical world, is only an image. As long as one has the inclination, however, to interpret the images in a rationalistic, purely intellectual way, so long does one also occupy an intellectual standpoint in regard to the dream life of sleep. What matters here is that we understand this dream life of sleep as the expression of a deeper spiritual life. Then only do we comprehend it imaginatively; then we grasp the pictures as something that stands in place of the content.

Then we shall not turn against something that is beginning for the human being today, namely, making inner soul demands out of sleep in a manner similar to the demands made by the imaginations prior to birth or conception. For today we are beginning to sleep differently from the way sleep was experienced in the regular life of the intellectual age since the middle of the fifteenth century. Man brought along into the waking state little inclination for faculties that wish to experience, rather than interpret, the images.

We have now reached the point in human evolution where, out of sleep as well, we draw imaginations that seek to indwell not only our ego, where rationality reigns supreme, but also our astral body. If we work against this, we once more reject something that is trying to rise into consciousness out of the depths of the human soul; we also work against the whole course of mankind's evolution, and what matters here is that we do not oppose humanity's development but work in harmony with it. We do this in the first place by permeating our culture once again with as many elements as possible connected in some way with the spiritual world. Naturally, in regard to external life, it is important for us to imbue ourselves with what is grasped from the spiritual world; hence, that we also imbue ourselves with a true spiritual insight, to fill ourselves with something that in this physical world cannot be comprehended in terms of the physical world. The whole past epoch of human life was actually opposed to this. Consider a case that I have already mentioned a number of times.

It is true that Christianity confronts human beings in such a way that they can only grasp its essence, especially the nature of the Mystery of Golgotha, if they come round to a comprehension of something supersensible. For one must envisage that Christ, a being Who formerly had not been connected with earth evolution, united with the human being, Jesus of Nazareth, and that supersensible events took place. One must conceive of the fact that in regard to the event of Golgotha, even birth and conception differed from the way they take place in ordinary human circumstances. In short, the demand is made by Christology to understand the Mystery of Golgotha in a supersensible sense.

There is an interesting passage in a book written by a modern naturalist[94] where fulminations are uttered against the Immaculate Conception, where it is said that it is an impertinent insult to human reason to claim that an immaculate conception can occur.

Well, a modern rationalist, a purely intellectual person, can't help feeling this way. In a certain sense, what is intended out of the spiritual life is indeed an impertinent mockery of human reason. But the point is that we now live in an age where we must gradually begin to bring into waking life what has been spiritually experienced between falling asleep and waking in such a manner that our astral body can be impregnated and permeated with a pictorial element—not merely our ego, which is the seat of rationality, of intellectualism.

It is interesting that even the theology of the nineteenth century developed in such a way that it opposed Christology with rationalism, with pure intellectualism. Increasingly, modern theology felt called upon altogether to deny Christ as such, and to describe the humble man from Nazareth, the mere Jesus, as a human personality somewhat more outstanding than other human beings. One did not wish to make the effort to comprehend something supersensible. What is to confront the human being supersensibly, what is to awaken him to the supersensible realm, this one tried to grasp with concepts gained here in the sensory world.

A Protestant theologian,[95] with whom I once discussed this matter, told me after we had talked about it for some time, "Yes, we modern theologians should really not call ourselves Christians any longer, for we no longer have Christ. If the name "Jesuit" had not been appropriated already, we should really claim it for ourselves." This is not something that I am saying; it is something that a Protestant theologian of the modern school said to me as a confession of his own soul.

One who has insight into the whole character of our time, however, will understand that we must advance to a comprehension of the Mystery of Golgotha. Just because it is the central manifestation of our human evolution, it will tear us away from the earthly manner of thinking, and will draw us with might and mean to understand something that is incomprehensible based on the earthly sense domain. Whoever wishes in everything to remain caught in the earthly sensory sphere would say, "The Immaculate Conception is an impertinent insult against human reason."

One who understands the task of present-day man will say: I must accustom myself to such ideas. In that case, I must emancipate myself from the customary use of words today. When somebody by the name of Smith or Miller announces himself, I must not assume that he is coming with a hammer in hand or overalls powdered with flour. I must expect something quite different from what I might deduce from the words. Thus, I have to become used to emancipating myself from what was ingrained into the words by the merely physical life of the senses.

Today, the Mystery of Golgotha is in fact the first test for us to see whether we are willing to go along with the comprehension of something that extends beyond the physical-sensory sphere. We, therefore, can no longer content ourselves with a merely traditional, historical description of Christianity, we need instead a creative understanding of the Mystery of Golgotha. Out of spiritual science, we need inner strength of soul which, in a new way, approaches the Mystery of Golgotha and is in a position to comprehend the Mystery of Golgotha as a supersensory fact. Then, having positioned the Mystery of Golgotha into the central point of human thinking and feeling, we must make a new beginning especially in regard to education, and prepare the child in such a way that it does not suppress, does not have to suppress, the imaginations that seek to arise from the depths of the soul. We must meet the imaginations halfway by making pictures of our conceptions.

This is the deeper reason why, in the last issue of *Soziale Zukunft* (Social Future),[96] which is a magazine dealing with education, I described education and instruction as an art in the most eminent sense. In the field of pedagogy, teachers and educators must actually proceed in the way an artist does—indeed, they must proceed in a style surpassing that of an artist. It does not do to impose abstract principles in an abstract pedagogical sense. What matters is that one penetrates the being of man, and, through this comprehension of man's nature, arrives at the point of reading from the inner human being what one has to do in each case. An artist who is creating something cannot go by abstract rules. The purpose of aesthetics is not that of establishing rules for the artists. An artist cannot even go by what he has created yesterday when he creates something today. At every moment he must endeavor to be creative and original. This is how the teacher must be, in a still higher sense. One must not say based on a certain attitude of mind: "Well, if we are looking for teachers like that, we have to wait another three to four hundred years." The only reason that we do not have such teachers as yet is because we say things like this. We can have them the very moment that we have the strong power of faith in it; but it is the strong, not the passive, power of faith that is needed here. Therefore, what is important here is that when we return from sleep, upon awakening, we truly experience in the astral body and imprint into the etheric body what the astral body experiences from the moment of falling asleep until waking up. It can only take place through pictorializing the whole cultural life.

This pictorialization of the whole life of culture, this pictorialization that is demanded by the laws of humanity's evolution, will come into being when the whole spiritual life is left to the decision of those who participate in the spiritual life; when no instructions, no school regulations are laid down by a government which by its very nature stands outside the spiritual life. It is important here that the state does not hand down pedagogical regulations, school curriculums, and such like in an abstract manner. What matters is that one has human beings in an emancipated spiritual life who act out of their own free personality, and that one accomplishes with them what one can or wishes to accomplish with them.

The fact that the human being is presently beginning to bring along through conception and birth something that differs from what he brought with him since the middle of the fifteenth century, and the fact that he also brings something different with him out of sleep, both these facts demand that careful attention be given such matters, and that one really permeates oneself with the knowledge of such decisive facts. But from where can this knowledge be gained, if not from spiritual science? The external culture, today's science, certainly does not deal in any way with these matters. It ignores them; indeed, its present methods compel it to do so. I feel obliged to say that the present situation becomes most poignant when one observes the frequent and strange discrepancy between the inner requirements of humanity's evolution and the way in which people meet them. In recent times, the need has arisen to reckon with what flows into the human being from the spiritual world. Those who were intellectual, who did not reckon with what flows out of the spiritual world, made hypotheses about atoms, molecules, and the like. It was thought that bodies possessing volume point back to an atomistic formation, and so on. Out of the root causes of mankind's evolution, the need arose to grasp spiritual facts. And this instinct to grasp the spiritual expressed itself also in something, for example, like the Theosophical Society. One of its heros is a certain Mr. Leadbeater who wrote an occult chemistry. What did he do in this book? He did something quite horrible, for he pictures the spiritual world in an atomistic sense; meaning, the materialistic manner of thinking is carried into the spiritual world.

I have recently mentioned this whole grotesque thing. Something very clever came about in the Theosophical Society. Someone wished to prove that here is one life; there is the next one (see drawing below). Now, it is so, isn't it, that something has to pass from the preceding life to the later one. One sees the body fall into decay. A proper materialist says that the body disintegrates and it is all over with man. A theosophist, however, wants another earth life to come; so,

something must pass from one life to the other! The proper materialist says that all atoms unite with the earth. The theosophist also does not think in any other way than materialistically, but at the same time he tries to think "theosophically." He wants something to pass from the first to the next life. So he says: "Of course, the atoms become one with the earth; one atom, however, remains and it passes through the whole period of existence between death and a new birth. There it appears again. This is the permanent atom." *One* atom! Oh, the theosophists were especially proud then, when they discovered this "permanent" atom! They had no inkling that in this way they were carrying materialism into the spiritual world conception! Materialism induced them to believe that something—they never said what it was—of the many atoms that sink down into the ground is saved; and this fortunate, saved, permanent atom then reappears in the next incarnation. Much has been written about this permanent atom. It is nothing more than an example of the fact that something was borne into spiritual science that people could not rise above, namely, materialism. It permeates, by the way, the whole description of man, in the way it is frequently presented in the literature of the Theosophical Society. As I have often pointed out, they present the physical body as dense, the etheric body as thinner, the astral body as still thinner. Then come degrees of thinness, where even thinking and conceptions become quite thin. Yet, one is still dealing with something substantial, like mist; hence, although Buddhi and Atma are mists, they are still tangible as mists. One does not have the will power truly to discard materialism even in one's conceptual life; to pass from concepts of matter to concepts of the spirit.

All these things prove how closely human beings are tied to the old ways of thinking. Out of such considerations, anybody who honestly wishes to acknowledge spiritual science should take up the inner challenge to test himself as to how far he has freed himself from the old materialistic concepts; or, when he turns to something spiritual, to what extent he imagines this spiritual manner in materialistic pictures, not being aware of the fact that they are just pictures.

It is always a matter of being conscious of this. For if, say, I were to draw a picture of one of you on the blackboard, the picture could mean a lot to me, if the person in question were no longer present. But if I were then to imagine that the person in the picture would shake my hand, or would speak to me, in other words, that he would be the actual person, then I would be suffering from illusions! Therefore, one may naturally sensualize the spiritual in pictures, but one must always be aware of the fact that they are nothing but pictures.

In the case of words, too, people must realize more and more clearly that language is on the way to turning the word into a gesture, and that we should go no further than to allow the word to indicate something to us that no longer is contained in the word. All words will have to take the same direction that proper names have taken.

For philosophers, I have something even better to say. Philosophers of recent times have set up any number of theories. When I say, "The child is small," they have a concept of "small;" they have a concept of "child." The "is," however, the copula of the two—what does it mean? Oh, much has been written about this copula even in the philosophical sense, not just from the grammatical or philological standpoint. Everything that has been written about it suffers from the fact that this verb, "is," no longer has the meaning of which people speak. It has already emancipated itself from its meaning and the soul content has become a different one. Thus, people in fact philosophize about something that no longer lives in the soul in an alive sense.

This is just an incidental philosophical remark which perhaps doesn't have much significance, but it is supposed to draw your attention to the fact that something that is not noticed by the outer world is by no means noticed immediately by the philosophers. Nevertheless, it is often true that the philosophers are the last to notice the things that really occur in the world, and many of our philosophical systems lag considerably behind what exists outside of themselves!

By proceeding principally from the example of language, however, I have tried to show you quite concretely how present-day human development presents itself. What actually takes place in regard to human development can really only be seen by looking at supersensible facts. Anthropology can no longer discover what actually takes place, only anthroposophy. This is the reason why anthroposophical cultural thinking must lie at the foundation of everything that constitutes work for the progress of mankind.

Address
*On the Occasion of the General Meeting
of the Berlin Branch*
Berlin, September 17, 1920

After a relatively long period of time, I am able to speak to you again today. It came about because of the importance of the General Meeting convening today, and the opportunity of my current brief presence in Germany. It has certainly already occurred to you that there must be a connection between my long absence and the nature of the time in which we find ourselves. The relationship between the events of the times and the very slight activity—if it is even possible to speak of such—that I can afford, particularly for the Berlin Branch, must be obvious to you.

Before entering into the order of business for today's session, I would like to make a few preliminary remarks. First, I wish to remind you of certain words I spoke in the early spring of 1914 in a lecture cycle in Vienna, which were intended to point to what then ensued. It was then that I spoke words which have since been printed. The words I uttered at the time indicated that civilized humanity lives in a kind of social sickness, in a sort of social carcinoma or cancer; that the whole way in which cultural, political, and economic matters are handled is such that it will undoubtedly lead to an outbreak of this creeping cancer, and that it will be bound to change from a chronic condition into an acute one. Of course, many clever people at that time took this statement, which I made out of a grief-stricken heart with regard to the immediate future, to be mere fantasy, an empty paraphrase of a pessimistic mood. At that time, the majority of people the world over naturally preferred listening to the sound of voices like the one, for example, of an official personage in the German Reichstag a short time after, who said that the relationships of the Central European governments to those of the other European countries were absolutely satisfactory, and that one could count on general lessening of tension in the near future. You may remember another remark made here in Berlin at a public session of the Reichstag —that the friendly, neighborly relations with the court at Petersburg were becoming more and more favorable, and that good relations with London existed as well, and so on. These were the words of "practical men," while those who spoke of the spiritual world had to speak of a sickness, of a slowly growing carcinoma. Actually those who claim to be practical men still speak the same way today, in absolutely the same way, although the results of their practicality have brought about the events of the most recent years. Such speaking continues, while what is brought forth from spiritual research and from social insight is either thrown to the winds or, as is the case in Germany, attacked. Furthermore, the worst is that what comes from spiritual research is being secretly persecuted and defamed, defamed in the worst way possible. Thus, anthroposophical spiritual science and everything connected with it today belongs among the most defamed matters in the world. Nevertheless, it can be assumed that today there already are a great number of souls who, out of the totality of the principles of spiritual science, have gained a feeling that only out of this science can arise what can save us from general disaster. One must say this today, even if foolish or malevolent people accuse one of vanity or ambition for saying such things.

    I can say—and I wish to keep these introductory words brief—that the whole attitude, the whole manner of discussions that I had to take part in during the actual wartime has not been understood. With the year 1914, a time came when considerations in the ordinary sense had to cease and what was supposed to occur through words had to turn into actions. Humanity, however, is used to taking words in the sense of the journalistic style, not in the style that should enter into mankind particularly through spiritual science. Thus, many things have been misunderstood during the so-called war years. Something that was of eminent importance to me was overlooked. It was probably known to most of you that before the first year of the war was over, I had a small book published, *Gedanken waehrend der Zeit des Krieges* (Thoughts During the Time of War).* It sold out rather quickly. If one would have considered the matter from the viewpoint from which, unfortunately, things are still considered today, despite the fact that the distress has become so great, it would have been a matter of course to publish a new edition. I opposed the printing of a new edition for the simple reason that the pamphlet had not fulfilled its task. This pamphlet—you can get hold of it again insofar as it is still available—was a question addressed to the German nation. It was not intended to be received in such a way as to lead one to assume the same tone which a great many members of the Central European countries had adopted during the war, and which is common today where surreptitious, poisonous defamations are leveled against anthroposophy. Nothing at all materialized of the expectation that I had concerning this pamphlet, the understanding that I had expected. A new edition would have been meaningful only if my expectation had been realized. So, it did not appear, but disappeared from public life, and in my opinion had to disappear. The proof of the lack of understanding given by this fact had to be taken very, very seriously. This was misunder-

---

*Contained in *Aufsaetze ueber die Dreigliederung des Sozialen Organismus und zur Zeitlage*; GA #24, Rudolf Steiner Verlag, Dornach.

stood in the same way many other utterances have been thoroughly misunderstood, utterances that were meant to elevate and ignite people's spirit in order to bring about what should have been made to prevail directly in Central Europe, namely, a reenlivening of the spiritual life that had been manifest around the turn of the eighteenth century. Spiritual science is basically the revitalization of this spiritual life in the form it must take in modern humanity.

Take everything that is written in the different kinds of newspapers today, in popular literature and even scientific popular writings; take what is written in Koenigsberg or in Berlin, Vienna or in Graz, in Munich or in Stuttgart, and compare it with what is written today in Paris, Rome, London, Chicago or New York—you will find a great similarity. You will find the same keynote in it, the same spirit that must be overcome. On the other hand, if we seek another similarity and compare what is written today in Berlin, Vienna, Dresden, Leipzig, Stuttgart, Munich, Hamburg, or Bremen with what such great minds as Herder, Goethe, Fichte and Schiller once proclaimed, then we must say that it is fundamentally different. All the declamations using quotations of sentences by Fichte or even Goethe that have taken effect, all that has been produced in this manner, resembles more what has been written in Chicago, New York, London, Paris and Rome than the spirit of Herder, Fichte, Schiller and Goethe. The tidal wave that has flooded Central European life from the West has also swept away what should have lived on in us. Nothing of the old spirit could be detected in what was prevalent in the last decades. This had to be shown to the world when the catastrophe fell upon Central Europe, and wrenched itself from my soul in the form of my "Appeal to the German Nation and the Civilized World" which I wrote then. What was connected with this could not simply be continued, as it was in the earlier form familiar to you, up till 1914.

At that time I could not appeal on the basis of something which one had to believe one could appeal to after 1918. One could not appeal to what is the proof of the decline of the general civilization—distress. Since 1918, one had to believe that the distress which had come over Central Europe would awaken the souls and make them receptive to the language intended in my "Appeal to the German People and the Civilized World." Certainly, the fostering of the Anthroposophical Movement could not go on as before. Earlier, one had to render the service which, naturally, always has to be rendered in the Anthroposophical Movement, and which has to be rendered today as well as in all future time: to foster the eternal in the human soul, the eternal which goes beyond birth and death and points beyond the merely sensory world into the supersensory world. Now one had to wait and see whether, from among the sleeping souls of the new civilization, souls would emerge here and there who really would have some understanding of what is meant by spiritual science. One could not yet appeal on the basis of circumstances brought about by the distress. Now, however, after 1918, the time had come when a quite different prerequisite had to be placed before the spiritual eye. Mankind could have realized where it had been led by the prevalence of materialism. For what we have experienced, what we continue to experience and will experience with more impact in the future, is the external karma of materialism in the cultural, political, and economic field. It is the consequence of neglect, because people do not wish to discover in themselves the active strength to foster the spiritual life in their souls. After the publication of the *Appeal to the German People*, the time came when it was, above all, important to work in a positive manner towards something factual. This arose purely out of the possibilities of life. I had to grasp the first hands reaching out to me, for each moment was precious. The first to reach out to me were from Stuttgart. It was a question of protecting and nurturing what could be fostered based on the initiative of some friends there. If mankind had understood at that time what was at stake, had it not failed even under the lesson taught by distress, it would have been enough to do something like this from one center, for it could have had an exemplary effect. But what happened?

In order that you can see how these matters must be understood, I would like to touch upon something else. Before I traveled in the spring of 1919 from Switzerland to Stuttgart for the first lecture tour, a well known pacifist came to me. Although he was willing to sign my *Appeal to the German People*, he hesitated and asked for more information about it. He asked me, "What are you counting on in Germany?" I believe he put it like this, "You are counting on the second revolution." This was in the spring of 1919 and people in many quarters in Germany reckoned with a second revolution after the first one in the autumn of 1918. He believed that what was supposed to come into being in the world through the Threefold Social Organism was only a kind of vehicle, a stepping stone, for the impulses of the second revolution. I said, "No! This is not at all my opinion. First, because I do not believe that those people who might bring about a second revolution in Germany will be able to develop the slightest understanding for the true meaning of the Threefold Social Organism, as long as the old leaders are still active. Secondly, because I do not at all believe in a second revolution. Rather, I believe that this second revolution will consist of a kind of chronic infirmity and will not reach an acute outbreak. What I am simply and solely counting upon is that as many souls as possible will associate themselves with what is born out of spiritual depths, souls who will accept it impartially out of the necessity of the times, quite part from the intentions of the old leaders."

So, I did not reckon with those things that many people

thought I was counting on. When I then arrived in Stuttgart, it stood to reason in a certain sense that the broad masses of people were addressed first. The broad masses of the people, though also partly paralyzed by the events of the war, were those who initially wished to hear something. In my innermost soul I knew how matters stood. For I knew that as long as the leaders who remain from the old days have the party leadership and the people firmly in hand—be they leaders of the parties to the right or the left, even those of the extreme left—nothing can be done with the people. But imagine what would have happened if I would have said that I was not in favor of addressing the masses. Nobody had to believe me, but if I had not addressed them, one would have said afterwards, "If only Steiner would have turned to the broad masses, everything would have turned out differently!" When one is dealing with realities, one must also give proof by means of realities. It had first to be proven by realities that out of all the left-wing parties, defamers and phrasemongers would rise up against what was just beginning by means of the concept of threefoldness to be comprehended by the masses of the people. We were well on the way. One could say that within a few days we had won thousands of people. But it was just this comprehension of threefoldness by the great masses of people that drove the old leaders to their defamations and phrasemongering. So it came about that from this side, seemingly at first, the ground was pulled from under our feet.

What could be hoped for from the other side? Well, it serves no purpose in regard to these matters to cling to illusions; the one and only thing that can help us in the present is to speak the truth. A leading personality who had come up in the party that called itself, by a strange interpretation of the words, "German Democratic Party," a person who had appeared at one of the meetings held at that time, said to me, "You know, if we were in a position to let more people capable of explaining matters in this manner speak to the broad masses, then well and good—one could go along with it. But one pair of hands is not enough and we therefore rely temporarily more on firearms, on force. For the next fifteen to twenty years, it will still be necessary to keep the masses down." This was essentially the predominant attitude of the bourgeoisie; the other was the activity of the proletariat.

So there really remains nothing else but to take what can be drawn out of the spiritual foundations and to represent it in such a way that more and more people can be found who will receive it into their minds. Back of this, we must have something that was born out of this insight and should have been fostered. Before the war, this building was set up on the border of Switzerland, France and Germany in order to look out from Central Europe into the wide world, in particular towards the West, and received the name it must rightfully have, the name Goetheanum. For, in regard to spiritual matters, we are facing worldwide tasks! Today, we cannot face spiritual matters as we would merely personal matters. To do that would lead us into ruin. This is the reason I had to limit my activity during recent times to southern Germany and Switzerland. Truly, I am longing for times when the horizon of my activity can widen again, but this does not depend on myself alone. It depends, above all, on the understanding that people will show toward this activity. I may perhaps find the opportunity in the next few days to point to a number of things which pretend to be "understanding" and which proceed from certain quarters, which work more in an underground manner by means of counterfeiting of letters, falsifying interviews, by defamations and lies.

For the moment, what I have said was merely mentioned in order to point out the reasons why it was necessary for us to abandon our activity in Berlin temporarily; to indicate the circumstances that made it necessary to appeal also in regard to Berlin to what must be appealed to in this age. Have we not been active anthroposophically for almost two decades over a large territory? Were we not justified in hoping that people would be found that could carry on the work independently? Well, they were found. They were found here in Berlin, too. And with the help of these friends the attempt must be made, first of all, to continue the work in Berlin. For this purpose we have gathered together here. In the General Meeting, we shall have to decide how to continue the work here in Berlin.

Lecture XVII
Berlin, September 18, 1920

Among the concepts of anthroposophically oriented spiritual science that must work toward the future development of man's soul being in the most fruitful, the most intensive, indeed the most necessary way, will be the concept of man's prenatal existence. Let us consider for a moment what will be added in this direction to those concepts and feelings that have for so long held sway in Western humanity. When anyone professing a faith, regardless of what religious denomination, speaks today of eternity, of the immortality of the human soul, he thinks mainly of nothing but living on after death, the continued existence of the human soul. In the future, when the viewpoints of spiritual science will have taken hold of a sufficiently large number of people, one will, above all, speak of the human soul's existence before birth. One will speak of the human soul's sojourn in spiritual worlds before it descended to physical earth existence. Mainly, one will speak of what takes place before birth or before conception, just as one speaks of what happens to the human soul after death. Today, one does not sufficiently realize the significance that such mention of prenatal existence will have for the whole of human life, not only for the inner but also external life.

Let us consider for a moment what this means when we look at the growing child; when we see how, from day to day, from week to week, from month to month, the physiognomy of the face assumes its outward form from within, how various features appear, smooth themselves out or recede, and so on. As yet, we really do not realize what secrets of existence we are looking into when watching such a developing human being. How great will be the intimate ardor with which such a developing human being will be viewed when one has the underlying awareness: Before this human being was conceived and born, its soul-spiritual entity was above in soul-spiritual worlds. There, it had experiences by means of soul-spirit organs, just as man during physical existence has experiences through his physical organs.

We can go a step further into the inner nature of the human soul and, from that standpoint, get some idea of the change of views in this regard. Take the various religious denominations that speak to people today in sermons and doctrine about eternity and the immortality of the soul based on their century-old traditions. One should not speak about these matters from a theoretical standpoint; one should speak from the standpoint of life itself. One should follow the nuances of feeling out of which flow most sermons and theological doctrines about the human soul's claim to eternity. I am not speaking about the content so much as the motives, intentions, and feelings that underlie what is being said in sermons and theological doctrine. It is a fact that, quite aside from what is true, a person can have the feeling, springing from an inner egotism of the soul, that the soul ought not to be destroyed along with the body! It is really an element of soul egotism that desires not to be destroyed. One cannot bear the event of dissolution; one thirsts for a continued existence of the human soul after death. It is this feeling of thirsting for immortality to which sermons and theological doctrines appeal. This gives the basis for what is spoken to people of various religious denominations about the eternity of the soul. One finds believers by making concessions to their hidden inner soul egotism. Actually, one tells such people something for which they thirst, the opposite of which they certainly do not wish to hear. By telling them of the continuation of life after death, one discovers the access to human faith. In no other way would one find this access to faith, if the human soul were not thirsting out of egotism for the soul's indestructibility after death.

Now we know from spiritual science that the human soul does, in fact, retain its existence after death. From the many descriptions that have been given in the course of the work in this movement, we could also see that one can speak with precision about the experiences after death based on the science of initiation.

To begin with, we will not speak about what really lies beyond death, only about the motives that underlie the preaching of the doctrine of immortality. Spiritual science cannot appeal to these motives. In fact, spiritual science will not make any appeal when it is supposed to speak of the human soul's existence prior to birth or conception, for it actually has nothing to do with the soul's egotism. As a rule, people give little thought to how they fared prior to birth or conception, as to what their experiences were before they descended into an earthly body. This leaves them more or less indifferent, and does not stimulate the same longing as does the question of life after death. An interest in this area will only be found in those in whom the desire is aroused to comprehend the human being in general, in whom exists a longing to discover that force in the human soul which, as an immortal force, actually lies at the basis of what we are in the outer physical world owing to our body. In our Western civilization, which is doomed to decline unless new forces are injected into it, we find little inclination and few concepts to which one might turn if one were to speak about this life of the human soul before birth. As you know, the churches view this teaching as heresy; they do not realize that in this they are not really teaching Christianity but Aristotelian philosophy. For when Aristotle's philosophy was included in the Church's philosophy in the Middle

Ages, the doctrine of the origin, of the creation, of each individual human soul at birth, or, respectively, with the development of the human embryo in the mother's womb, gained ground increasingly in the philosophy of the Church. Thus, gradually, the belief arose that this denial of the human soul's preexistence was part of the true doctrine of the Church, of Christianity. It was not part of it. To the real practical teaching of Christianity belongs the penetration of the spiritual worlds. Penetration into the spiritual worlds cannot exist without the insight into the preexistence of the human soul.

Western civilization, however, is infected by the various creeds. Things have gone so far that we do not even have the means in our language to express what is the truth in this area. If we still adhere to a religious world concept, or to some kind of rational philosophical world view, we speak of the immortality of the human soul. In that we have this word "immortality" of the human soul, we point to the fact that with this word we actually negate only dying, not birth; for what word could we use with which we could indicate preexistence in the same way that the word "immortality" points to postexistence? Why should we not use a word like "unbornness" which, in the face of true spiritual knowledge, has as much justification as does the word "immortality?" This can be your best evidence of what has been lost in the West directly through the activities of the various religious denominations: the truth about the being of man. This truth has been lost even in regard to language. And even insofar as language is concerned, we must bring about the awareness that the human soul is eternal, that it exists *before* birth as much as it exists *after* death. We need a word for the condition of "unbornness" just as much as for "immortality." Now, however, when you think of an existence before birth, and turn to really sound logic, logic that makes you capable of thinking something through to its conclusion, ask yourself if you are then still capable of *not* speaking of repeated earth lives. Of course, if you speak only of immortality, of postexistence, you can believe: Here is one earth life, then follows an eternity of a totally different kind! Logically, you will no longer be able to do that when you speak of preexistence. For, otherwise, you would have to ask yourself: Well, how is it that I now find that the soul is not created at birth? Why should it be created somewhere along the way before birth? In short, you absolutely arrive at repeated earth lives when you speak of preexistence. It is a fundamental fact that never in earthly civilization has one come to the view of preexistence without also speaking of repeated earth lives.

But consider what it will mean for the whole approach to this earthly existence if this teaching of repeated earth lives is not to be proclaimed as a mere theory, if this view finds its way into all the feeling life and also the will life of people, if man experiences himself as a being that has descended from spiritual worlds and has embodied himself in a physical body. Then, you know that here on this earth you are a messenger of the divine spiritual world; you know that this life here is a continuation of a spiritual life. Everything that we bear in ourselves as a sense of duty, as abilities, is illuminated and energized by such an awareness, for we know that the gods have sent us down into this physical existence. Only then will this physical existence receive a task not set by itself, but set for it by the heights of heaven. This is what is special about spiritual science—it does not just speak *against* the intellect, it must speak *to* the intellect, for these matters must be *comprehended*. Yet, insofar as we take up the concepts derived from initiation science, these concepts penetrate the whole of our human nature; they penetrate not merely our thoughts; they penetrate feeling, our emotions; they penetrate our will and give us an awareness of the nature of our whole human condition. The manner in which one places oneself in the world in awareness of this preexistence of the human soul will be especially important for the civilization of the future. This manner will penetrate human beings with the light and with the power that is needed to struggle free from the powers of decline that otherwise will, without fail, drive civilization into barbarism at the beginning of the third millennium.

Indeed, all the segments of life take on special form when one has such an underlying view. You have often heard me speak here of the Waldorf School that was founded in Stuttgart. In teaching and education, this school is in a certain sense supposed to make practical use of anthroposophically oriented spiritual science. The abstract guidelines that you normally find in pedagogical textbooks, or in teaching regulations approved by the state, are by no means particularly important in the pedagogy of Waldorf School teachers. Instead, the feelings with which a teacher enters the classroom, for instance, are among the especially important things effective there. One of these feelings that is especially effective pedagogically—a feeling that every teacher is permeated with because he has been led into his calling from this aspect—is the reverence for the divine seed that, from day to day, from week to week, from month to month, is blossoming forth from within the entity that has come down from the eternal spiritual world into this physical world. The awareness, possessed by the teacher, that, through the gate of the physical body, he is dealing with a being that has descended to him out of spiritual worlds, is the basis of the deep reverence the teacher has for that human being, which, as a soul-spirit being, increasingly takes on form in the physical body. One may or may not believe it today—a teacher who has this reverence for the developing human being possesses a secret power within himself by means of which he teaches and educates quite differently from a teacher who does not have this reverence, and who believes that the human being comes into existence at the moment his physical body is released from the mother's body. For one teaches and educates not only by means of concepts and ideas. Above all, one educates with the mysterious powers and forces that pass as imponderables from teacher to child.

An example can be cited for this that can be mentioned as an especially important one. As a teacher, one may ponder over how one might give this or that child the idea of immortality. Today, of course, the usual way of thinking is that the teacher is the clever one and the child the dumb one. The clever teacher thinks: How do I teach this dumb child something of the idea of immortality? He might say to the child: Look at the chrysalis of the butterfly! Inside is the butterfly; it emerges and unfolds after the chrysalis bursts open. It is just like this in the case of the immortal soul in your body—the body bursts open. The immortal soul is just not as visible as the butterfly, but it is visible to supersensible perception, and it flies into spiritual worlds. Certainly, one can think up something like that and teach a child the concept of immortality by means of such a comparison. In my opinion, the child will not gain much this way when the idea of immortality is taught to him by the type of teacher who is clever by today's standards. This is because he does not believe in it himself! He only thought it up. When any one of our Waldorf teachers teaches a child the idea of immortality in this way, it is quite different. For he himself believes in this picture; he is permeated with the truth that the chrysalis and the butterfly that crawls out of it were ordained by the gods to represent the picture of the human soul's immortality. He is permeated by the thought: This is the same phenomenon—the emerging butterfly on a lower level, on a higher level the soul that comes out of the body. I did not make up this picture; it has been placed into nature by the divine-spiritual powers themselves. He believes in it with the same fervor with which the child should believe, and this faith is what matters. If the teacher has this belief, then he can also secure it in the child; if he does not have it, or if he has it only as an abstract idea in himself, this idea will not have a fruitful effect. For it depends upon the feelings that flow into the classroom, upon the feelings that are kindled in our own soul out of the knowledge of preexistence.

Only if one takes seriously all that follows from preexistence will one gain an accurate concept of the connection between the human soul and the human body. If you take any handbook of knowledge concerning the soul—one calls this psychology—you find all kinds of theories on how the soul works upon the body, and so forth. You would not become very knowledgeable through these theories, for they are abstract webs of thought, and when you are finished with them you don't know much more than you did before. For, in psychology, all kinds of hypotheses are merely set forth on how the soul affects the body.

If one knows how the prenatal human being incarnates itself in a physical body, then one follows the developing human being in the child quite differently. We find that there are two stages in the developing human being. The first stage is indicated by the change of teeth around age seven. What does this change of teeth signify? It is a much more powerful change in the whole human organism than one usually believes. Today, however, one only observes these things outwardly. When people eventually accustom themselves to consider these things on the soul level in the way it can be done through spiritual science, what will they realize? They will say: Strange! Until the change of teeth the child does not really form solid, contoured concepts; to be sure, the child remembers a lot but does not retain its memories in concepts; actual intelligence does not yet appear. Just observe a child carefully and notice how, during the time when the teeth change, the faculty of actual intelligence increasingly emerges. Today one has no sense of the difference existing between a seven-year-old and a five-year-old regarding the development of intelligence. If one would only observe how the soul gradually emerges after age seven —the Waldorf School teachers must observe it, for their whole teaching and education is based upon it—one would immediately understand in which direction one has to look in order to answer the question: Where was the element of intelligence that emerges after the seventh year? Where was it concealed? It was within the body; it was active in the organism. The same element that emancipates itself at age seven and turns into intelligence was within the body, was forming the body, and the culmination point of its activity of shaping the body is reached when the second teeth appear. The power that thrusts itself into being with the second teeth has been active in the whole organism. It is, however, a power that is active in the body only up to the seventh year. After that it has nothing more to do with the body; it then becomes intelligence. It already was intelligence earlier; as such, however, it was at work in the body. Look at what takes place in the child's body up until the seventh year. Next, look at what the child has as intelligence after age seven. You are looking at the same thing. Through birth, intelligence descended. At first it was not active as intelligence, as soul being; it becomes active in this way gradually after the seventh year. Here you have a concrete view of the working together of the soul with the body. Now you are able to see what was mainly at work in the human body until age seven. You do not have the foolish abstract concepts, fabricated and put into our textbooks and handbooks, concerning the interaction of body and soul. You have the concrete views of what works throughout seven years in blood and nerves, in muscles and bones, and then becomes the child's intelligence.

In this way, when one gradually penetrates into what spiritual science is able to give, one comes to know the human being in the totality of his nature, in his soul and bodily being. Now, man stands before us in a completely different way. It is strange—materialistic science aimed at knowing what matter was, and yet could not know anything, for example, of the nature of the forces that are active in the child's body until the seventh year. Now comes spiritual science and teaches how one really comes to know matter; spiritual science penetrates right into the material element. This is the tragedy of materialism—it becomes more and more abstract and no longer teaches what matter really is. What does the modern physician really know of the liver and kidney, of the stomach and lungs—that is, of the material structures? One day when the insights attained through spiritual science are applied to medicine and natural science, when something of what I tried to show in the course held in Dornach this spring[97] penetrates modern science, one will see that spirit insight is called upon to throw light even into the essence of matter, while the materialist confronts the whole world like a blind man standing before color. Material existence is just what the materialist never comes to know.

A second stage in the life of the human being is puberty; in the male sex it is marked by the change of voice, in the female by changes in the body that spread over the whole organism, not focusing on one organ as clearly as does man's change of voice. In both sexes the changes fall somewhere around the fourteenth year. Once again, this is an essential change in the organism. What is really happening there? What is different after puberty? The whole life of will of the human being is quite changed! Try to compare a nineteen-year-old with a thirteen-year-old, directing your attention to the concrete life of will. The whole life of will becomes quite different; otherwise feelings of love could not enter the life of will. Again, a transformation in the soul life! When through spiritual science we investigate what is going on, we come to the following: We increasingly grow together with the outer world, especially in the time between the change of teeth and puberty; we grasp more and more of this outer world; our will becomes more and more oriented and we learn to bring it into harmony with the things and events of the external world. When one really studies the whole complex confronting us here, one finds that during this time the human being acquires for himself the will element, not from within, but through contact with the outer world. It was out of deep intuition that Goethe said, "A talent is formed in the stillness, a character in the stream of life."[98]

Talent springs from within. Character, that is, the element of will, is formed in the stream of the world, in the exchange between inner and outer forces. The human being always has to defend himself against all that comes toward him from the outer world; the inner being has to react; it has to resist what comes from the outer world. This will-developing element, which approaches man through the alternating communication with the external world, is confronted by an inner force from the opposite direction. This force accumulates in the larynx of the male, in the female in other organs. This accumulation, this collision between the outer element of will and the inner will element, is expressed in the transformation of the larynx or similar organs. Here you even see the spiritual of the outer world working on the human being.

Now bring all this together with the views of spiritual science with which you are already familiar. We know that we descend from the soul-spiritual world into the physical world through conception or birth. We know, on the other hand, that with our astral body and ego we enter a spiritual world every time we go to sleep. The spiritual world, which gives us our soul, works upon the shaping of our form until the seventh year, but after that it becomes our intelligence. Now this intelligence is confronted by the will element— actually, from birth onward, but especially so at puberty, because the interchange between them takes place then. This struggle between the external will element and the inner element of intelligence; between that spirituality we sleep through—passing through it from the moment we fall asleep until we awaken—and the particular realm of the spiritual world that we went through before our birth and conception respectively; the struggle between what we have brought along and what we sleep through each night expresses itself in the development of the larynx, in the development of what occurs in the organism during puberty. A spiritual element works with another spiritual element. We go through a spiritual world between falling asleep and waking up. Concealed in this spiritual world is the will that is communicated to us; concealed in our organism is the intelligence that we bring through birth into physical existence. We can understand the human body when we experience it as an outer revelation of something taking place out of the spiritual domain.

Everywhere we look, and especially when we look upon the human being, we find that spiritual forces are the basis of the world. We only begin to understand man when we actually envision the interchange between these spiritual forces. Mankind will take up all of this in the future. Then, humanity will find it incomprehensible how a certain age could once have come to the point of saying: There is the sense world; in it work atoms, molecules, tiny particles whose collision with each other is supposed to be brought about through certain movements of light or electricity. No, it is not the effects of atoms and molecules; spiritual forces are at work there! Behind all that is perceived by the senses, spiritual forces are at work. The dramatic reversal will be that man no longer will believe he is walking through a mist of atoms and molecules; he will be aware that with every step he is going through spiritual worlds. It is spirit worlds that dwell in him, and spirit worlds that build him up, that transform him. Just as our materialistic faith, the mere postmortem doctrine, has, in its final consequence, led us into what is now happening in the East of Europe, so the teaching of the spirit will lead us in the future into an existence truly worthy of man. But only this spirit teaching, only this, can lead to a real social reconstruction, and not until mankind comprehends this can things improve; they will only get worse and worse.

Certainly, all of you have often allowed a saying by Christ from the Gospel to pass through your souls: "Heaven and earth will pass away, but My words will not pass away."[99] What does this word of Christ mean? It has no meaning for the person who believes in atoms and molecules because he assumes that, prior to this earth existence with its animals, plants and human beings, there was a nebulous formation, and that out of it, the sun and the planets gradually developed; then, along with the conglobulation and constant rotation, plants, animals and human beings eventually originated. Right-feeling people go along with what the famous historian Hermann Grimm[100] said: "Future ages will have difficulty explaining the nonsense of the Kant-Laplace theory, for a carrion bone being circled by a hungry dog is more appetizing than this theory!" This is what a person with healthy feelings says. For when we look out into the world of the senses, what is behind the colors, what is behind the sounds? Not atoms and molecules, but spiritual forces that collide with our own spiritual forces and so form the carpet of color, the network of sounds, and the sphere of warmth that spread out around us. If, then, this is what is in truth around us—I have already identified it in the eighties of the last century in my introduction to Goethe's natural-scientific writings—namely, metamorphosing sensations and behind them a spiritual world, then we shall experience what one would see if one could travel from earth to a distant star and from there look back at the earth. From there, one would not see what is in our surroundings—trees, clouds, plants and animals—one would only behold what is contained within the human skin. What *you* see in the star is not what the beings of this other star see, for that has no meaning for a strange star. The light that streams toward you from other stars is not a process in the external world; it is a process within the beings that inhabit these stars, just as what is within your skin becomes visible only when earth is viewed from another star. When you grasp this you will no longer say that the world came into being out of a multitude of atoms that conglobulated. Human beings form ideals; what is to become of such ideals if earth turns again into nothing but a heap of atoms? The whole moral world, all ethical, moral and religious ideas that ever arose, would be lost, forgotten and destroyed, if only matter and energy were everlasting. Energy and matter resolve themselves into sensations. The spirit that we bear within us is eternal, and this spirit also appears physically on another celestial body. What exists outside the human skin is in no way present for that other heavenly body. Therefore we can say that a certain nature surrounds us now; we are born again and again; this nature will no longer be there in the future; it will have been replaced by a different nature. Of everything that is present now, only what dwells within the human skin will still exist in future times. It was therefore out of a profound intuitive knowledge that Christ Jesus said, "Heaven and earth will pass away, but My words will not pass away!" He meant, All that you see around outside will pass away, but the words that issue from My mouth will not pass away; they will endure!

Now let us look from this point of view at the lies of today's world. We hear it proclaimed from the pulpits that the human soul is immortal; we hear it proclaimed from the universities that matter and energy are everlasting. Then come the cowardly compromisers who try to fit these two concepts together. It would only be honest if those who believe in the eternity of matter would say that there is no immortality of the soul, and if those who believe in the soul's immortality would deny the eternity of matter. They would then have to confess to the truly Christian saying, "Heaven and earth will pass away, but my words"—meaning, the content of my soul—"will not pass away!" The two concepts are incompatible; if people had courage, the materialistic university professors would admit that Christianity has no validity for them. Those whose task it is to proclaim Christianity would have to fight against the materialism of the universities for the sake of Christianity. The fact that this is not done, that people try to glue the two viewpoints together—this is the great lie in our time regarding life. Where the attitude of falsehood prevails, its seeds come up; the germ of lying proliferates and creeps into the other aspects of life. It has done so extensively in the course of time because men did not try to appeal along with postexistence to a knowledge that would unconditionally point to preexistence, to a life before birth. All untruthfulness of life, prevalent today in so many areas, springs from the fact that so many wished to speak only of postexistence—something that appeals merely to soul egotism, not to knowledge. The spirit of untruthfulness cannot be halted if it takes hold of the best in us, namely, our innermost conviction.

These matters can only be rightly and fully evaluated, however, in connection with the whole of human life. Throughout the Middle Ages and right into our time, one spoke only of "right" and "wrong." Everyone, of course, believed he had hit upon the right thing and whatever did not conform with that was wrong. When people spoke of right and wrong they spoke from the standpoint of logic. Logic was the great pride of mankind. It is already hardly the case today. From America, a teaching has come that has already taken hold of philosophy and, in Germany, has assumed an especially grotesque form. This is no longer the logical teaching of true and false; it is the so-called pragmatism, the teaching of what is useful. One believes that something is true, not because one has perceived it logically, but because people like William James[101] and others say that true and false are merely other expressions for what is useful or damaging. We notice that something is useful; therefore we say it is right; we note that something is damaging to us; therefore we consider it wrong. In Germany, this has asserted itself as the "as-if" philosophy. There actually exists a thick book on this by a certain university professor, Vaihinger,[102] who taught philosophy for a long time in Halle. This "as-if" philosophy goes something like this: One does not know whether atoms or molecules exist, but it is useful to explain the world as if there were atoms. One does not know whether the good has any everlasting significance, but it is useful to explain the world as if this were so. One does not know if there is a God, but it is useful for humanity—more useful than the opposite—to view the world as if there is a God, and so on. I am only expressing this with a few paradigmatic words. This "as-if" philosophy is the German version of the American teaching that what is useful is true and what is damaging is false.

Beside these viewpoints there existed yet another in all the old cultures. In the late Greek culture, it was already no longer present, but it was still noticeable in more ancient Greek times by those who study this era not in a professorial manner but according to truth. In those times one did not say of a viewpoint in the logical sense that it was "true" or "false"; one said of it that it was "healthy" or "sick." That signified something! Today we really talk of health or sickness only when we refer to physical man, for in ordinary life we refer to nothing any longer but him. We know that from somewhere in the cosmos come the forces that make us healthy or sick. But when we speak of soul and spirit, we no longer refer to health or sickness; for there we have changed over to abstractions, to mere theory. In the cultures of antiquity, when somebody said something that was correct, one had the feeling that this organized his spirit in a correct sense and he was healthy. When he said something that was awry and what we today abstractly call "false," people sensed concretely that this came from a sick soul mood. "Healthy" and "sick" were terms that were applicable also to the soul; actually, above all, one felt this way about the soul. Out of this feeling originated a word about which scholars have later written long philological treatises—the word "catharsis" in Greek tragedy, a word that comes out of the Mysteries. According to Aristotle, catharsis takes place in the human soul when it watches a tragedy. Fear and compassion are stimulated in the soul, leading to a kind of crisis, to catharsis, and the human being in turn is purified by fear and pity. Thus, the process that occurs in the human soul when it looks upon a tragedy is described as a healing process occurring in the strengthened soul. There, in aesthetics, in art, you still have the concept of a curative element and of an element that causes an affliction.

We must return to this! We must once more regain the concept that what we now abstractly call "right" comes about because the soul, descending from prenatal existence, gains control over the body and organizes it so that it will submit as malleable substance to the soul forces that make it healthy. This is the truth. It is the sick soul element which comes from a soul that is unable to use its body as an apparatus, a soul that expresses itself obliquely and darkly through its body. We must once again learn to replace the concepts "true" and "false" with "healthy" and "sick." We must again experience an inner pain that can overcome us when somebody expresses wrong views; we must again sense inner satisfaction over truth. Not until we speak equally of prenatal existence and postmortem existence, however, not until we learn to use a word like "unbornness" just as we use the word immortality, shall we feel that way.

The fact that we do not feel this now shows how far we have strayed from the knowledge of that spiritual world from which the human being actually comes.

You will find that those matters I have only briefly summarized today are described in more detail in numerous published cycles of my lectures and books. From such descriptions you can realize what a change it signifies in the whole constitution of the human soul when spiritual science will be the very nerve center of human feeling; when human beings will go about in the world with an awareness of their being such as the one attainable from spiritual science. People today indulge only the egotism of the soul that wishes to cling to a postexistence; they do not want to press onward to a real comprehension of the human soul which had experiences before birth, just as it will have experiences after death. The whole, complete eternity of the human soul is only grasped by one who can not only speak of immortality but, based on insight, of "unbornness," too. We can *believe*, because belief always comes from a desire for life after death. We can *know* of the life before birth and the life after death as two things that are inseparable. Knowledge takes in the total being of the human soul; belief is concerned only with the postmortem existence. Knowledge of the spiritual is what the human being must struggle to acquire, but this is what people today strongly resist. Real knowledge of the spiritual world can only flow out of spiritual science. Out of spiritual science will come a constitution of the human soul that is healthy, not only true, and physical healing will be a necessary consequence of spiritual healing. Then man will not view the earth in the manner of modern geology as a huge mineral globe; he will view it as a spiritual being of which he himself is a member. That is what we must work toward.

This was meant to be the first part of my observations today.[103]

Notes

1. Reference to Rudolf Steiner's return from Stuttgart where, from July 24 until August 1, 1920, he had been giving lectures for the teachers of the Waldorf School, for the general public and the Anthroposophical Society.
2. The Waldorf School: Founded by Emil Molt (1876-1936) in the year 1919 for the children of the workmen in the "Waldorf-Astoria" cigarette factory and the public as a coeducational elementary and high school under the leadership of Rudolf Steiner, who had also appointed the teachers and had given them preparatory courses.
3. Dr. Walter Johannes Stein: 1891-1957, Dr. Caroline van Heydebrandt: 1866-1938; both teachers in the Waldorf School from 1919.
4. See Preface and Introduction to *Goethe's Naturwissenschaftliche Schriften*, edited by Rudolf Steiner. Introductions to all the volumes written by Rudolf Steiner under the same title, Dornach, 1926.
5. Rudolf Steiner: "The Portal of Initiation," contained in *Four Mystery Plays*, GA 14 (Toronto, Steiner Book Centre, 1973).
6. "Stimmen der Zeit," Freiburg i. Br., 1918-1920, Otto Zimmermann SJ, Josef Kreitmaier SJ, Konstantin Nopels SJ.
7. Max Kully: 1878-1936, Catholic minister of Arlesheim near Basle. Reference to a calumnious article against Rudolf Steiner that he wrote in a Catholic Sunday paper, July 6, 1920.
8. Rudolf Steiner: *The Mission of the Folk Souls*, GA 121 (London, Rudolf Steiner Press, 1970).
9. Lenin: 1870-1924, founder and leader of Bolshevism; Trotski, 1879-1940, Lenin's closest associate.
10. Rudolf Steiner: *From Jesus to Christ*, GA 131 (London, Rudolf Steiner Press, 1973).
11. Rudolf Steiner, *Occult Science, an Outline*, GA 13 (Spring Valley, Anthroposophic Press, 1972).
12. Ludwig Buechner: 1824-1899, doctor of medicine; Jacob Moleschott: 1822-1893, physiologist; Carl Vogt: 1817-1895, zoologist.
13. Rudolf Steiner: *Towards Social Renewal*, GA 23 (London, Rudolf Steiner Press, 1977).

14. Words by Pylades in Goethe's play, "Iphigenie auf Taurus."
15. Rudolf Steiner: *The Wisdom of Man, of the Soul and of the Spirit*, GA 115 (New York, Anthroposophic Press, 1971); *Human and Cosmic Thought*, GA 151 (London, Rudolf Steiner Press, 1967); *Kosmische und menschliche Geschichte*, Vol. I and II, GA 170/171 (Dornach, Rudolf Steiner Verlag, 1964). Not translated.
16. Rudolf Steiner: *Knowledge of the Higher Worlds and Its Attainment*, GA 10 (Spring Valley, Anthroposophic Press, 1983).
17. Mechthild von Magdeburg: 1207-1290, mystic; St. Theresa, 1515-1582, Spanish saint; Johannes vom Kreuz (Juan de la Cruz): 1542-1591, mystic and theologian, reformer of the Carmelite Order; Meister Eckhart: 1260-1327, Dominican mystic; Johannes Tauler: 1300-1361, student of Meister Eckhart, mystic, Dominican preacher.
18. Charles Webster Leadbeater: 1847-1934, prominent personality of the Theosophical Society.
19. Oswald Spengler: 1880-1936, *The Decline of the West*, Munich, 1922.
20. Dr. Roman Boos's descriptions, given on August 13, 1920, were not recorded. He reported orally on them to Dr. Steiner.
21. Refers to a news report carried by the French, German and Swiss press, according to which the German Foreign Minister, Simons, had supposedly told a reporter of the "Impartial" that he was a follower of the reforms suggested by Rudolf Steiner (the threefold social organism). See, among others, "Basler Nachrichte," 1920, #345, August 14, in which an article is quoted from the "Vossische Zeitung" of August 6. In the lecture of April 22, 1921, in answer to a particularly crude article in which Simons was described as "the favorite disciple of the Theosophist, Steiner," Rudolf Steiner made the following comment: "In the weekly magazine which is primarily the mouthpiece of widespread public opinion, we note in the last issue that public sentiment was being worked up against Simons' policies. It goes without saying that neither anthroposophical spiritual science nor the threefold movement have anything to do with Simons' politics. It is out of a spirit of deep untruthfulness that anthroposphical spiritual science is lumped together with Simons' policies."
22. See Lecture III of this volume.
23. See the lecture of March 18, 1920; printed in "Menschenschule," Pamphlet 6, 1958.
24. Hermann Grimm: 1828-1901, *Goethe-Vorlesungen*, Vol. 2, Berlin, 1877.

25. This law was first proclaimed by Julius Robert Mayer (1814–1878), doctor and scientist. See Rudolf Steiner: *Erdensterben und Weltenleben*, GA 181, Lecture XII (not included in English translation of this cycle). Dornach, 1967.
26. Adolf von Harnack: 1851–1930. The quotation literally says: "Not the Son, but only the Father belongs in the Gospel, as Jesus proclaimed it." In *Das Wesen des Christentums*, Leipzig, 1900.
27. Rudolf Steiner: "Durch den Geist zur Wirklichkeits-Erkenntnis der Menschenraetsel: Philosophie und Anthroposophie. Vier Maerchen (aus den Mysteriendramen). Anthroposophischer Seelenkalender. Der Seelen Erwachen, 7.u. 8. Bild," Berlin, 1918. Compiled upon requests by friends and published in book-form for the German soldiers on the front.
28. See Lecture III of this volume.
29. See Note #4.
30. See Lecture II of this volume.
31. See Note #17.
32. See lecture by Rudolf Steiner, "Urteilsbildung in den drei Gliedern des sozialen Organismus" in *Gegenwart*, 1950/51, #7 and 8/9. Not translated.
33. Johann Gottlieb Fichte: 1762–1814. The quotation literally says: "The kind of philosophy one chooses depends . . . on what kind of human being one is . . . A philosophical system is not just a pile of inanimate household goods that one can either dispose of or accept any way one likes; it is ensouled by the soul of him who has it." In "Erste und zweite Einleitung in die Wissenschaftslehre und Versuch einer neuen Darstellung der Wissenschaftslehre," 1779.
34. Rudolf Steiner: *Spiritual Guidance of Man and Humanity*, GA 15 (New York, Anthroposophic Press, 1970).
35. Max Dessoir: 1867–1947. Compare this with Rudolf Steiner: *Von Seelenraetseln*, GA 20 (Dornach, 1960). Not translated.
36. Hans Vaihinger: 1852–1933, *Die Philosophie des Als-Ob*. System der theoretischen, praktischen und religioesen Fiktionen der Menschheit auf Grund eines idealistischen Positivismus. Berlin, 1911.
37. Wilhelm Jerusalem: 1842–1910, who in 1908 published a translation of *Pragmatism* by William James.
38. Rudolf Steiner: *Zeitgeschichtliche Betrachtungen*, Part I, GA 173 (Dornach, Rudolf Steiner Verlag, 1966). Not translated.
39. Appeared in "The Morning Post," London, July 12–30, 1920. Also published in pamphlet form, *The Causes of World Unrest*, London, 1920.

40. Bimetalism: The policy of using two metals (mostly gold and silver) jointly as a monetary standard. In most cases, replaced by the gold standard since the second half of the nineteenth century.
41. Rudolf Steiner: *Egyptian Myths and Mysteries*, GA 106 (New York, Anthroposophic Press, 1971).
42. See Note #4.
43. Rudolf Steiner: *Inner Nature of Man and the Life Between Death and a New Birth*, GA 153 (London, Anthroposophical Publishing Co., 1959).
44. Scotus Erigena: 810-877 A.D. Translator of the writings by Dionysius Areopagita; author of "De divina praedestinatione," "De divisione naturae." In 1225, the Vatican ordered all his writings burned.
45. See Note #13.
46. Sophie Cheftele, "Les forces morales aux Etats-Unis (l'eglise, l'ecole, la femme), " Paris, 1920.
47. The source of this quote could not be found.
48. Rudolf Steiner: *Oswald Spengler, Prophet of World Chaos*, in GA 198 (New York, Anthroposophic Press, 1949).
49. David Lloyd George: 1863-1945, British statesman, prime minister from 1916 until 1922.
50. Eugene Clemenceau: 1841-1929, French statesman.
51. Philipp Scheidemann: 1865-1939, German secretary of state, later minister president.
52. Gerhart Hauptmann: 1862-1946, playwright; "Die Weber," Berlin, 1892.
53. Johann Gottlieb Fichte: *Appellation an das Publikum ueber die ihm beigemessenen atheistischen Aeusserungen*, 1799.
54. Rabindranath Tagore: 1861-1941, Indian poet and religious philosopher.
55. Francis Bacon: 1561-1626, English philosopher and statesman, founder of empiricism; Thomas Hobbes: 1588-1679, English philosopher; Adam Smith: 1723-1790, English philosopher and sociologist; John Stuart Mill: 1806-1873, English philosopher and political economist, one of the founders of positivism; Henry Thomas Buckle: 1821-1862, English writer on social history.
56. David Hume: 1711-1776, English philosopher and statesman; John Locke: 1632-1704, English philosopher.
57. Rudolf Steiner: *The Riddles of Philosophy*, GA 18 (New York, Anthroposophic Press, 1973).
58. Mary Baker Eddy: 1821-1910, founder of Christian Science.
59. Herbert Spencer: 1820-1903, English philosopher; Jeremy Bentham: 1748-1832, English jurist, founder of philosophy of utilitarianism.

60. Ralph Waldo Trine: 1866–1958, American author.
61. Woodrow Wilson: 1856–1924, president of the USA from 1913 until 1921. In an address to Congress on January 8, 1918, he outlined a "Program of World Peace," condensed in fourteen points.
62. Prinz Max von Baden: 1866–1929, became German chancellor in the fall of 1918; on October 5, 1918, he directed a peace offer to President Wilson based on the latter's "Fourteen Points."
63. Georg Wilhelm Friedrich Hegel: 1770–1831; complete edition of Hegel's works, Berlin, 1832–1844.
64. Eduard von Hartmann, 1842–1906.
65. Reference to Alfons Lehmen, SJ: 1847–1910, and his book *Lehrbuch der Philosophie auf aristotelisch-scholastischer Grundlage*, Vol. I, Freiburg i. Br., 1917. Compare with this the lecture of July 10, 1920, reprinted in "Blaetter fuer Anthroposophie," September, 1953. Not translated.
66. Heinrich Marianus Deinhardt: 1821–1879, "Beitraege zur Wuerdigung Schillers. Briefe ueber die aesthetische Erziehung des Menschen." Published by G. Wachsmuth, Stuttgart, 1922.
67. Orison Swett Marden: 1850–1924, American author.
68. Reference to the first Course of the School of Spiritual Science at the Goetheanum from September 26 until October 16, 1920.
69. Ludwig Graf von Polzer-Hoditz: 1869–1945; his lecture was later published under the title, "Der Kampf gegen den Geist und das Testament Peters des Grossen," Stuttgart, 1922.
70. Friedrich Wilhelm Schelling: 1775–1854.
71. Friedrich Hoelderlin: 1770–1843.
72. See Lecture IV of this volume.
73. Karl Rosenkranz: 1805–1879, philosopher and literary historian. *Hegel's Leben*, Berlin, 1844.
74. Rudolf Steiner: *Der Baugedanke des Goetheanum*, Gesamtausgabe Stuttgart, 1958.
75. Literally, this sentence says: "What is rational, is real; and what is real is rational." From preface to Hegel's *Grundlinien der Philosophie des Rechts*, 1821.
76. Professor Paul Menzer: "Abbau der Universitaeten?" in "Hallische Nachrichten," August 18, 1920.
77. Ludwig Plate, 1862–1937.
78. The Phyletic Museum of the University of Jena was founded in 1907, and according to its foundation-charter was "intended for the development and dissemination of the teaching of evolution as well as morphology and anthropology." Already in 1886, Ernst Haeckel had tried to realize the plan of the museum with the help of the so-

called Ritter-Foundation, but had failed because of the opposition of the donor, Paul von Ritter. It is quite possible that on the occasion of his sixtieth birthday, Haeckel talked about this planned museum in Dr. Steiner's presence. For Haeckel's birthday, his students and friends collected money for a marble bust. More money was collected than was needed. In 1894, this surplus of 10,000 marks still existed when the museum was established. It was then included in the capital of the foundation. In a footnote to a letter from Haeckel to Carneri on March 23, 1907, the publisher of the letters writes, "The construction of the Phyletic Museum in Jena was of great significance for the popularization of the teaching of evolution. For a long time, Haeckel had been envisioning such a 'public-spirited center of education,' namely, a collection . . . in which the most pertinent facts of phylogeny would be suitably placed together, . . . preparations, pictures and explanations would aid the public's understanding. The necessary financial means came together through donations." Rudolf Steiner was aware of all these matters.

79. Refers to the article by E.F.: "Haeckel und — Plate," in the "Berliner Tageblatt," evening edition of August 19, 1920.

80. The writer of the article, E.F., bypasses the true facts with his report. Compare with this Heilborn's description on pp. 12 and 13 of his pamphlet, *Die Lear-Tragoedie Ernst Haeckels:* "One of Plate's first official actions after his move was the demand that Haeckel immediately clear out his study in the zoological institute. The elderly scientist was at that moment suffering from severe rheumatism. In order to be able to comply with Plate's request, Haeckel had to have himself carried into the institute . . . This hasty move then took place in the custodian's and Haeckel's daughter's presence; a move that required the transport of letters, documents and books across to the Phyletic Museum. In two days, this was accomplished. Haeckel was just surveying his new workroom when the recently appointed director of the museum, Plate, appeared, announcing that he was requisitioning the assistant's room for his . . . 84 cages of live mice that he had brought with him . . . for the purpose of genetic tests. Haeckel . . . protested against this because of the unavoidable dirt and smell of such a breeding center and asked whether the mice couldn't be housed somewhere else in Jena besides the brand-new museum. Haeckel suggested . . . a room in the zoological institute for this purpose. Plate, however, did not like this, because the foul smell would be too irksome for him in the adjacent laboratory. When Haeckel remarked that surely *he* had a voice in the matter of the ar-

rangements in the Phyletic Museum, which was to serve purposes other than the raising of mice, especially since the museum had cost him two years of work and a great part of his own financial resources, Plate declared as if with the full weight of his office, 'I am sole director of the Phyletic Museum since April 1 and you have to submit to all my orders without exception.' A bitter exchange of words ensued and the elderly Haeckel finally said, 'You treat me like an assistant who is twenty years younger, not like your teacher who is thirty years older!' Plate left without a word . . . This was the first tribute of gratitude on the part of the 'sincerely devoted old pupil' and the first expression of his 'special joy over furnishing the museum together with Haeckel according to the latter's intentions!' "

81. Ottokar Lorenz: 1932-1904, Austrian historian.
82. Friedrich Wilhelm Nietzsche: 1844-1900.
83. See Note #9.
84. See Lecture VII of this volume.
85. See Note #54.
86. Thomas Huxley: 1825-1895.
87. Friedrich Hegel: *Grundlinien einer Philosophie des Rechts*, 1821.
88. Johann Gottlieb Fichte: *Grundlage des Naturrechts*, 1796.
89. A.W. Lunatsharsky: 1875-1933, Russian author and politician.
90. In Matthew 24:35; Mark 13:31; Luke 16:17.
91. Thomas Aquinas: 1226-1274; compare Rudolf Steiner: *The Redemption of Thinking*, GA 74 (Spring Valley, Anthroposophic Press, 1983).
92. Erich Ludendorff: 1865-1937, German general.
93. Alexander Helphand, died in 1924, Russian socialist, for a time a political refugee in Germany. He played an important role in bringing about the Bolshevic revolution as well as the peace of Brest-Litovsk (1918).
94. Ernest Haeckel: *Anthropogenie oder Entwicklungsgeschichte des Menschen*, Leipzig, 1891, p. 871.
95. Max Christlieb: 1862-1916.
96. In "Soziale Zukunft," #5-7, Dornach, 1920.
97. Rudolf Steiner: *Spiritual Science and Medicine*, GA 312 (London, Rudolf Steiner Press, 1948).
98. Goethe: *Tasso* I, 2.
99. See Note #90.
100. See Note #24.
101. William James: 1842-1910. American psychologist and philosopher.
102. See Note #36.
103. The second part is unknown.

www.ingramcontent.com/pod-product-compliance
Lightning Source LLC
Chambersburg PA
CBHW020942230426
43666CB00005B/127